To all wonderful, kind people doing great things on the web, challenging the status quo and sharing what they've learned.

Abbes Bessrour	Arun Agrawal	Christos Keramitsis	Elena Salaks	Heather Sigler	Joanna Cymkiewicz	Kevin M. Kelly
Abhishek Prakash	Asha Baker	Claudine Vallee	Eli Levit	Helena Hajsek	Joao Salazar	Kevin Van Ransbeeck
Adam Wills	Astrid Schildberger	Claudio Götz	Elikem Jason Daniels	Henry Lawrence	Joel Gerhold	Khalid Jalingo
Adriana Lafarga	Ava Salazar	Courtney Brillhart		Iain Heath	Joel Villamil	Kim A Dyrby
Afiq Hazwan	Azure Wordsworth	Craig Taylor	Elina Dorokhova	Ian Craddock	Joelene Weeks	Kim Lee
Alberta Soranzo	Balanarayanan	Crancis Fabrel	Eliza Struthers-Jobin	Ichsan Fachreza	Joey Kidd	Kirsten Blocker
Alberto Trivero	Bálint Marietta-Timea	Cristián Sepúlveda	Elvir Zekic	Imam Firmansyah	Johannes Schröder	Kole Krstev
Alejandra Chevey		Cristian Teichner	Emmanuel De Roo	Immo Junghärtchen	John Fischer	Konrad Kęska
Alejandro Pascual	Bartosz Kaszubowski	Crystal Grace So	Epochial Hank	Irakli Simonishvili	John William	Kostas Chantzis
Becerra Sarmiento		Dan Hayes	Eric Ziegler-Snover	Isabela Nastasa	David-Thomson	Kraig Walker
Aleksandar Perisic	Becca Muir	Daniel Grima	Erin Thompson	Isfahan Ashraf	Jon Mulligan	Kris Kong
Aleksandr Fesenko	Ben Callis	Daniel Robles	Ervin Chua	Iulia Oprea	Jon Shaffer	Kristen Watson
Aleksey Pastuhov	Ben Seymour	Daniel S Blanes	Erwin Liemburg	Ivan Andhika Chen	Jonathan Frutos Rodrigo	Kristine Mauric
Alessio Vertemati	Benjamin Blake	Daniel Schmidt	Fahad Ibnay Heylaal	Jaci Aricheta		Krzysztof Kominiak
Alex Baar	Benjamin Laible	Daniel Senn	Farah Alaoui	Jack Sutherland	Jonathan Gall	Lakshmi Mareddy
Alex Barsukov	Benjamin Martin	Daniel Zenzen	Fardeem Munir	Jacki Jorgensen	Jordan Moore	Lara De Domingo
Alex Graham	Benjamin Rancourt	Danielle Kloots	Farid Ben Kacem	Jai Soni	Jorge Arturo Galicia Ramos	Lau Vi Ee
Alexander Kozyrev	Bernard Gannon	Danijela Filip	Felix Bengtsson	Jakub Kolář		Lauren Balloch
Alexander Mikhailovsky	Binu P	Danny Dickson	Felix Catwoord	James Grima	Jørn E. Angeltveit	Lauren Paul
	Bjorn Passchier	Dario Calonaci	Fernando Fernandez	James Myers	José Manuel Pérez Pérez	Leah Garber
Alexander Nuzhnyi	Bob Farrigan	Darrell Arjune		James Noble		Leanne Mclaughlin
Alexander Romano	Boonsuen Oh	Darren Odden	Filip Zrnzevic	Jamie Ferguson	Jose Vieitez	Lee Griffiths
Alexis Colin	Bora Volkan Güler	Dave Blake	Flint Johnston	Jamie Holden	Joséphine Kurvers	Lenny Peters
Alfredo Rodríguez Joya	Bria Mears	David Dogneton	Florencia Rosenfeld	Jamo Hutcho	Josephine Seyfferth	Leo Melo
	Brian Dorey	David Fowler	Florin-Alexandru Ilinescu	Jamshid Hashimi	Josip Kraljevic	Leonardo Pessoa
Alvin Tan	Brian Fernandes	David Helebrant		Janel Thomas	Joy Azajar	Ljubisa Stojanovski
Alysa Mccall	Bryan Colle	David Henrich	Fulvia Di Fortunato	Jannis Schäfer	Juanjo Melgar	Lucy Eru
Amir Zare Pashaei	Bryan González	David May	Gabriele Canepa	Jared R Davis	Juha Snellman	Luis Carlos Tapia Sandoval
Amrita Mayuri	Alcibar	David Politi	Gabriele Coroniti	Jared Smith	Julie Gadoury	
Anders Engan	Bugz Bayfield	David Reed	Gauthier Geerolf	Jason Bennefield	Julius Danilevičius	Lukas Heuser
Andi Saleh	Bui Hai	David Roessli	Geert Jansen	Jason Birnie	Justin Maestri	Lukáš Kraft
André Lang	Cain Gillis	David Watson	Geoffrey Pearson	Jason Featheringham	Justin Mcdonald	Łukasz Rysiak
Andreas Helge	Calle Hunefalk	Davide Lanfranchi	Gerardo Rodríguez Silva		Justin Rains	Luke Dewitt
Andreas Hengl	Calvin Szeto	Davit Bitsade		Jason Gradwell	Justyna Senska	Luuk Leijtens
Andreas Kolli	Carl Woolley	Deanna Wong	Gerd Wippich	Jason King	Jyotsna Clarkin	Lynda Wilson
Andreas Nebiker	Carmen Ansio Ruiz	Deepak Anupalli	Gerry Rohling	Jay Allen	Kai Radanitsch	Maciej Teodorowski
Andreas Seebald	Casey Smith	Delia Maria Mija	Ghis Bakour	Jay Wrkr	Kaitlyn Thul	Maggie Cheung
Andreas Van Nuffelen	Catarina Nunes	Dennis A Cooper	Ginés Arabi	Jean Paul Torres Neumann	Kamil Górny	Małgorzata Iwańska
	Cathy Clarke	Denys Ambrosevych	Giorgos Katsiampas		Kamil Grzegorczyk	
Andrei Marante	Cédric Aellen	Diederick De Geest	Giovanni Guarino	Jean-Francois Potvin	Kanakamani	Manfred Oeding
Andrés Laplace Kellogg	Charlie Schmidt	Dillon Jones	Girish B		Karolina Werynska	Manik Singh
	Chen Hui Jing	Diomari Madulara	Gopinath	Jean-Marc Buytaert	Kasper Mikiewicz	Manjusha Anuragh
Andrew Morgan	Cheryl Oberholzer	Dmitry Shamonov	Goran Mitic	Jem Bezooyen	Kat Garsi	Manoj Kumar
Andris Klaipins	Chetika Chawda	Dominic Colaso	Graham Martin	Jennifer Broman	Katarzyna Grabowsk	Marat Faizov
Andy Fuchs	Chiara Veronica Señires	Donna Lynn Smith	Gregory Bowrin	Jeremy Bell		Marc Schappach
Andy Mortimer		Donnell De Leon	Grzegorz Wójcicki	Jeremy Foster	Kate York	Marc-Antoine Aubé
Ania Pietras	Chinmay Pandey	Dorsa Giyahi	Guido Schmidt	Jeremy Madrid	Kathinka Martinsen	Marco Hagemann
Anita Kiss	Chris Stauffer	Dr. Jörg Naumann	Guram Kashmadze	Jeremy Sarber	Kathryn Carruthers	Marco Kotrotsos
Anna Puchalska	Christiaan Nieuwlaat	Dustin Goodman	H. Kamran	Jeribeth Stevens	Katie Nelson	Marco Slusalek
Anthony Devine		Eddie Choi	Hanif Nouhi	Jesse A. Dugas	Katrin Krieger	Marcus Herrmann
Anthony J J Norton	Christian Althoff	Eddy Tseng	Hannah Sharp	Jessica Komene	Keith Leow	Margaret Leonny
Anthony Ugas	Christian Hegedüs	Edward Ronald Calugtong	Hapiuc Robert	Jessica Vandusen	Kelvin Travers	
Antonio Marugán	Christian Stuff		Harald Bröcker	Jesús Cortés	Kenneth Abad	
Areejh Lee	Christina Balda	Efren Castillo	Harshit Purwar	Jitendra Berde	Kevin F.j. Harris	
Arkady Kuznetsov	Christoph Sippel	Efthimis Katsanos	Hazem Farahat	Jo Minkwon		
Arkka Pradipta	Christopher Beard	Egbert Woerdeman	Hazem Hisham	Joan León		
Arne Eitel	Christopher Demicoli	Eileen Phan	Hazim Sami			
Arshabhi Rai		Eileen Xue	Heather Oneill			
Arturo Jofré	Christopher Serna	Elco Klingen				

Biggs
Maria Cristina
Maria Mosesku
Marijana Pivac
Marin Knežević
Mario Rader
Mark Casey
Mark Learst
Mark Mcmurray
Mark Seymour
Mark Smith
Marko Bodrozic
Marouane Rassili
Marta Teixeira
Martin Collazo
Martin Hahn
Martin Hairer
Martin Starosta
Martinko Hoško
Martino Stenta
Martins Grudups
Marvin Santiago
Matias Niemela
Matt Desailly
Matt Mcalexander
Matthew Keelan
Max Antonucci
Maya Shavin
Mayur Kshirsagar
Meenakshi Sharma
Megan Macnaughton
Melanie Linares
Melanie Witzmann
Melissa Harris
Mia Lee
Micael Andrei Diaz De Rivera
Michael Anthony Sosa
Michael Nichols
Михаил Просмицкий
Michael Pyrkh
Michael Staudenmann
Michelle Thatcher
Midori Kocak

Miguel Muñiz
Mihail Stamenov
Mikhail Delport
Mikhail Nechaev
Milan Nohejl
Miroslav Hornak
Mišel Tekinder
Mohamadrafiq Jakate
Mohammed Munawar Ahmed
Mona Alexandra Hirsch
Monisha Rajeesh
Monozona Web Tech Studio
Muhammad Yousuf Tafhim
Mylène Gaultier
Nadav Blum
Nadia Sidko
Nadja Gimaletdinow
Nagaraj Chandran
Nancie Kelly
Naresh Babu Baleswaran
Natalie Sanderson
Natasha Fenech
Nathalie Vidon
Nathan Schmidt
Nathan Woulfe
Nathaniel Albrecht
Naweed Chougle
Neil Mckay
Nelson Carvalho De Jesus
Nguyen Khang Ninh
Nhi Nguyen
Nicholas Wright
Nick George
Nico Schober
Nigel Duckworth
Nikki Goel
Nina Pruchay

Numa J. Quevedo-Castro
Oghenemaero Ezarevah
Oliver Beckenhaub
Oliver Hunziker
Oliver Ochs
Oluwafemi Epebinu
Osamah Mohammed
Oscar Björn Gren
Oti Kelechi
Pablo Picasso
Pablo Tamarit
Panos Makrostergios
Papageorgiou Nikolaos
Pasquale Bucci
Pat Yuen
Patima Tantiprasut
Patricia Grace Y. Recto
Patrick Mennen
Paul Cushing
Paul Pinier
Paulo Gomes
Pavel Matarevic
Pavlo Pochapsky
Pedro C Palomino
Peggy Lee Oster
Pervez Choudhury
Peter Mcgrath
Peter Mézeš
Peter Pirc
Peter Schotman
Peter Swiek
Petra Gregorová
Pham Quoc Cuong
Pham Quynh Huong
Pham The Anh
Philipp Christen
Phonbopit Sahakitchatchawan

Pierre Jeunejean
Pieter Daveloose
Pixeldeluxe
Prajesh Ghimire
Quan Pham;
Rabie Abbas
Rae Tan
Rafael Gerena
Rafal Kociatkiewicz
Rahul Kapoor
Rahul V
Rajan Creative
Rajeesh Pk
Thalassery
Raquel Plaza
Ratan Mondal
Rayana Verissimo
Rebecca Cox
Reghupathy
Reid Mirre
René Berger
Renellyn Talabucon
Rich Cook
Rihnna Fe Macasaet Jakosalem
Rob Portil
Robert Hertel
Robert Marsland
Robert Nicholls
Robert Schneider
Robert Scully
Robert Sekulic
Robin Pietersen
Romain Pennacchio
Romain Verbeke
Romanos Tsouroplis
Ronie Eduardo Meque
Roscoe Beretta
Ryan Lockhart
Sachin Dangol
Sachin Sharma
Saini Deepanshu

Samantha Campbell
Samantha R Wilz
Sampsa Kuronen
Samuel Gyger
Sandra Wendeborn
Sascha Müller
Sascha Toussaine
Sascha Wolff
Saskia Bouten
Saunier Elodie
Scott Gruber
Scott R Schafer
Scott Whitehead
Sean Hester
Sean Porter
Sebastien Dufresne
Sergey Bekker
Sérgio Santos
Shawn Cicoria
Shaza Hakim
Shirley Allaway
Sibren Missiaen
Silvère Duplan
Silvestar Bistrović
Silviu Scutariu
Simon Kastenhuber
Simon Ramsay
Simone Moneta
Soufiane Ghzal
Souheil Mechlawi
Soumil Roy
Stef Spakman
Stefan Dourado
Stefan Gräwe
Stefan Günther
Stefan Meier
Stefan Osorio
Stefan Santana
Stephane Boudreau
Stephanie Frieze
Stephen Krupa
Steve Baker
Steve Perron

Steven Carter
Steven Hassall
Steven Stowers
Steven Woodson
Stian Kristiansen
Stuart Mcmillan
Sue Delsol
Sue Runkowski
Suné Du Preez
Sunny R Gupta
Swapnil Sidram Bandagi
Szabolcs Kertész
Tabytha Rourke
Taeyuun Thomas Min
Tammi Relles
Tania Pigem
Tarun Agrawal
Temmuz Kindermann-Güzel
Thomas Blaymire
Thomas Filius
Thomas Weitzel
Thomas Wilz
Tibor Vizi
Timo Rinta-Aho
Timon Borck
Timothy Burnett
Titti Filomeno
Tobias Alvik Hagen
Tobias Burkart
Toby Plewak
Tokiko Miyazato
Tom Arnold
Tom Frauenfelder
Tomas Miskerik
Tomasz Zwierzchoń
Torsten Stern
Tracey Wong
Tricia Smith
Tuukka Uskali
Uliana Spivachuk

Valerio Francescangeli
Vasileios Mitsaras
Vassilis Galopoulos
Veronika Brezovnik
Victor Baroli
Viktor Kalinin
Villaceque Jonathan
Vincenzo Landi
Vineesh Venugopal
Vineet Chaudhary
Ving Kris Saliendra
Vinodh Barnabas
Viren Jhonsa
Vishal M N
Vít Pečeňa
Vitalii Dvoretskyi
Vitalii Petrenko
Vlad Kyshkan
Vu Nguyen
Waheed Imran
Wahyu Goenawan
Wang Lei
Warren Laine-Naida
Wiktor Chojnacki
Will Sutton
William Goss
Wilma Warchol
Wiwat Ruengmee
Wojtek Zając
Wokoro Douye Samuel
Xinyi Hu
Yamil Arroyo
Yassir Yahya
Younes Adil
Yow-Long Lee
Yuniar Setiawan
Zachary Dalgleish
Zack Ward
Zell Liew
Ziad Naseriddin
Zoltan Veres

Dedicated to the wonderful Smashing Community — kind and generous people who have been supporting us over all these years. This book wouldn't be possible without your support. You are truly *smashing*.

YOUR JOURNEY STARTS HERE

Table of Contents

Making Design Systems Work In The Real World 11
Laura Elizabeth

Accessibility in Times of Single-Page Apps 47
Marcy Sutton

Production-Ready CSS Grid Layouts 81
Rachel Andrew

A Strategy Guide to CSS Custom Properties 137
Mike Riethmuller

Building an Advanced Service Worker 183
Lyza Gardner

A Guide To Loading Assets On The Web   235
Yoav Weiss

On Designing Conversations   319
Adrian Zumbrunnen

UX Design Of Chatbots And Virtual Assistants   365
Greg Nudelman

Crafting Experiences for AR/VR/XR   431
Ada Rose Cannon

Bringing Personality Back to the Web   469
Vitaly Friedman

Foreword

by Vitaly Friedman

Imagine you were living in a perfect world. A world where everybody has fast and stable connections, reliable and powerful devices, exquisite screens, and capable yet resilient browsers. The screens are diverse in size and pixel density, yet our interfaces adapt to varying conditions swiftly and seamlessly – not least due to the revival of design systems and advent of universally accepted design patterns. A world in which interfaces are predictable and intelligent, customers are delighted and respected, and even clients seem to allocate enough time and budget for both exciting and challenging projects.

What a glorious time for all of us — designers, developers, project managers, senior Webpack configurators and everybody in-between — to be alive, wouldn't you agree?

Well, we all know that the reality is slightly more nuanced and complicated than that. (Sorry for crushing your dreams at this point.) Yet why is it, when designing and building interfaces today, we often shoot ourselves in the foot, assuming a bit too much about everything from network conditions to screen resolutions to user behavior? Why is it, as we craft those precious pixels on our ultra-wide screens and fiber connections, we often fall into the trap of creating for a perfect, spotless world – one not unlike the world depicted above?

It's not for lack of willingness or empathy that we end up there. It's just infinitely difficult to keep all those unknowns and variabilities in mind when being on a tight deadline.

When setting out to create this book, our goal was to provide a highly practical guide – for designers and developers alike – with actionable insights to help all of us get better at our work right away. The book explores *new frontiers in web design*: new challenges and opportunities for more reliable and more flexible web experiences. But most importantly: it's the book about problems in the fragile, inconsistent, fragmented and wonderfully diverse web we find ourselves in today.

We'll explore how to make design systems work in the real world, and how to keep single-page apps accessible. We'll look into production-ready CSS Grid layout, CSS custom properties and service workers. We'll also establish guidelines for better performance of our websites and applications. We'll study how to design and build better conversational interfaces, chatbots, and virtual assistants, as well as AR/VR/XR experiences. The last chapter will guide you through some practical strategies to break out of generic, predictable, and soulless interfaces.

All of these chapters were written with care and thoroughness by active members of the wonderful web community. As you read them, think about how you could apply all those techniques to your ongoing and perhaps upcoming projects. I can only hope that the insights you'll read in this book will help you become better and smarter at your work.

We might not be able to reach that perfect world we can only dream of, but if this book manages to provide you with real value for your ongoing projects today, it will have served its purpose. With this in mind, flip over this page and dive in – just be sure to have your coffee ready next to it.

Happy reading!

CHAPTER 1

Making Design Systems Work In The Real World

Laura Elizabeth

Making Design Systems Work In The Real World

by Laura Elizabeth

Many of us have been there before: at some point, somebody in the company suggests we build a design system. It sounds pretty straightforward: the team creates a group of reusable components that everybody can mix and match to build reliable, consistent interfaces faster. In fact, it also sounds like a great tool to improve the workflow: the team stops wasting time reinventing the wheel with every new feature. Instead, everybody can use previously tested code with baked-in accessibility, visual language, functionality, and naming conventions — we all can focus on the bigger picture.

It's no wonder that according to UXPin's 2017–2018 Enterprise UX Industry Report,[1] 69% of enterprise companies either actively use a design system or are currently working on one.

Why, then, are we still struggling to make a design system stick? What seems to be the main problem? Is it that working with a component-driven workflow is too difficult, or that maintaining the design system feels like too much work? I wanted to find the answers. I spoketo many different companies, large and small, and there are a few key reasons kept cropping up:

1. The team didn't use it.
2. Management didn't support it.
3. After a while, the system stalled and it never recovered.

[1] http://smashed.by/uxpinreport

The interesting thing to note here is that none of these are technical issues. Many people I spoke to during my research for this chapter did articulate issues with the tech, but as it turned out, the tech wasn't *really* the problem. As we'll find out in this chapter, despite their robotic name, design systems are predominantly about one thing: people.

Roadblock #1: The Team Isn't Using The Design System

If you go to any conference or meet-up about design systems, I guarantee this question will come up at least once: "How do I convince other people in my organization to use the pattern library we created?"

It's an important question because no matter how grand your design system is (whether it's a pattern library with shareable components, editorial style guides, and so on), if people don't use it, there's not much point to it being there.

What stands in the way of people using a design system? I spoke to a developer who has been working on a small system in his spare time to help him and his team members produce website templates with already tested and quality-assured components. He felt like he was solving a real pain, not only for himself but also for his team. Working quickly with untested code is hard, not to mention risky, so he offered a solution to help. But he met with resistance:

> *I thought the team would pick it up instantly. But I found there were a lot of roadblocks stopping people from using it, like needing to switch to different naming conventions. People were used to doing things a certain way, and didn't want to spend time changing their process, which, for all intents and purposes, works perfectly fine.*

It turned out he needed a way to make the design system easier for his team members to adopt. As it stands, they don't have much of an incentive to use it. As far as they're concerned, their process is fine, albeit a little inefficient.

This is something they're still working on, but to understand why people don't use your design system, you first need to understand people and their motivations. Una Kravets argues that we need to be more empathetic to what people are being judged on at work.

> We're all being judged on different things. Most people aren't being judged on clean code. The engineers we're building this for are being judged on their ability to build the product and ship features quickly.

This can be applied to other disciplines, too. Designers aren't being judged on their articulation of design principles, or the use of symbols or smart objects in their tools. They're being judged on making great-looking products that are easy to use and increase conversions.

Ultimately, if your design system doesn't help your team meet *their* goals, you're going to have a hard time convincing them to use it.

Why Are You Doing This?

The first question you need to ask yourself is why you even want a design system in the first place. Or, more accurately, how will a design system help your company and its team members?

You could argue that *every* company would benefit from a design system. And there's truth in that. If we could flick a switch and suddenly have a design system, it would no doubt be beneficial.

But you don't make a design system by flicking a switch or pressing a button. A design system often takes an extraordinary amount of work, effort and time.

The benefits, or at least the promise of benefits, need to be worth the headaches of systemizing your website. It needs to be worth the change in process and workflow that your team will go through.

So how can you find out whether a design system is really something your team needs? Nathan Curtis from EightShapes recommends starting every design system with a phase of discovery:

> *A design system doesn't start with choosing a first color. Instead, ground a system in a strategy that discerns customer needs, sets objectives, explores and converges on a design direction, pitches a strategy, and obtain an organization's commitment.*
>
> — Nathan Curtis, "Starting a Design System"[2]

Before you even begin putting together your design system (or even if you've already started), you need to understand how your team currently works and what the biggest struggles are.

You can do this by talking to people directly, or sending out an anonymous survey. I find keeping questions fairly broad and open yields the best results. We're not trying to steer their answers in any way; we just want to find out how they work and what they'd like to change.

[2] http://smashed.by/startds

We can ask questions like:

1. What is your favorite part of your job?
2. What is the most frustrating thing about your day-to-day work?
3. If you could get rid of one aspect of your job, what would that be?
4. What are the main inefficiencies in your design/development process?
5. How can your company improve in terms of enabling people to get their work done more effectively?

It's important to note that we haven't mentioned design systems at all. We're not asking "Would you find a design system helpful?" or "Do you wish you were more efficient?" because most people want to be more efficient. What we want to find out is whether efficiency is *the* problem that's keeping them up at night.

With this exercise, we're looking for any commonalities that people are struggling with. What do people want to fix in their jobs? What will make them happier, more effective people?

Once you've collected the data, whether it's a survey or transcripts of conversations, you can start to normalize the data. I usually do this by creating a spreadsheet with different category headings based on feedback. So maybe "lack of efficiency" is one, or "difficulty in collaborating."

Beneath these you can paste the exact words people have used. For example, a developer's problem might be that they're under pressure to keep building new features, but they're getting complex and inconsistent styling from the designers for each new component. The codebase is becoming messy and they're struggling to meet the deadlines.

Feedback	Lack of efficiency	Need core styling	Can't build fast enough	Lack of shared vocabulary	Lack of collaboration
Every time we launch a new feature, I have to create a new component. I can't meet the deadlines!	x				
We have to wait too long to launch new features or they are sub-par		x			
Developers are never happy with what I give them but I don't understand what they want from me			x		
I'd be more effective if I could work closely with designers on new features out			x		
I never have enough time to get everything done				x	
The code base is a mess and it's making me inefficient					x
The shared workspace is counter-productive. I wish there was a quite zone I could go when I need to get some focused work done.			x		
Inconsistent styling makes it hard for me to know which bits of design is 'our' design.		x			

Then you you could have a product manager who is frustrated because they feel like they're waiting too long to launch new features. They also think that these features end up nothing like they had envisioned or talked about at the start.

And then you have designers; maybe they're frustrated because developers never seem happy with what they give them but they don't understand how they can be more helpful to them. These could be problems that are cropping up over and over in your company.

From these issues we can categorize them: whether it's creating core styles so developers don't have to code new styles for every new feature; or saving time by being able to launch faster using previously tested components; or even just creating a shared vocabulary so people can talk to one another and work together more effectively.

This will give you a good overview of the current problems in your company. The idea is that you'll use this to decide whether a design system is really what your company needs *right now*, or if there's something else you need to fix first.

If the answers show you could benefit from a design system, it'll also give you reasons why. Some companies might feel pretty efficient in their work, but team members struggle to collaborate with one another. Maybe testing is a big roadblock for your company – you're having to spend too long testing every component, which means you can't push out features fast enough.

This exercise will help you build your design system because you'll have a better understanding of *why* you're doing it. You'll be working towards what's best for your team, making the design system work for them and their needs, which will help with adoption.

Getting Your Team To Adopt The Design System

Unfortunately, it's all too easy for us to declare: "Our process is inefficient. We're solving a real problem" and expect that alone to be enough to ensure the survival of our design system.

In her book *Thinking in Systems,* Donella Meadows states that "information about the existence of a problem may be necessary but not sufficient to trigger action – information about resources, incentives, and consequences is necessary too."

Let's look at these one by one.

RESOURCES

People are busy. No matter how much technology advances to make our lives more efficient, we always find ways to fill that time. Most people aren't sitting around at work, twiddling their thumbs, looking for projects to work on. We have deadlines, meetings, and the allure of Twitter vying for our immediate attention.

How can you demonstrate to your team members that you have the resources available to put this into action without adding to their already full plates?

The developer I mentioned earlier in the chapter tried to convince his coworkers to stay behind after hours so he could run a workshop on how to use the design system he was working on. But because management hadn't provided any additional resources to do this during the day, he had a very low turnout: "I found it tough getting people to stay after hours. If management allowed a workshop in working hours I think I'd be more successful in showing people how a design system could help them."

Expecting people to spend their already limited free time learning about design systems sets the wrong precedent. You're already selling the design system as extra work from the get-go. It's important to make sure your team has the resources needed for a design system without putting the burden on your teammates.

INCENTIVES

We've already identified key problems a design system could solve in your company, and hopefully you've got a clear idea of what your coworkers desperately want fixed. In most cases, promising these pains will be solved is enough incentive.

When it doesn't work, the most likely cause is that you're not solving a problem painful enough for them. Sure, your coworkers want to be efficient, but is that enough? After all, they're getting paid the same amount each month no matter how efficient they are.

People are typically resistant to extra work. As Scott Berkun points out:[3]

Designers love to draft design principles, rules for their coworkers to follow to 'do good design' – this rarely works. […] The principles always create more work, or at least demand more thinking. But humans avoid work. […] There is little motivation for anyone to change their own behavior.

If you're finding team members still aren't motivated, you may need to dig deeper. James Ferguson from Skyscanner knew that different teams had each spent weeks or months creating various date pickers for their website. He knew these were a massive pain for people to create, and that it was unnecessary to create so many different variations when one would do.

If James could take away the need for all these teams to create their own date pickers and have a single, tested component, that would solve a huge problem for them:

[3] http://smashed.by/designprinciples

Our job is to be a pain killer, if you like. A lot of stuff we do isn't sexy work. It's a total pain in the ass, but we're doing it so that other people don't have to do that multiple times.

James wasn't selling being more efficient. He was selling no longer needing to recreate a date picker over and over again. It may sound trivial to some, but for his team this was a huge incentive to get some kind of system in place.

Find out what people are *really* struggling with, the kind of thing they'd pay someone to solve for them. Solve that first.

CONSEQUENCES

The last element mentioned is consequences. What will happen if a team doesn't get behind a design system?

Often, this is just a reverse of the incentives plus one additional caveat: the longer you wait before starting to systemize your website, the bigger the job is going to be.

Building a working system around your website isn't something that happens overnight. For many people, it's like organizing your home: you know you're going to have to tackle it at some point; but the longer you leave it, the more you're going to have to clean up.

Getting Your Team to Adopt the System Organically

When we talk about incentivizing your team to get behind a design system, often there's an obvious question in the back of people's minds: why not just impose a design system top-down?

It's a valid question. But if there's one theme that's cropped up again and again with companies that are successfully using a design system it's that you can't police a design system. What this means is, you can't create a library of reusable components, for example, and expect everyone to use and contribute it because you said so. Any type of design system is only as good as the people using it; if the people using it do so out of obligation, your design system is not going to be as stable.

This is something Brent Hardinge understood and took measures to curb during the creation of the design system for the Seventh-day Adventist Church.

> *We always knew organic growth was going to be better than having forced growth. We spent a lot of time building relationships with people who would benefit from the system. We'd meet them in person, talk to them and try to get to a certain level of trust before moving forward."*

Brent admits that this is a slower process, but he's found it to be far more lasting because through meeting people and talking to them, he's been able to create a deeper understanding of what a design system is and why it will benefit them.

Getting your team to use and contribute to a design system may not happen quickly, but as long as you're making their lives easier it will happen. Instead of taking a top-down approach and requiring every team member to use the design system, try taking a more collaborative approach – show them the benefits and let them decide whether this is something they want to get involved in.

Roadblock #2: Management Doesn't Support Your Design System

In our industry, we talk a lot about whether designers should learn to code, or whether developers need to learn design principles. One subject which doesn't get spoken about enough is business. One way or another, we're all invested in business. Whether you work in-house at a company, at a web agency, or you're a freelancer, we're all hired for the same reason: to make a company more profitable.

Yes, on the face of it we've been hired to improve the user experience, or to build out new features. But the end goal is still to make a profit. It doesn't have to be in a cutthroat, "we will make more money, no matter the cost" way. Increasing revenue means creating more jobs (and thus, supporting more families), better equipment and facilities, higher paychecks, and so on.

Those who immediately understand that make themselves more valuable to their employers. Not only that, they'll know exactly how to ask for what they want and get a positive response. This is important when talking about design systems because, as we mentioned earlier, we rely on getting support and resources from management to help us do the best jobs we can without sacrificing our personal time.

Ryan Rumsey wrote a great article about how he managed to get buy-in for his design system at Electronic Arts. With previous projects he had struggled with this, so he understood the value of putting together a case for a design system up front:

> *I've learned first-hand, through my experience, friends, and the design community at large, that asking for up-front buy-in on many projects is difficult. There's a certain amount of research and analysis needed to be done to get a good proposal together. It's made an even more difficult if data to evaluate the potential gains on efficiency is not available.*
>
> — Ryan Rumsey, "Selling a Design System before asking for buy-in"[4]

He found that asking for additional time or resources, without anything tangible in terms of what the business will see for it, meant the conversations often turned into subjective opinions, which is something management will struggle to sign off.

So how can we get them on board? From my research, I've seen two approaches:

1. Create a small, working pattern library or style guide — then use the results from that to ask for support later.
2. Ask for permission to start sytemizing your website upfront before you do any work on it.

---

4 http://smashed.by/askbuyin

Create A Small System First And Ask For Support Later

Many teams have had great success creating a working design system, using that to prove it's value, and then asking for additional resources later. Wolf Brüning from the German online retailer OTTO went down this route when his UX lead brought together a small team of three (himself, a front-end developer, and an external UX consultant) to start researching the best way to put together a design system.

They ended up bringing on one front-end developer from each of their product teams and ran a tightly scoped workshop, which resulted in a small, working pattern library. Adoption of the pattern library happened slowly, but organically. By simply referencing the pattern library instead of giving detailed specifications when asked about a component, they encouraged their team members to use it. And as their team members started to see the benefits, they began using it independently. This had a knock-on effect with management. Wolf noted:"As management saw the benefits of saving time, cleaner code, better UI quality, and reducing complexity, we also got buy-in from there."

Dedicating a set amount of time to try out a small style guide or pattern library and measuring its effects across your team is the simplest way to get buy-in. If you've already created something and it's proving to be effective, you'll be hard-pressed to find a manager who isn't willing to help sustain the efforts.

WHAT IF YOU DON'T HAVE THE RESOURCES JUST YET

Creating even a small pattern library can be a time-intensive process. Sometimes you simply don't have the resources at your disposal to be able to assemble a team, put one together *and* stay on top of your workload.

Not only that, involving a small portion of your team can actually impede adoption by alienating other people from the system. This is what Donna Chan and Isaak Hayes from AppDirect found during their early attempts at a design system:

 Upon completion, many of the style guides were basically put in the trash and not adopted, in the sense that they were unusable for the intended users. We heard comments like "They were a waste of time" and "All these resources were put in and what came of it?"

They learned that by trying to implement a design system on their own, they weren't helping the very people who were meant to be using it. Without support from management to work with everyone on the team, they were creating a system useful to only a handful of people.

In these cases, it's more effective to spend some up-front time ensuring you get buy-in from management so you get the resources you need to create something useful for your team. Which leads us to…

Asking For Permission Up-Front

The second option is asking for permission in advance, before you do any work on a design system. This has some obvious advantages, mainly that you can get the time and resources you need to work on the system; you don't need to try to fit it around your current workload.

But getting permission for such a mammoth task is notoriously difficult. Many stakeholders won't necessarily know what a design system is, so there's an educational element. Then we have the problem of a design system *sounding* simple ("We're just making our website reusable – like Lego!"); stakeholders may find it difficult to understand why you need a whole team just to work on the design system.

And when we try to talk about metrics, we usually want to see either an increase in efficiency, saving money, or making a profit. In other words, we want to see a return on our investment (ROI). Is the time and money that we need to put in to create a design system going to be less than what we get out of it? Not necessarily, says Alla Kholmatova in her book *Design Systems*:[5] "Some teams struggle for a while to see a return on investment in a modular system, which makes it hard to justify the investment in the first place."

An ROI assumes that the design system is adopted by the team, used consistently, and enables them to get results faster. None of this can be guaranteed but, as we'll see later in the chapter, there are things we can do to dramatically increase its chances of success.

5   http://designsystemsbook.com/

When approaching management, it's best not to go in with a full five-year roadmap for a design system. Instead, it's easier to get approval if you start small and low-risk. Remember, at this stage you're still researching whether a design system is the best option for right now. For some teams, a style guide and basic pattern library might be enough. A full-fledged design system might be too much work for too little reward *right now*. And if that's the case, don't force it until your company is ready.

So what exactly do management need to see in order to invest in the project? At a minimum, you'll need to be answering questions like:

- What is a design system and why would our company benefit from one?
- What kinds of results have similar companies been getting from implementing their design system?
- What resources do you need?
- What do you hope to achieve with a design system?
- What's your roadmap for getting one off the ground?
- How will you measure results and stay on track?

The first three points are pretty straightforward to get together. It's the last three I'd like to focus on now.

Setting Goals, Coming Up With A Roadmap, And Measuring Results

When it comes to goals, our last exercise gave us a start. The pains we identified are what we are aiming to eliminate. Now we need to go a bit deeper and turn those problems into something we can work toward solving.

One goal-setting solution gaining popularity is objectives and key results (OKRs). What I really like about OKRs is that they're used with team members, not just management. They empower every team with tasks that contribute to the higher-level business goals of an organization. A study by Sears Holding Company in 2013 found that OKRs have been shown to improve staff efficiency and the bottom line with their sales teams:[6]

For the group who used OKRs we saw an increase in their average sales per hour from $14.44 per hour to $15.67, or an average increase of 8.5%. This increase is not only statistically significant, but practically significant.

— Chris Mason, Senior Director,
Strategic Talent Solutions at Sears Holding Company

An OKR is essentially a framework of defining and tracking objectives and their outcomes. Honestly, it seems pretty similar to most goal-setting techniques, but I think OKRs just give a really simple, no-fluff framework, which is:

1. Where do I want to go? (the *objective*)
2. How will I know if I've got there? (the *key results*)

6   http://smashed.by/sears

You can use OKRs in any aspect of an organization (like the sales team example above), including your design system. The reason OKRs are great for design systems is because you're treating the system as a means to an end. In other words, the result isn't having a design system. The result is improving efficiency, or shipping more products.

This works well for management because instead of saying "This design system will absolutely make us more efficient, which will enable us to release more products and features, which will save us money," you're saying "We think this will help us do the former, and here's how we're going to test that hypothesis. We'll keep you in the loop the whole way and will only ask for more budget **if we can prove to you that this is effective**."

In doing this, you're reducing the risk for management. Instead of asking for half the team to create something which may or may not ever be adopted, you're asking for a few people in a limited time frame to test something that could drastically improve the company.

Let's look at an example of a company which has used OKRs successfully with a design system. Brent Hardinge from the Seventh-day

Adventist Church worked with Dan Mall from SuperFriendly on their design system (Adventist Living Pattern System: ALPS[7]), and they outlined exactly what they wanted to get out of it, and how they would measure whether it had been successful or not.

Their primary goal was to create a pattern library team members could use to envision what they wanted to build. It also needed to contain the code that could help their developers quickly bring their ideas to life.

That was their *why*. This will be different for every company. What's important is that they clearly defined what the goal was. They then split this into three objectives that helped them achieve this goal and laid out exactly how they'd measure it:[8]

1. **"Create a foundational, deeply-rooted pattern library."**

   - 1,800 Adventist websites (15% of the 12,000 sites) make obvious use ALPS.
   - 57 websites made by the General Conference (50% of the 114 sites produced by the GC) make obvious use of ALPS.
   - The first Adventist websites built for certain languages report 0 issues when building.

2. **"Allow for customization and individuality in the new pattern library."**

   - A trained person can build a site with the new design system in two days.
   - 2,400 Adventist sites (20% of the 12,000 websites) use one of the color preset options.

7 http://smashed.by/alps
8 http://smashed.by/adventist

3. **"Involve the community in the creation and adoption of the pattern library."**

    - 18 unions (30%) register in a feedback program.

    - 3 ideas originating from the community not included in the initial delivery of the design system have been adopted.

    - Design system adopted by 3 customers that weren't part of the initial interviews or any feedback program.

They kept track of each goal as they progressed with their design system, and it gave them the motivation to keep going and get the results they hoped for. Some they achieved, others they didn't, but OKRs are meant to be adapted as you learn more about what's achievable. This means if you set the bar too low or high, or are tracking the wrong metrics, you can change them.

On reflection, Brent found the OKRs essential: "The project is so broad, so the OKRs really helped us narrow down on what we were building and doing." When the time came to review their goals, they could celebrate the ones they achieved and, more importantly, review the ones they hadn't before setting new goals.

HOW TO MEASURE WHEN THE DATA IS SUBJECTIVE

A design system's effectiveness is notoriously difficult to measure. When I first started selling a systemized solution (like a pattern library) to clients, I tried to focus on the financial benefits; the reason being, if you can prove something will either make more money or save money, it becomes the easiest thing to sell.

Laura Elizabeth
@laurium

How much money do you think style guides and/or pattern libraries save your clients in the long run?

- **38%** A bucket load
- **42%** Maybe a little
- **9%** Stays the same
- **11%** They probably lose money

1,239 votes • Final results

However, just *saying* a pattern library would save money wasn't enough. I always felt a bit icky making a claim I didn't know was true. So I decided to go out and look for evidence.

A Twitter poll drew over 1,200 responses: a whopping 80% said they think style guides and pattern libraries save money; 9% said it made no difference; and 11% said they probably lose money.

But when I tried to dig deeper I found that nobody seemed to have any proof that money was saved. Their answers were based on intelligent reasoning, not evidence.

The issue is that a design system is always interconnected with other projects and improvements. A company doesn't shut down to build a pattern library. This makes it nearly impossible to define exactly which figures the design system is responsible for, and which were from an entirely different change.

But there are other benefits to a design system, Including some that would appeal directly to management. Here are four benefits that will get your managers or stakeholders on board:

1. **Getting new features into production much faster.**
   Management like to see movement. They like to see their company progressing and feel like they're keeping up with their competitors. Getting new features shipped faster would be a great incentive for most managers.

2. **Makes their company more attractive when hiring.**
   Managers deeply understand the importance of hiring the right people for a job. They put a lot of stock into making sure their company is attractive for potential employees. The benefits of a more systemized way of working has been gaining traction in the last few years and many of the top designers and developers are specifically looking for roles in companies that prioritize this. If a systemized way of working makes their company more attractive to exceptional employees, they'll more than likely listen.

3. **Saves the cost of a redesign every other year.**
   Redesigns or rebrands are always going to happen. But if you have a large website, a redesign is not only going to be incredibly time-consuming, but it'll cost the company an awful lot of money. To make matters worse, giant overhauls can have a negative impact on both SEO and user experience. In my mind, a redesign is far more risky than a design system!

   When you have a design system, you'll still be able to rebrand, optimize for conversions and improve the UX but you'll be doing it in a more sustainable and more effective way. You can work on and test small chunks of the website over time, rather than trying to overhaul the entire thing. Unlike a redesign which decreases in value over time, a design system has the opposite effect: it continuously increases in value.

4. **Everyone else is doing it!**
   Yes, managers experience FOMO too. Often, just knowing that this is something a handful of their competitors have bought into is enough to get them to listen up and take your request seriously.

This all goes back to what we talked about earlier. Ask yourself, "What is my manager being judged on?" Are they being judged on how well designers and developers work together? Not exactly. They're being judged on how they fare next to their competitors; they're being judged on profit, jobs being created, growth.

Now we know the outcomes we're looking for, we can get a better idea of how to measure those effects. We can split these into two categories: measuring based on shipping, and measuring based on time saved. Let's look at two case studies that have made these work.

Amazon Web Services Increased the Amount of Features They Shipped by 98% in One Year

Thomas Lobinger leads the team responsible for the design system at Amazon Web Services (AWS). Thomas noticed that since launching they went from releasing 722 new services and features in 2015 to a whopping 1,430 (around four per day) in 2017: an increase of 89%. Today AWS offers over 100 services with thousands of features. Each service team develops its own service's UI, so having a central system where everybody could use previously tested and approved components and user flows was a huge factor in releasing so much, so quickly.

Not only that, they found that with the design system they were continuously improving the UX, accessibility, and conversion rates throughout the AWS suite. When something worked, they could apply it elsewhere and dramatically improve their services in a fraction of the time.

When talking about the success of the system, Thomas said:

We were able to sell and grow the team because of the already apparent side effects from the simple UI components that we developed in the first weeks. From the very beginning, there was already customer value created. I would advise teams to start even if they don't feel like all the conditions are met. A small team and system can already provide huge benefits.

FutureLearn Found That a Component Had to Be Used Just Two or Three Times before It Became a Net Positive

At FutureLearn, Alla Kholmatova and her team did some experiments to measure the effect systemizing their components had on staff efficiency. She found that on average a reusable component took around two to three times longer to create than a one-off alternative – but the time was made up when they reused a component twice or more. This provided a good baseline as to when it would make sense for the team to create a reusable component or a custom one.

There is one small caveat to measuring a design system based on saving time: you can inadvertently have a negative effect on the user. As Alla and her team discovered, the increase in productivity they enjoyed led them to proactively try to reuse a component as many times as possible. After all, the more they used it, the more cost-effective it became.

However, this didn't always give the best results:

 We then found we were reusing components for the sake of it, to fit it into our pattern library, even if it wasn't the best solution for the user. Now we're spending time redoing components to make them more usable.

By all means, encourage and celebrate efficiency with your design system; just make sure you do what FutureLearn did and keep an eye on your users. Make sure your reusable components aren't detrimental to their experience.

Now we've managed to get management on board, and we're clued up on how to encourage your team to use the design system, what happens after the initial rush wears off? What happens if (or more likely when) you stall?

Roadblock #3: Your Design System Stalls

Pretty much every design system stalls at some point. No matter how motivated you are at the start, progress is going to feel slow and frustrating at times. It's simply part of creating a design system.

When you first start work on the system, there will probably be a ton of excitement. People will be motivated, and you'll feel like things are going to move very quickly. Then you'll get hit with roadblock after roadblock. You'll end up in these long, drawn out discussions about naming conventions, or trying to work out some problem you hadn't foreseen.

Before you know it, weeks have passed and your boss is asking to see progress on the design system. You don't have anything and you're essentially spinning your wheels and the program risks getting axed.

This is a pretty pessimistic outlook but not uncommon. Fortunately, there's a fix. The problem isn't that you're not cut out for systemizing your website. It's not that your company is too complex to make a design system work. It's usually just a misalignment between strategy and implementation. These are two very different but equally important tasks, and it's important to understand and recognize the difference.

What tends to happen is that we mix up these two tasks. We're implementing something and the conversation turns to strategy. We get on tangents, we find new issues that we hadn't considered before; and then at the end of the day, week, or month, we realize we're no farther along. We've made no measurable progress, aside from a lot of conversations.

What we need to do is give ourselves dedicated time for each task. Save up all the big-picture conversations for a strategy day, when you get together the key decision-makers in your design system team and iron out all the high-level details that have cropped up. It also gives you a chance to reassess your goals and make any adjustments before the next strategy day.

Conversations could include things like:

- Should our components follow naming conventions based on a particular theme?

- Should we open-source or build a marketing website around our design system?

- How should we accept contributions to the design system? Can anybody contribute or should we have an application process?

These are questions that are probably going to require a lot of discussion. Saving them up for when you have time to address them is going to be a huge help for you and your team. It leaves you free to work on making measurable progress with the design system, without being held back by too many roadblocks. When you're working on your day-to-day stuff, if you find a conversation turns to strategy, you can simply delay talking about it until your next strategy session.

This is simply an exercise in learning to identify the difference between strategy and implementation, noticing it, and being able to compartmentalize it. If you do this, you'll find your design system makes progress and you'll be far less likely to give up out of frustration.

If you still find yourself stalling and your team lacks motivation, Alan Wilson, a designer at Adobe, suggests getting past a stall is often as simple as taking a break:

I find that I need occasional breaks – sometimes just an hour or a day, sometimes longer, like a week – to work on other (non-design system) things. For instance, it's nice to design a product using your design system, which means you come back to design systems with more empathy for your customer.

He finds that switching from working on a design system to working *with* a design system can be enough to step back, see it with fresh eyes, and understand what needs to be done next to keep it progressing.

Above all, we need to remember that stalls are natural, and they don't necessarily mean your system is broken. But they can also indicate that there's something wrong with the direction you're going in. Some companies find they can't progress until they change how the system is governed. Others find they can't move forward until they change how components are organized.

It doesn't mean you've failed, but it does mean that you need to take a step back and try to figure out why your system is stalling. Is it because the effort you're putting in isn't equal to the benefits? (And if so, why?) Or is it just because you haven't seen tangible progress for a few weeks?

A Roadmap For A Successful Design System

Now we've gone over the three main roadblocks to making a design system stick (team members didn't adopt it, management didn't support it, and it stalled and never recovered), let's look at a roadmap for how you can start a design system and give yours the best chance of succeeding.

1. FIND YOUR PURPOSE

The first thing is to find your motivation for having a design system. Why do you want one? What will that do for your fellow team members? How will this serve your users? And how will it help grow your company?

It's important not to gloss over this stage and come up with vague principles. Dig deep into your company's culture and find out whether a design system is what's needed right now. (If it's not, don't do it yet.) As you'll come to realize, if you haven't already, a design system is not about technology. It's about people. A big part of this journey is going to be spent talking to people and helping solve their problems.

2. START SMALL, WITH AN EXPERIMENT

There's a lot of risk in creating a design system. What if nobody uses it? What if we put in all this work and we don't see any benefits? I wouldn't recommend anyone going all in on systemizing all your flagship projects at once.

It's much safer to test the waters with something small. Maybe there's a new feature you can test your system on? Perhaps there's a particular flow that (if you did nothing else) would benefit a large amount of people. Even a simple style guide is a good exercise to start seeing how this could help your company.

When starting a design system, look for something small you can test the system and its adoption on. The goal is to help people do their jobs better and more efficiently. If you do that, you won't get any backlash. If you encounter resistance or people aren't interested, you may need to go back and assess why.

3. GET PAST THE STALL (AND HAVE REGULAR CHECK-INS)

Setting up regular check-ins to focus on the goals and strategy of a design system will help reduce the likelihood of a stall halting work on it. Spend at least one day at regular intervals (say, every four to six weeks) taking a high-level look at your design system and reassessing your goals. This frees up your day-to-day work and enables you to focus on getting things done, as opposed to being stuck in long conversations about the overall strategy.

4. DON'T FOCUS ON WHAT EVERYONE ELSE IS DOING

It's easy to get caught up in what other companies are doing with their design systems. Every day, it seems, bigger, better, shinier design systems are unveiled. Focusing too much on this can end up crippling your efforts to create a useful design system. You'll see things other companies are doing and think, "We need to do that too!" But remember that a design system's success is measured by how many people it helps, not how many claps you get on Medium.

A great example of a team who did their own thing despite everyone else doing it another way is WeWork. When they built their design system, Plasma, they assumed they would create a dedicated website to show the system, specs, examples, and guidelines because it was the done thing. They started a Google doc to get all their components documented before pushing it to a live website, but over time they realized the doc had everything they need to document a design system. It has built-in navigation, the ability to add comments and collaborate, it's accessible to everyone on their team, and doesn't need any special skills to update it.

Andrew Couldwell, the design lead on Plasma said about the success of the Google doc:

> As the document grew, I realized it did exactly what we needed it to – the only reason to create a public, branded website for this would be as a "pride project" for WeWork Digital, or as a resource if we open-source the system.
>
> — Andrew Couldwell, "Plasma design system"[9]

9   http://smashed.by/plasma

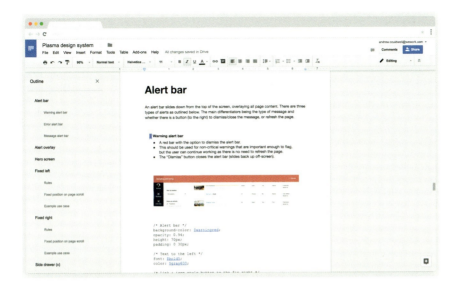

There are many benefits to creating a public design system (accountability, PR, education) but WeWork's ability to look past what everyone else was doing and make a judgement on whether this was the best solution for them, right now, ended up paying off. So don't worry about what you feel like you *should* be doing, just work on what's going to be most effective for your company.

5. BECOME AN EVANGELIST...

Having at least one person in charge of keeping the design system front-of-mind is going to be a huge help when working on a design system. When you're starting out, it's not likely that you're going to have a full-time role for a design systems lead (though as you grow, this becomes a necessity), but you will benefit from somebody who will act as an evangelist for the system.

The evangelists job is to be in charge of the design system, acting as a go-between for everybody using it. For that reason, it's important to have someone who can easily speak to designers, developers, marketers, editors etc. You're looking for a people person who's incredibly enthusiastic about systems – not necessarily the most technical.

The evangelist's job is to be in charge of the design system, acting as a go-between for everybody using it. For that reason, it's important to have someone who can easily speak to designers, developers, marketers, editors, and so on. You're looking for a people person who's incredibly enthusiastic about systems – yet not necessarily the most technical.

These people are also in charge of educating the team about design systems and keeping everyone updated with progress. Alan Lindsay from Experian organized an entire conference called One UX for their team members around the world to learn about design systems and get excited about using them.

Even though Experian has incredible design talent and has always been a very innovative company, prior to the conference they operated in disparate design teams that sometimes didn't even know of one another's existence. Alan ended up becoming "chief evangelist." He uncovered pockets of amazing talent all across the globe, and organized a community to discuss challenges. They eventually met together at One UX to work out solutions, including creating the global design system they enjoy today. Considering so many people contribute to the design system, they found having at least one person in charge of evangelism a huge help:

Given our current situation, evangelism was absolutely essential – someone had to dedicate time and back this vision to make it real and it was my privilege to start a conversation and gather these incredible people in the same room so we could elevate the company together. Now we're in the process of formalizing several roles that naturally emerged through this journey because the business recognizes how valuable managing this collaboration is. It's not always easy – there are challenges with evangelism like every other area of business – but the payoff is completely worth it!

To have a successful design system, at least one person must be in charge of keeping it in people's minds, making sure everyone is happy with it, collating feedback, and educating others.

6. …BUT DON'T MANDATE

Perhaps the most important thing to remember if you want a successful design system is that no matter how much you believe in it, don't force anyone to use it. You shouldn't have to persuade anyone to use a design system. The benefits should be so clear that people will want to use it. As Wolf Brüning said, "The most evangelizing is done by our library itself, as it provides a great way to save time and build better product by not reinventing the wheel again and again."

If getting people to use your design system is like pulling teeth, it's not doing its job.

A Design System Is About People

Design systems are often presented as a technical challenge. What tech stacks should we use? How do we make it "living? Is this a molecule or an organism? These are certainly valid questions but not the most important ones. Design systems that succeed are not the ones with the best tech, they're the ones that help the most people.

As James Ferguson puts it:

> "It's not about your design skills, it's not about your engineering skills, it's about your problem and people skills. Trying to find that level of people skills **and** engineering is difficult. You need to get out there and speak to people, help people out and be really proactive. That's the hardest problem. It's always people."

If your design system improves efficiency, team collaboration, user experience, and even impacts the bottom line, you're onto a winner. But at the same time, no design system is perfect. Striving for perfection is admirable but unrealistic. Perhaps we need to learn to be OK with imperfection because the most successful systems are the ones that can embrace those imperfections, adapt quickly, and have a clear purpose that benefits not just businesses, but people.

About The Author

Laura Elizabeth is a designer turned product creator. She predominantly helps developers conquer their fear of design and runs *designacademy.io*, a training platform where developers can learn how to design.

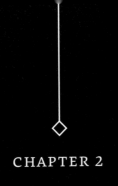

CHAPTER 2

Accessibility in Times of Single-Page Apps

Marcy Sutton

Accessibility in Times of Single-Page Apps

by Marcy Sutton

An increasing number of web applications and websites are architected and rendered entirely with JavaScript these days, both client- and server-side. Accessibility is as important as it's ever been, as more of the products and services users depend on move online – things like paying bills, shopping, education, and more. Without accessibility, people with disabilities will likely encounter barriers preventing them from using your shiny new web application.

Imagine using a screen reader to navigate a checkout form and finding you cannot complete the transaction, meaning you have to share your bank details with someone to complete it for you. Try using a web application with only a switch device powered by moving your cheek: would you be able to watch your favorite TV shows without the use of your arms? There are so many scenarios[1] where people encounter barriers to using the web – when holding a baby, when moving from one place to another, or when carrying a heavy bag, for example. Some scenarios are minor inconveniences, others require a high amount of responsibility and attention, while other problems are severe enough to compromise someone's independence and privacy. Even if you don't think accessibility applies to you now, it's important to recognize that life can change in an instant for anyone.

1 http://smashed.by/a11yscenarios

Fortunately, we can apply web accessibility basics[2] to our websites and web applications, and start to make a huge impact. However, when developing single-page apps (SPAs), there are some unique accessibility requirements we must consider to avoid constructing barriers for users with disabilities. And designing and developing inclusively not only benefits the roughly 15% of people with some kind of disability[3] – it benefits absolutely everyone.[4]

The Gist of Accessibility in SPAs

When a traditional web page reloads, it causes a user's keyboard focus to go to the `<body>`; screen readers will also announce the page `<title>`. When views change in a web application or site delivered with JavaScript, there typically isn't a traditional page reload. Instead, views and subviews are updated dynamically and the user's focus point is often left in the same place. To improve usability for someone who can't use a mouse, the keyboard focus must be explicitly handled to guide them through the application. Screen reader users also need to be informed of visual changes.

It's possible to implement proper accessibility with frameworks like React, Vue, and Ember. With development so heavily focused on JavaScript, however, it's too easy to implement HTML experiences without proper semantics or keyboard interactivity. Making matters worse, framework documentation and UI libraries are chock full of accessibility anti-patterns, and bad practices spread far and wide.

2   http://smashed.by/a11ybasics
3   http://smashed.by/15perc
4   http://smashed.by/allbenefit

It's critical for users with disabilities that collectively we do better at this. Fortunately, there are techniques and tools you can use to encourage better coding practices, catching accessibility violations before they ship.

To help you work through these challenges and provide more accessible user experiences, in this chapter we'll dive in to the aspects of single-page apps that impact accessibility, including HTML and ARIA semantics, keyboard interactivity, focus management, screen reader announcements, and tooling. By the end of this chapter, no matter which framework you use (if any), you should have enough knowledge and skills to work accessibility into a modern JavaScript web application.

Semantic Structure in JavaScript Apps

H1-H6 headings are extremely important for any web app or web page. These elements not only create an informational hierarchy for your content, but they also provide helpful navigation for screen reader users. In the JAWS and NVDA screen readers, users can hit the **H** key to cycle through headings in browse mode.[5] By starting your HTML hierarchy with an `h1` for the most important heading and following with `h2`–`h6` tags in order, you can create a healthy content structure. CSS classes can help when selecting the appropriate heading level for your content, while fitting in with an established brand guide.

HTML5 landmark elements such as `header`, `nav`, `footer`, `section`, `article`, `main` and `aside` group content into areas more easily discovered by screen readers. In a JavaScript application where subviews are split into separate component files, landmarks chunk nicely into vari-

5   http://smashed.by/srmodes

ous includes and templates. When rendered, these come together with headings to form a complete page structure that's helpful for blind users to understand and navigate.

For example, here's a main UI component from a React.js application:

```
// component-main.js
import SubnavView from "./subnav-view.js"
import ContentView from "./content-view.js"
export default function MainView (props) {
  const { view, className } = props
  return <main tabIndex="-1" {...props}>,
    <h1>{i18n`My Single Page App`)}</h1>,
    <SubnavView className="panel-subnav" />,
    <ContentView className="panel-main" />,
  </main>
}
```

In the above code snippet, `MainView` ultimately returns a `main` landmark with `tabIndex="-1"`. Focus management can then script the user's focus to or into `<main>`, but that `main` is also discoverable as a landmark with its own screen reader shortcut. Inside `main` are an `h1` heading and a few subviews, pulled in as child components, each with their own logical landmarks and `h2`–`h6` headings. Depending on which part of the app you're working on, you'll need to select the most appropriate landmark and heading levels for your content. This example uses `main` only, but for a larger application it might be more appropriate to use `header`, `main`, and `footer` as top-level landmarks.

In reusable UI components, making heading levels configurable with a prop is a nice touch – especially if it renders real `h1`–`h6` heading elements, as opposed to the ARIA `heading` role and level (which is less widely supported).[6]

6 http://smashed.by/html5ally

Customizable components can fit easily into any content hierarchy without a headache.

Semantics are all about choosing the best candidate element for the the job, while crafting an informative page structure for an accessible user experience. Start with native HTML elements that give you the most appropriate functionality for free; if you're having to reimplement a lot of the same features as links, selects, or inputs, take a closer look at the native HTML elements. You can also get pretty far with the blessed style patterns on *WTFForms*.[7]

If there's still something you can't style, open an issue in a browser or web standards bug tracker (seriously – you'll do us all many favors. Reach out to the author if you need help!). In many cases, completely custom user interface components aren't worth the hassle of maintenance or the technical debt accrued with lacking accessibility.

Need more convincing about the importance of semantics in modern web applications? Consider alternative ways of consuming content, which will only increase as technology continues to evolve. Not only do browsers and search engines use semantic structure for parsing and ranking, but screen readers and voice interfaces make use of it too. This shared language enables many technologies we already use today, and can lead us to even more robust, innovative, and inclusive technologies tomorrow.

7   http://wtfforms.com/

Interactivity

There's a lurking misconception we should clarify right off the bat: unless explicitly turned off by the user in their web browser, screen reading software *does* use JavaScript when announcing content. In fact, this is a helpful reality when coding JavaScript applications for both blind users and sighted keyboard users.

Interactivity in an application built with React, Vue, Angular, Ember, or a newer kid framework on the block has the same requirements as a regular webpage. As a single-page app developer, you are tasked with including interactive UI controls that can be reached and operated with the keyboard, no matter how they get included in your app. Elements might be referenced as JSX objects with a DOM factory, like in React (prior to version 16.0.0),[8] or with regular HTML in a template.[9] There are lots of different flavors, but the requirements for accessible *rendered* HTML are always the same.

When compared to unreachable `<div>` soup, making something keyboard-interactive goes a long way towards web accessibility. A good rule of thumb for coding interactivity is that if something is operable with the mouse, it must also work with the keyboard. Typically, the best approach is to make controls multi-modal,[10] rather than implementing separate affordances[11] for keyboards or screen readers.

An exception is made when a click event is redundant, such as a larger hit area on a card pattern[12] that also contains a focusable link going to the same place (this redundancy also benefits touch users). When your

8 http://smashed.by/domfactory
9 http://smashed.by/userinputangular
10 http://smashed.by/multimodal
11 http://smashed.by/affordances
12 http://smashed.by/a11ycards

carpal tunnel or developer elbow flares up and you can't use a mouse anymore – like many of your disabled users – you'll be grateful you made keyboard navigation central to your app's experience.

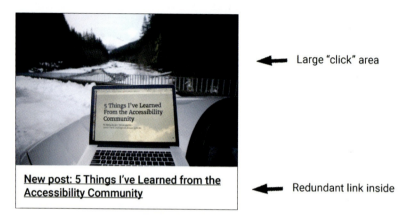

Card pattern with link

USING THE TABINDEX ATTRIBUTE

By starting with natively focusable elements such as buttons, links, and inputs, you'll get functionality for free: both keyboard interactivity and accessibility information from their implicit roles, states, and properties. You can make a custom UI control like an ARIA checkbox accessible with the tabindex attribute (along with the necessary role="checkbox", aria-checked state[13] and an accessible name,[14] plus JavaScript to respond to user events). But in doing so, you can quickly see how custom controls snowball into something more complicated.

Be careful not to abuse tabindex on non-interactive elements, as too many extra tab stops can be a keyboard user's productivity killer.

13 http://smashed.by/ariacheckedstate
14 http://smashed.by/a11yname

Screen readers also have functions to navigate text content, so you don't have to make non-interactive content part of the tab order.

For custom widgets with ARIA, start with `tabindex="0"`[15] and avoid positive integer values unless you're dying to manage an entire application's tab order (spoiler: it's highly error-prone, and your footer should absolutely not come first in the tab order). You can remove a keyboard-interactive element from the tab order using `tabindex="-1"`. This also has the effect of making any element focusable by script, such as a focus management target (see the upcoming section for more information).

FOCUS STYLING

No matter what element or technique you use for keyboard interactivity, it's critically important to include visible focus states so users know where they are on the screen. Resist using the horribly exclusionary sledge hammer `* { outline: 0; }` in your CSS, which removes focus outlines for everyone. Instead, for truly picky users[16] you can employ tools to be more specific with input styling, such as What Input,[17] or the proposed CSS4 pseudo-selector `:focus-visible`.[18]

Including `:focus` alongside your `:hover` CSS styles is also a good way to go – it highlights that something interactive by mouse should be focusable too. However, if you're using custom `:focus` styles as a replacement for the browser's default focus style (often a blue ring or dotted border) on everything, make sure you've tested every user interaction for a visible and contrasting focus style.

15 http://smashed.by/tabindex
16 http://smashed.by/buttonfocus
17 http://smashed.by/whatinput
18 http://smashed.by/focusvisible

```
// styling focus and hover at the same time
a:link {
  color: black;
  text-decoration: underline;
}
a:hover, a:focus {
  color: white;
  background-color: black;
  text-decoration: none;
}
```

A debugging strategy: tabbing through any kind of web page or application, you should be able to reach and operate every interactive control using only the keyboard. Sighted users should also see where they are on the screen. Provide a better keyboard browsing experience by preventing focus in non-visible content like inactive sidebar menus with CSS `display: none` or the default HTML `hidden`. See "Disabling Background Content" later in the chapter.

THE "<DIV> BUTTON"

The biggest, most obvious interactivity offender in single-page apps and UI libraries is what I like to call "the `<div>` button."

```
<div onclick="doTheThing()">Click here</div>
```

You can bind a click event to any element, including a `<div>` (and in rare cases, this is fine), but the problem is that a `<div>` isn't focusable by default. We have to do a significant amount of work to make it accessible.

```
<div role="button"
    onclick="doTheThing()"
    onkeydown="alsoDoTheThing()"
    tabindex="0">
    All this work just to make a DIV accessible
</div>
```

Or, we can just use a `<button>` element and be done with it:

```
<button onclick="doTheThing()">Much easier</button>
```

If styling is your reason for using a `<div>` button, here's some common reset CSS so you can put that argument to rest:

```
button {
  background-color: black;
  border-radius: 0;
  border: none;
  color: white;
  -webkit-appearance: none;
}
```

Focus Management

In the absence of traditional page reloads, it's critical to manage the user's keyboard focus to guide them through your JavaScript application. Views are updating; UI components are toggling with the mouse; modal windows are opening and closing; items are being deleted from the DOM.

Can you guess what happens to the user's keyboard focus in these scenarios? If you don't explicitly handle it, focus can be lost or do absolutely nothing; these are huge barriers to someone relying on the keyboard to navigate.

It's worth mentioning that not every situation calls for managing focus with JavaScript. Later in this chapter, we'll discuss screen reader announcements for the times a user's focus shouldn't be moved, but they still need to be notified that things are happening.

These are two different tools at our disposal for creating accessible experiences. But in general, focus management is the more common and better supported technique of the two. Plus, it impacts all keyboard users – not just screen reader users.

UPDATING VIEWS

As mentioned above, when a user clicks a link going to a different page in your single-page app, they are usually taken there asynchronously, without a traditional page reload. Sighted mouse users can see the transition, navigate the page, and continue on their way. However, for a keyboard or screen reader user, their focus is often left in the same place: the link they clicked with the **Enter** key. If this link is inside of a navigation drawer that opens over the content, the drawer may stay open until they tab through the page and click elsewhere. For these users, we can create a more accessible keyboard experience by sending focus to the new content and closing any side navs or component layers.

Let's look at a basic React component to help explain this scenario:

```
class App extends Component {
  pageFocus() {
    this.setState({menuOpen: false});
    this.main.focus();
  }
  isMenuOpen(state) {
    if (state.isOpen) {
      setTimeout(function() {
        this.firstMenuItem.focus();
      }, 100);
    }
  }
  constructor (props) {
    super(props)
    this.firstMenuItem = React.createRef();
    this.main = React.createRef();
    this.state = { menuOpen: false }
```

```
    }
    render() {
      return (
        <Router>
          <div className="App">
            <div className="menu-wrap">
              <Menu
                isOpen={this.state.menuOpen}
                onStateChange={ this.isMenuOpen.bind(this) }>
                <ul>
                  <li><Link
                    to="/"
                    ref={this.firstMenuItem}
                    onClick={this.pageFocus.bind(this)}
                    >
                      <i className="fa fa-fw fa-home" aria-hidden="true" />
                      <span>Home</span>
                  </Link></li>
                  <li><Link
                    to="/gearlist"
                    onClick={this.pageFocus.bind(this)}>
                      <i className="fa fa-fw fa-suitcase" aria-hidden="true" />
                      <span>Gear Packing List</span>
                  </Link></li>
                  <li><Link
                    to="/trips"
                    onClick={this.pageFocus.bind(this)}>
                      <i className="fa fa-fw fa-plane" aria-hidden="true" />
                      <span>Trip Suggestions</span>
                  </Link></li>
                </ul>
              </Menu>
            </div>
            <div className="primary">
              <main id="main" ref={this.main} tabIndex="-1">
                <Route path="/" component={Home} />
                <Route path="/gearlist" component={GearList} />
                <Route path="/trips" component={Trips} />
              </main>
            </div>
          </div>
        </Router>
      );
    }
  }
export default App;
```

In this example, our app instantiates a menu component with an unordered list and links inside. Those links hook into React Router, which outputs accessible anchor elements with `href` attributes and proper client-side routing. We can provide additional interaction support for keyboard users by layering on click events that do two things:

1. Close the open menu when the view changes (if not already handled)
2. Send focus to the main element, putting keyboard and screen reader users in the appropriate place in the page

Rather than leave them in the same spot without a page reload, we know where their focus should be sent by the link they clicked. (The new *createRef API*[19] in React 16.3.1 makes this easy.) By handling focus gracefully, users aren't forced to tab through the entire app looking for the right spot.

TOGGLING UI COMPONENTS AND LAYERS

Focus management is a critical technique for accessibility with the way HTML is appended and removed in JavaScript-heavy apps. When interactive widgets like dropdown menus or modal dialogs are opened, we have to send focus to the first focusable item to get keyboard users to the right spot for additional interaction. This also has the effect of announcing new content in a screen reader.

For widgets and overlays that appear over the content, managing focus is especially important if the trigger (usually a link or a button) and the widget contents are in different areas of the DOM. Hitting the **Tab** key to reach something seemingly close by can have unexpected results,

19 http://smashed.by/reactref

depending on the source order. In these scenarios, a keyboard user can easily get lost and not be able to find their way back. How much time would you spend before giving up and leaving the site?

As a convention, use JavaScript to send focus into new layers when they open, putting the user's focus in the right place. Also be sure to wire up the **Escape** key to provide an easy exit, sending focus back to the triggering UI control. This common navigation paradigm applies to multiple patterns, including modal windows, custom listboxes, and tooltips.

You can read more about common keyboard navigation in the *ARIA Authoring Practices Guide*.[20]

From a UX point of view, it sometimes makes sense to add a different affordance for keyboard and screen reader use, such as a button alternative for a discoverable swipe gesture (which isn't truly discoverable for some mobile users). Many users with cognitive disabilities can also benefit from more explicit and keyboard-accessible controls. The *"Offer choice" principle of inclusive design*[21] explains this nicely.

SKIP LINKS

A common convention of large applications is to provide one or two skip links to the most important HTML sections. An unordered list of links can point users to the major landmarks of your app, using in-page links and the `tabindex="-1"` attribute (needed to catch focus in some browsers):

---

20 http://smashed.by/waiaria
21 http://smashed.by/offerchoice

```
<ul class="skip-links>
  <li><a href="#globalNav">Global navigation</a></li>
  <li><a href="#main">Main content</a></li>
  <li><a href="#footer">Footer</a></li>
</ul>
<header aria-label="Global" tabindex="-1">
<!-- navigation links here -->
</header>
<main tabindex="-1">
<!-- main content here -->
</nav>
<footer aria-label="Global" tabindex="-1" role="contentinfo">
<!-- global footer here -->
</footer>
.skip-links {
    list-style: none;
    margin: 0;
    padding: 0;
    position: relative;
}
.skip-links li a {
    background-color: #fff;
    display: block;
    left: -600000px;
    padding: 0.5em;
    position: absolute;
}
.skip-links li a:focus {
    left: 0;
}
[tabindex="-1"]:focus {
    outline: none;
}
```

DISABLING BACKGROUND CONTENT

One of the most frequent focus management issues seen on the web is when focusable controls in background layers aren't properly disabled. Keyboard or screen reader users can get lost navigating through content that's visually hidden or obscured, but not actually disabled. This applies to side navs, modal windows, tab switchers, dropdown menus, navigation takeovers, and more.

To properly disable a control, you have a number of options, some more complex than others. Let's narrow it down.

- **Is the inactive content hidden from everyone?**
- Use CSS `display: none`. This turns the display off *and* disables all focusable items inside. If you have to animate it, you can transform `opacity` and set the `display` on the last keyframe of a CSS animation or after a `setTimeout` in JavaScript.
- **Is the background layer visible but dimmed, and/or covered with an overlay?**

Traditionally, the steps required to disable a background layer include:

- Using a focus trap with JavaScript[22] to keep the user's focus inside the active content. But this isn't always enough, especially in mobile screen readers. You also need to:
- Walk the DOM[23] for your inactive content and put `tabindex="-1"` on each focusable item inside to remove it from the tab order. (Check out the helpers from ally.js.)[24]

---

22 http://smashed.by/focustrap
23 http://smashed.by/walkthedom
24 http://smashed.by/focusable

- Put `aria-hidden="true"` on the inactive content to remove it from assistive technology. This must be paired with the `tabindex="-1"` to avoid "ghost controls" with no accessibility information.

Here's what a snippet of background HTML should look like when properly disabled:

```
<body>
  <main id="app" aria-hidden="true" class="dimmed">
    <h1>My App</h1>
    <p>You've come to the right place. <a href="/about" tabindex="-1">About the author</a></p>
    <button onclick="openModal()" tabindex="-1">Sign up for updates</button>
  </main>
  <dialog aria-labelledby="modal-header">
    <button class="close" aria-label="Close modal" onclick="closeModal()">
       <span aria-hidden="true" class="icon-close"></span>
    </button>
    <h2 id="modal-header">Sign up</h2>
    <form></form>
  </dialog>
  <script>
  var app = document.querySelector('main');
  var triggerBtn = app.querySelector('button');
  var dialog = document.querySelector('dialog');
  function focusTrap(state) {
    if (state.active) {
      // enable focus trap
    } else {
      // disable focus trap
    }
  }
  function openModal() {
    app.setAttribute('aria-hidden', 'true');
    focusTrap({ active: true });
    modal.setAttribute('open', '');
    modal.firstChild.focus();
  }
  function closeModal() {
    modal.removeAttribute('open');
```

```
    focusTrap({ active: false });
    app.setAttribute('aria-hidden', 'false');
    triggerBtn.focus();
  }
  </script>
</body>
```

In reality, achieving the markup above can be quite advanced, especially for large pages – and particularly the focus trapping portion cross-platform. For this reason, I highly recommend using the HTML5 inert attribute being reproposed through web standards.[25] With a polyfill, you can disable an entire region of an HTML page with a single attribute and no DOM walking. Just like with `aria-hidden="true"`, which can't be overridden further down the tree, it's easiest to set inert on a sibling to your active content. Even with a polyfill, I can guarantee it's a lot less work than the alternative of manipulating aria-hidden and tabindex on every focusable control.

Here's the same example with `inert`, which requires less work than handling both `aria-hidden="true"` and `tabindex="-1"` on each interactive element:

```
<body>
  <main id="app" inert>
    <h1>My App</h1>
    <p>You've come to the right place. <a href="/about">About the author</a></p>
    <button onclick="openModal()">Sign up for updates</button>
  </main>
  <dialog aria-labelledby="modal-header">
    <button class="close" aria-label="Close modal">
      <span aria-hidden="true" class="icon-close"></span>
    </button>
```

[25] http://smashed.by/inert

```
      <h2 id="modal-header">Sign up</h2>
      <form>...</form>
    </dialog>
    <script>
    var app = document.querySelector('main');
    var triggerBtn = app.querySelector('button');
    var dialog = document.querySelector('dialog');
    function openModal() {
      app.setAttribute('inert', '');
      modal.setAttribute('open', '');
      modal.firstChild.focus();
    }
    function closeModal() {
      modal.removeAttribute('open');
      app.removeAttribute('inert');
      triggerBtn.focus();
    }
    </script>
  </body>
```

DELETING ITEMS FROM THE DOM

Some user interfaces provide a way to delete items inline; for example, in a sortable list. If the user's focus is on something to be deleted (because that's where the delete button is), their focus can get lost.

What happens next exactly depends on the user's browser: in some cases they'll have to start over from the top of the page, an unforgivable pain in a large web application. Chrome handles this more gracefully with a sequential focus navigation starting point,[26] but you can't rely on it. Instead, handle the interaction by sending focus to a neighboring focusable item.

[26] http://smashed.by/focusstart

Focus Management

Main content

A link.

Basic sorting interface with items that can be deleted. © 2018 Rainier McCheddarton.

```
// Simple jQuery focus management example
var DeletableList = (function() {
    var list, listItems, deleteBtnSelector, deleteBtns;
    function init() {
        list = $('ul.list');
        listItems = list.find('li');
        deleteBtnSelector = '.btn-delete';
        deleteBtns = $(deleteBtnSelector);
        deleteBtns.on('click', handleDeleteClick);
    }
    function handleDeleteClick(event) {
        removeItem($(event.target).parent());
        api.focusItem(list.find(deleteBtnSelector).first());
    }
    function removeItem(target) {
        target.remove();
    }
    function focusItem(target) {
        setTimeout(function() {
            target.focus();
        }, 1);
    }
    var api = {
        init: init,
        deleteBtns: deleteBtns,
        focusItem: function (target) {
            focusItem(target);
        }
    }
```

```
        return api;
});
// usage:
var list = new DeletableList();
list.init();
```

DEBUGGING FOCUS

A focus management tip: add a native `focusin` JavaScript listener to log the currently focused element with `document.activeElement`. Open your favorite browser's developer tools console and tab through the whole page with your keyboard. Since the `focusin` event is bound to the `document` instead of `focus` on individual UI controls, this technique is very effective for finding elements you forgot to disable for keyboard and screen reader users. You might be surprised at what you find!

```
document.addEventListener('focusin', function() {
  console.log('focused:', document.activeElement);
});
// focused: <button>Close Menu</button>
// oh, my focus went inside of the inactive sidenav! OOPS!
```

Notifying Users

Although focus management is effective at announcing content, sometimes changes occur in your app away from the user's keyboard focus point and it would be horribly disorienting to send them over there. An example would be if a screen reader user was typing in an auto-saving form, and a visual alert calmly popped up every so often saying, "Content saved!" – it would be pretty infuriating to have your focus moved to announce that alert as you were typing. Or, if the view changes after they click a link in your single-page app, you might want to send focus to the `main` element *and* announce the overall page change (including the `header`, above `main` in the DOM).

In those scenarios, it might make more sense to use ARIA live regions to announce new content in screen readers. They're decently supported, although, by design, repeated announcements of the exact same message (like "Content saved!") won't be announced. In those cases (and in the event of stubborn, not-happening announcements), you might try using two regions and trading off, like in ngA11y[27] or react-aria-live.[28]

Live regions can be applied in HTML using `role="alert"` or `role="status"`, each with a different impact level (`alert` will interrupt other messages, while `status` will wait). These same screen reader behaviors can be applied with the `aria-live="assertive"` and `aria-live="polite"` properties respectively, along with other attributes.[29]

Here are some guidelines for using ARIA live regions effectively:

- Don't disrupt a screen reader user's flow while typing with assertive or too many alerts.
- Always test the behavior in multiple screen readers, such as NVDA, and iOS/macOS VoiceOver.
- Using live region roles along with `aria-live` properties will maximize compatibility.
- Try trading off between two live regions of the same politeness level if different messages aren't being announced.

27 http://smashed.by/whatinput
28 http://smashed.by/reactaria
29 http://smashed.by/liveregions

```
// Maximizing compatibility with aria-live and role=status
<div aria-live="polite" role="status"><!-- append messages here --></div>
```

Here's an example of announcing a form save action in Vue.js,[30] using the status role to invoke an ARIA live region:

```
<section id="app" class="section">
  <form>
    <h1 class="title is-1">
      {{form.formName}}
    </h1>
    <div class="field">
      <label class="label" for="name">Name</label>
      <div class="control">
        <input class="input" id="name" type="text"
        v-model="form.userName" />
      </div>
    </div>
    <div class="field">
      <label class="label" for="color">Favorite Color</label>
      <div class="control">
        <div class="select">
          <select id="color" v-model="form.favoriteColor">
            <option v-for="color in ['Red', 'Blue', 'Green']"
 :value="color">
              {{color}}
            </option>
          </select>
        </div>
      </div>
    </div>
    <fieldset class="field">
      <legend class="label">Favorite National Park</legend>
      <div class="control">
        <label>
          <input type="checkbox" value="olympic" v-model="form.natlPark" />
          Olympic National Park
        </label>
        <label>
          <input type="checkbox" value="n-cascades"
          v-model="form.natlPark" />North Cascades National Park</label>
        <label>
```

30 http://smashed.by/vueform

```html
          <input type="checkbox" value="glacier-natl"
v-model="form.natlPark" />Glacier National Park</label>
      </div>
    </fieldset>
    <fieldset class="field">
      <legend class="label">How many hours a week do you play?</legend>
      <label class="control title">
        {{form.playHours}} / 40
        <input type="range" min="0" max="40" v-model="form.playHours"/>
      </label>
    </fieldset>
    <input class="button is-primary margin-bottom" type="submit"
@click.prevent="fakeSubmit" />
  </form>
  <transition name="fade" mode="out-in">
    <div role="status">
      <article class="message is-primary" v-show="showSubmitFeedback">
        <div class="message-header">
          <p>Fake Send Status:</p>
        </div>
        <div class="message-body">Successfully Submitted!</div>
      </article>
    </div>
  </transition>
</section>
```

```javascript
new Vue({
  el: '#app',
  data: {
    form: {
      formName: 'Tell Us About Yourself',
      userName: '',
      favoriteColor: 'Red',
      natlPark: [],
      playHours: 0
    },
    showSubmitFeedback: false
  },
  methods: {
    fakeSubmit(){
      this.showSubmitFeedback = true;
      setTimeout(() => {
        this.showSubmitFeedback = false;
      }, 3000);
    }
  }
});
```

Putting an ARIA live region role on an existing element means it can act as a screen reader announcement center. Make sure the live region exists when the page loads, and doesn't have CSS hiding its display from everyone. By using visually hidden (or screen reader-only) CSS[31] instead, you can render content to screen reader users while not displaying it for sighted users. Be sure to test in multiple screen readers, including JAWS, NVDA, and VoiceOver for both macOS and iOS. Live regions can be a little tricky sometimes, so test in the major screen readers for browsers your team supports.

Putting It All Together

Earlier in this chapter, we saw a non-standard, fancy `<div>` masquerading as a custom text input. If you chose a `<div>` element in that scenario because you needed to build in an edit mode with JavaScript, it is possible to do this more inclusively with accessible defaults. You could always bind custom JavaScript functionality on a neighboring `<button>` element to change the input to and from `readonly` mode.

Here's an example:

```
<div class="custom-input">
  <label for="input0">
    Content title
    <input type="text" readonly placeholder="I love dogs" id="input0" tabindex="-1">
  </label>
  <button aria-describedby="input0">
    <span class="edit">Edit</span>
    <span class="done">Done</span>
  </button>
</div>
```

31 http://smashed.by/hiddencontent

```html
<live-region role="status" aria-live="polite"></live-region>
```
```css
.custom-input {
  /* default styling goes here */
  button {
    .edit {
      display: inline-block;
    }
    .done {
      display: none;
    }
  }
  &.edit-mode {
    /* edit mode styling goes here */
    .edit {
      display: none;
    }
    .done {
      display: inline-block;
    }
  }
}
live-region {
  display: block;
  position: absolute;
  left: -500000px;
}
```
```js
var customInputWrap = document.querySelectorAll('.custom-input');
var liveRegion = document.querySelector('live-region');
for (var i=0; i<customInputWrap.length; i++) {
  var el = customInputWrap[i];
  var customInput = el.querySelector('input');
  var customInputBtn = el.querySelector('button');
    el.addEventListener('keyup', function(event) {
      if (event.keyCode === 27) {
        disableInput(el);
      }
    })
  el.addEventListener('click', function(e) {
    if (e.target !== e.currentTarget) {
      el.classList.toggle('edit-mode');
      if (customInput.hasAttribute('readonly')) {
        enableInput(el);
```

```
        } else {
            disableInput(el);
        }
    } else {
        customInputBtn.focus();
    }
  });
}
function enableInput(el) {
  var input = el.querySelector('input');
  input.removeAttribute('readonly');
  input.removeAttribute('tabindex');
  liveRegion.textContent = 'Now Editing';
  input.focus();
}
function disableInput(el) {
  var btn = el.querySelector('button');
  var input = el.querySelector('input');
  input.setAttribute('readonly', '');
  input.setAttribute('tabindex', '-1');
  btn.focus();
  liveRegion.textContent = 'Done editing';
}
```

In the code example above (available as a CodePen[32]) we use HTML, CSS, and JavaScript to create a custom widget using accessible defaults. While the text input is only focusable in edit mode, the "Edit" button is always focusable, and it transforms the widget between edit mode and "Done." Triggering edit mode gracefully sends the user's keyboard focus to the active text input, and triggers announcements to alert screen reader users of changes through an ARIA live region. With some creative CSS styling, this edit control could be transformed into a more accessible version of the Pen title component on *codepen.io*.

32 http://smashed.by/customedit

Editable Pen title component on CodePen.

The fun of using JavaScript means we can craft highly interactive web applications and components. By truly recognizing how our HTML, CSS, and JavaScript come together to improve web accessibility, we can learn how to create higher-quality user interfaces that enable users rather than get in their way.

Maintaining Accessibility in Your Single-Page App

These are all cool techniques to play with, of course, but how can developers and designers embed accessibility for long-term support, especially when working with team members who might not be as curious or passionate? Some of the techniques suggested here can easily be broken with one wrong implementation, and further degraded over time (à la *broken windows theory*[33]). How do you go about making accessibility changes stick? Humans are indeed human and we break things; fortunately, the answer can be found with accessibility testing.

AUTOMATED ACCESSIBILITY TESTING TOOLS

The good news is that accessibility tools can be integrated into a build routine to help spread the knowledge around your team. Linters like eslint-plugin-jsx-a11y[34] for React projects can warn you about missing form labels and some basic HTML accessibility fails. More generic

33 http://smashed.by/brokenwindows
34 http://smashed.by/eslintplugin

tools like axe-core[35] and Tenon.io[36] can integrate into your automated tests and continuous integration server, no matter which templating library or framework you're using.

It helps to have CSS and JavaScript applied to your markup when testing for accessibility issues, so you don't encounter red herrings. You'll want to write tests to assert behavior and quality in all of your app's various states, including opening menus and modals. Using headless browsers like Chrome or PhantomJS (where there is no graphical user interface), or real browser instances using Selenium WebDriver,[37] you can script a lot of this behavior. Write tests that assert keyboard functionality in your own app, including focus management. You can cover even more ground with common accessibility issues using an accessibility API like axe-core, or its `iframe`-friendly Selenium integration, axe-webdriverjs.[38]

By using an accessibility API in your tests, you can catch a lot of common accessibility issues without having to maintain the infrastructure for them yourself:

- poor color contrast (the number-one accessibility fail)
- misspelled or misused ARIA roles, states and properties
- unlabeled UI widgets, including form controls, links and buttons
- missing image `alt` text
- abused `tabindex`
- incorrect use of landmarks and heading structure

35 http://smashed.by/axecore
36 http://smashed.by/tenon
37 http://smashed.by/selenium
38 http://smashed.by/webdriverjs

WRITING AUTOMATED ACCESSIBILITY TESTS

APIs for accessibility testing can help prevent you having to keep tabs on the latest ARIA and HTML specs, and from writing complicated testing algorithms. But there are some areas where automated testing can't make guarantees, either due to testing constraints in browsers, or the possibility of producing false positives which you'd likely ignore over time.

Some items could be tested manually, and perhaps that's the best place to start for harder to assert items like *visible focus* states. However, at some point it's a better return on investment to automate testing so you don't have to spend human energy repeating the same tasks over and over.

Key accessibility requirements that would benefit from coverage in your automated test suite:

- Focus management: not dropping the user's focus when views change and items are deleted from the DOM.

- Keyboard support for interactions: **Tab**, **Space**, and **Enter** keys, arrow keys, **Escape** key

- Component-specific APIs: that is, hooks and attribute values that must land somewhere internal to the component to be accessible

- Watched ARIA properties

- Interaction APIs, like focus managers

- Visible focus states

When writing your automated tests, some of the items above are best covered with small units, while others might be more suited to browser integration tests; it depends on the task at hand. Are you asserting something that can remain isolated with no dependencies in a unit test, or does it require integrating UI components to more closely mimic the user's experience? Learn more about the answers to these questions in my blog post, "Writing Automated Tests for Accessibility."[39]

ACCESSIBLE STYLE GUIDES AND PATTERN LIBRARIES

We've talked a lot about accessibility in the coding process. However, it's worth noting that a healthy accessibility practice truly starts with UX and design. To avoid being set up to fail repeatedly as a developer trying to implement accessibility, it helps to bake it in to interactive style guides and pattern libraries.

Without presenting accessible examples in your online style guide, you force the responsibility on every consumer downstream – and they'll likely forget accessibility or get it wrong. On the contrary, having examples of styled but accessible heading structures, interaction states (including keyboard focus), and accessible UI widgets can help show team members how successful implementations should work. By putting some effort into accessibility at the style guide or pattern library level, you get to say how it should be implemented (Is this a tab switcher? What are the roles, states, and properties? How do I label an icon button?). Everyone using your patterns and styles will benefit – an especially important consideration for all the teams depending on your hard work.

[39] http://smashed.by/a11ytests

Accessibility Rules of Thumb in SPAs

- It's easier and less costly to incorporate accessibility the earlier you tackle it, starting with UX and design.

- Prototype complex or custom interactions early, and include accessibility.

- Check out the *ARIA Authoring Practices*[40] for known interaction patterns.

- Be generous with color contrast; it not only helps people with low vision and color deficiency, but also low-contrast projectors and outdoor displays.

- Screen readers have ways of navigating other than using the **Tab** key, so you don't need to make *everything* focusable.

- Interactive widgets ("controls") should be designed to work with the keyboard, not just on hover or swipe.

- Get comfortable with focus management in JavaScript, and write it into your automated tests.

- Test with accessibility browser extensions and automated testing tools for extra muscle.

- Test your app with real users, including users with disabilities. Organizations like Knowbility's *Access Works*[41] can help.

---

40 http://smashed.by/ariapractices
41 http://smashed.by/accessworks

Conclusion

Developers are capable of so much with JavaScript these days – we can learn new APIs and build complex applications that look great on our resumés. But who are you building those apps for? If you're selling a product online or trying to expand reach, doesn't it make more sense to include as many users as you can? People with disabilities want to participate in life online along with everyone else. By building inclusive design into your apps and really baking it in with automated tests, you'll raise the bar for quality software and be the hero of so many users.

About The Author

Marcy Sutton works on web accessibility tools at Deque Systems, a company focused on digital equality. In 2016, O'Reilly gave Marcy a Web Platform Award for her work in accessibility. She loves co-leading the Accessibility Seattle meetup and is starting a code club for *Girl Develop It Bellingham*. When away from the keyboard, Marcy can be found hiking with her dog, riding a bicycle, or snowboarding.

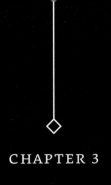

CHAPTER 3

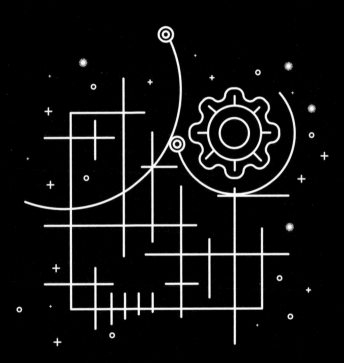

Production-Ready CSS Grid Layouts

Rachel Andrew

Production-Ready CSS Grid Layouts

by Rachel Andrew

CSS Grid Layout launched in the majority of browsers during 2017, with Chrome, Firefox and Safari all shipping their implementations of the specification in March, and Edge following up with an updated implementation in October. In this chapter I'm not going to attempt to teach all of the specification; instead I'm going to assume that you have followed some of the existing tutorials referenced at the end and are ready to get started using Grid in production.

I'll cover some of the main things that trip people up when starting to use Grid Layout. I'll also look at some fundamental parts of CSS that become very important when using layout methods such as Grid and Flexible Box Layout (Flexbox). Key to both of these methods are concepts of sizing, space distribution and alignment. My hope is that by reading this chapter, and building the examples, you'll have a better understanding not only of Grid, but of CSS layout as a whole.

Getting Into a Grid Mindset

To understand Grid Layout, and become confident with the methods it enables, you need to make a shift in thinking. This involves no longer thinking about creating layout by giving sizes to items and lining them up with one another, and instead thinking about creating a grid on the container and placing the items into it.

Consider a float-based layout. The main layout method since responsive design arrived on the scene had us assign a percentage width to floated items. We carefully calculated our percentages, making sure we didn't end up with more than 100% per "row," and achieved something that looked like a grid, and that maintained the correct ratios as the available width changed.

```css
.wrapper {
  max-width: 980px;
  margin: 0 auto;
  padding-right: 2.093333%;
}
.col {
  margin-bottom: 1em;
  margin-left: 2.093333%;
  width: 6.20%;
  float: left;
}
.row::after {
  content: "";
  display: block;
  clear: both;
}
  .col.span2 { width: 14.493333%; } /* total of 2 column tracks plus 1 margin-left */
  .col.span3 { width: 22.786666%; } /* total of 3 column tracks plus 2 margin-left */
  .col.span4 { width: 31.079999%; } /* total of 4 column tracks plus 3 margin-left */
  .col.push2 { margin-left: 18.679999%; } /* total of 2 column tracks plus margins */
```

We can create something that looks like a grid using floats.

We then gained Flexbox. However this one-dimensional layout method isn't suited to grid-based design either. While you declare `display:flex` on the parent, to make things line up in rows and columns we have to return to adding percentages to our items and their margins to achieve something that looks like a grid.

```css
.wrapper {
  max-width: 980px;
  margin: 0 auto;
  padding-right: 2.093333%;
}
.col {
  margin-bottom: 1em;
  margin-left: 2.093333%;
  width: 6.20%;
  flex: 0 0 auto;
}
.row {
  display: flex;
}
.col.span2 { width: 14.493333%; } /* total of 2 column tracks plus 1 margin-left */
.col.span3 { width: 22.786666%; } /* total of 3 column tracks plus 2 margin-left */
.col.span4 { width: 31.079999%; } /* total of 4 column tracks plus 3 margin-left */
.col.push2 { margin-left: 18.679999%; } /* total of 2 column tracks plus margins */
```

Grid behaves differently. We define our grid on the container and, while doing so, also define *tracks* for columns and rows. We assign the sizing of these tracks from the container, rather than adding sizing to the items. As we shall see, this doesn't mean items cannot affect the track sizes. But sizing *starts* with the grid container. In this way, Grid Layout is unlike previous layout methods. The only layout method that behaves similarly is Multi-column Layout.

Once we have our track sizing, all that needs to be added to rules on the items is a description of how many column or row tracks the item should span. That might start from a fixed position on the grid, such as the item in the code below with a class of `special`, which starts on line 3 and ends on line 7. Or we might use auto-placement, asking items to start where they would be placed with `auto` and span a certain number of tracks.

```
.wrapper {
  max-width: 980px;
  margin: 0 auto;
  display: grid;
  grid-gap: 20px;
  grid-template-columns: repeat(12, minmax(0,1fr));
}
.col.span2 { grid-column: auto / span 2; } /* start where grid would place the item, span 2 tracks */
.col.span3 { grid-column: auto / span 3; }
.col.span4 { grid-column: auto / span 4; }
.col.special { grid-column: 3 / 7; }
```

With a layout method unlike anything that came before, a number of new ways to define sizing have been created. They allow us to distribute space in proportion, to set minimum and maximum track sizes, to indicate that we want the size of the content to dictate track size, and to mix fixed-size tracks with flexible ones. It is with these new sizing methods that I want to start, as I believe that a lot of the apparent complexity of Grid is because we see all of these new methods, and wonder why things got so complicated.

Existing Length Units

We can start very simply with sizing we are familiar with. Grid tracks can be created using existing length units, which are specified in the CSS Values and Units specification.[1] You can create tracks with pixel-sized widths, ems or even the ch unit, which denotes width by number of characters.

In the following example, I have created a grid with one column set to 20ch; a second column is defined in pixels and a third as ems. The first column will be as wide as 20 characters of the character 0 (zero) in the font size used for the grid container. The second is 400 pixels wide and the third 8em. I have added a second row of grid items to demonstrate that this sizing continues to the next row of the grid. It is vital to remember that Grid is a two-dimensional model. If you set sizing for a track, it takes effect all the way down the columns and along the rows.

```
.grid {
  display: grid;
  grid-template-columns: 20ch 400px 8em;
  grid-gap: 20px;
}
```

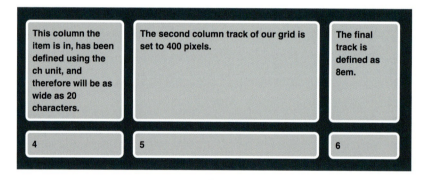

Grid tracks defined using length units.

1 http://smashed.by/lengths

You can also use percentages, just as with a float-based or flex "grid." This approach can be useful if you are trying to ensure that a grid component introduced into an existing design lines up with other elements, which likely have percentage-based sizing. As we shall see, however, using percentages for sizing and having to work out the math yourself is something we'll probably need to do less of in the future.

```css
.grid {
  display: grid;
  grid-template-columns: 22% 50% 22%;
  grid-column-gap: 3%;
  grid-row-gap: 2em;
}
```

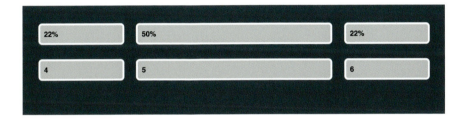

A grid with tracks sized in percentages.

PERCENTAGE SIZING AND GRID-GAP

The `grid-gap` property is a shorthand for `grid-column-gap` and `grid-row-gap`. It enables the creation of gaps between grid tracks. If you use percentage sizing for your gaps, this will work as you would expect for column gaps. The gap essentially acts like any percentage-sized track: you need to make sure you do not end up with a total of more than 100%.

With row gaps, what the percentage resolves against is less obvious. Should it use the width, so that a gap of 10% is the same for rows and columns, or should it use the height? Currently, results across browsers are not the same, so you should avoid using a percentage value for `grid-row-gap`. In the example above I used em instead.

Sharing Space with the fr Unit

The unit that will save us from the need to calculate percentages is the fr unit. The fr unit is described as a *flexible length* in the CSS Grid Specification,[2] and is not part of CSS Values and Units as it is not a length unit. This is helpful to remember as fr cannot be combined with other units in `calc()` because it doesn't represent a length in the way other length units do.

The fr unit allows us to distribute space in the grid container, and to do so in proportion. If you have used Flexbox, and distributed available space by giving flex items a different `flex-grow` value, then you will find the behavior of the fr unit very similar.

In the example below I have a grid container with one `1fr` track, and two `2fr` tracks. This means that the available space in the grid container is divided into five: one part given to the first track, and two parts each to the second and third tracks.

```
.grid {
  display: grid;
  grid-template-columns: 1fr 2fr 2fr;
}
```

2   http://smashed.by/frunit

The first track is `1fr`, *the next two are each* `2fr`.

To achieve a similar layout using Flexbox, you would use the CSS below. Using the flex properties I set my first item to a flex-grow factor of 1, and the next two items to have a flex-grow factor of 2:

```
.flex {
  display: flex;
}
.flex > :nth-child(1) {
  flex: 1 0 0;
}
.flex > :nth-child(2),
.flex > :nth-child(3){
  flex: 2 0 0 ;
}
```

This example also highlights the point made earlier about Grid working on the container and Flexbox on the items. With Flexbox you target only that individual item; we have to go to each item and decide how much it can grow or shrink in proportion to the others. With Grid we size the full track, which means that every item in that column will go into the track created by the fr unit sizing.

It would be possible to get the above Grid layout using percentages. What would be harder when using percentages, though, is when we want to mix fixed-length and flexible tracks.

We can see a very simple example of this if we add 20-pixel gaps to our grid. Before the fr units are calculated, the amount of space required for the gaps is taken away from the total available space.

```
.grid {
  display: grid;
  grid-template-columns: 1fr 2fr 2fr;
  grid-gap: 20px;
}
```

The fr units share out the space after accounting for the gaps.

The fr unit shares out *available space*, which means you can ask it only to share out space left *after* fixed-size tracks have been created. So if your layout requires some fixed-size elements in it, this is not a problem. In the next example, I have a first track of `10ch`, one of 200px, and then two flexible tracks of `1fr` and `2fr`. The available space the flexible length tracks have to play with is whatever is left after the two fixed tracks have been laid out.

> *Note:* The `ch` unit is relative to the size of the character `0` (zero).

This available space is then shared into three parts: one part given to the first track, and two parts to the second track.

```
.grid {
  display: grid;
  grid-template-columns: 10ch 200px 1fr 2fr;
  grid-gap: 20px;
}
```

Fixed and flexible tracks in the grid definition.

Content-Sized Tracks

In addition to tracks using familiar length units, and those using a flexible length, we also have ways to allow the content to dictate the track sizing. When we start to do this, we have to keep in mind the two-dimensional nature of a Grid layout. If an item in a row or a column track is able to change the size of the track, it will change the size of that track all the way down the column or along the row. This is essentially the big difference between Grid and Flexbox. If you do not want items to change the size of entire rows in *both* dimensions, a flex layout is probably what you're looking for.

auto Track Sizes

The simplest way to allow content to change track sizing is to use a value of `auto` for grid tracks. This is the default for grid tracks and something you will be familiar with if you have created a grid and specified only the column sizes, allowing rows to be created using auto-placement. Those rows are `auto`-sized by default. This means that whatever content is placed into them, the row will grow to be the height of that content.

If `auto` is used for column track sizing and you have not used any of the CSS Box Alignment properties discussed later in this chapter, the column will stretch to take up available space in the grid – so the track may end up larger than is required for the content inside. In the next example, I have set `justify-content` to `start` in order that the tracks do not stretch.

```
.grid {
  display: grid;
  grid-template-columns: auto auto auto;
  grid-gap: 20px;
  justify-content: start;
}
```

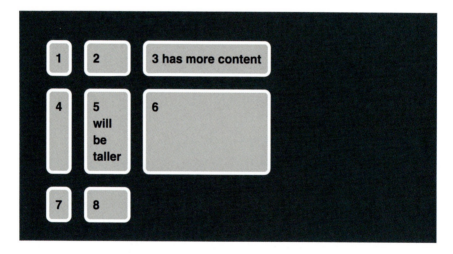

All of the columns as `auto` sized.

Content Sizing Keywords

Using `auto` for track sizing tends to be what we want for rows, but for columns we often want a little more control. This is where the new keyword values for `width` and `height` defined in the CSS Intrinsic and Extrinsic Sizing specification[3] come in very useful. These new keywords are `min-content`, `max-content` and `fit-content`.

These keywords are not specifically for Grid layout. They can be used anywhere you might use a width or a height (although browser support is currently limited outside Grid). For example, we can look at how `min-content` behaves by giving a `div` which contains a string of text a `width` of `min-content`.

```
.min-content {
  width: min-content;
}
```

The element displays on the page with a width defined by the longest word in the string. The text takes all possible soft-wrapping opportunities, becoming as small as it can be.

If we were instead to use the keyword value `max-content`, the element would become as large as it could possibly be, taking none of the possible soft-wrapping opportunities. This could cause overflow as the item now does not wrap to fit into the container.

```
.max-content {
   width: max-content;
}
```

3   http://smashed.by/minmaxcontent

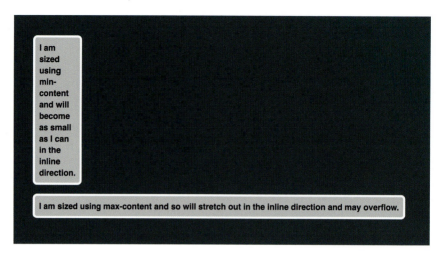

The first box has a width of min-content, and the second a width of `max-content`.

If we bring these keywords into our `grid-template-columns` and `grid-template-rows` definitions, we can use them to help define track sizing based on the content of the tracks.

In the example below, I am using `min-content` and `max-content` to define column tracks. You can see how the tracks are sized based on the content, and that this sizing happens all the way down the column track.

```
.grid {
  display: grid;
  grid-template-columns: min-content max-content min-content;
  grid-gap: 20px;
}
```

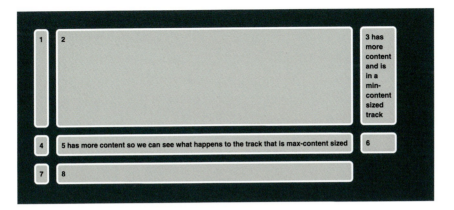

Using min-content *and* max-content *for grid tracks.*

Using max-content to force a track not to wrap at all has the potential to cause overflows. There is a final new keyword of fit-content that we can use to get the best of both worlds. It provides a defined limit to the maximum size a track can reach.

The fit-content keyword can be passed a value that becomes the maximum size of the track. The track behaves as though sized with max-content, becoming as big as it can and not taking advantage of soft-wrapping opportunities. However, once it reaches the value entered it stops, and then text inside wraps. In the next example, I have three tracks: the first two use fit-content(200px), and the last track uses fit-content(15ch).

```
.grid {
  display: grid;
  grid-template-columns: fit-content(200px) fit-content(200px) fit-content(15ch);
  grid-gap: 20px;
}
```

In the first column track there is nothing that makes the track wider than 200 pixels, so the track uses `max-content` sizing. The second track has a long string of text, so when it hits 200 pixels, the track stops growing and the content wraps. The same is true for the third track sized at `15ch` (15 characters). There is a string in that track longer than `15ch` and so the track maxes out and the content wraps.

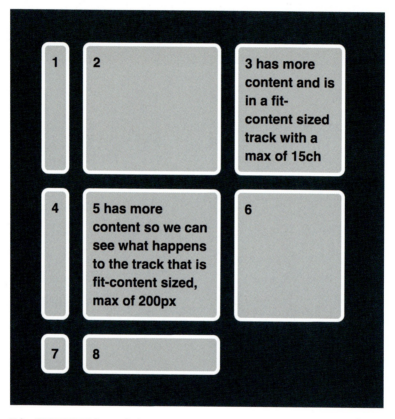

Using `fit-content` for track sizes.

This allows some interesting use cases. For example, I might want to have a media object that sometimes contains an icon and other times a larger image, which might need to be scaled down inside the container depending on the available width.

If I use `fit-content` for the track size of the image, I can show the image at full size if it is smaller than the maximum specified, but clamp the track at a maximum so a large image does not spread out too much, leaving no space for my text. The column for the text is set to `1fr` so takes up whatever space is left.

```
.media {
  width: 500px;
  display: grid;
  grid-gap: 20px;
  grid-template-columns: fit-content(250px) 1fr;
}
```

Don't forget these content-sizing keywords as you think about the grid for your design: they can be incredibly useful. In production, I tend to use these for small components, like our media object above. The keywords mean I can have fewer individual design patterns for components, allowing Grid to do a lot of the work when figuring out how big things need to be.

We should eventually have these keywords available for us in `flex-basis` too. For now, to use them as in our example above, you will need to use Grid Layout for the component, where there is good support. All browsers that support Grid Layout also support `min-content`, `max-content` and `fit-content` for track sizes.

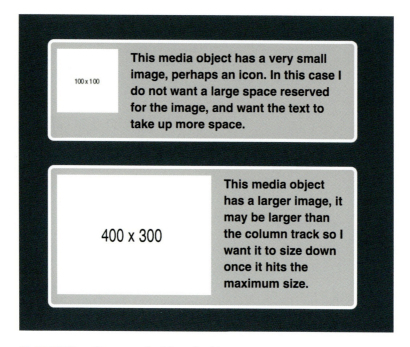

fit-content *used to create a flexible media object.*

minmax()

The content-sizing keywords – and fit-content in particular – help you define tracks that base their size on their content. We also have another flexible way to define track sizing: using the minmax() function. This track-sizing function defines a track with a minimum and maximum size.

I find this particularly useful when defining rows, or when specifying the size of rows created in the implicit grid. As we have already learned, a row track with a size of auto will expand to accept whatever content is placed into it. If we use auto as the value for `grid-auto-rows` (the default value) then row tracks will be created and content will not overflow the track.

```
.grid {
  display: grid;
  grid-auto-rows: auto; // this is the default value
}
```

In some designs, you might need to create row tracks that are always a minimum height. If you were to use a fixed-length unit for that height (for example, 100 pixels), then content would overflow the fixed-height track if more content than you designed for was added. If we know anything about designing for the web, it is that at some point more content will *always* be added!

This type of situation is one that `minmax()` deals with very well. In the example below, I have set up a grid with rows created in the implicit grid with a minimum of 100 pixels and a maximum of `auto`.

```
.grid {
  display: grid;
  width: 500px;
  grid-template-columns: 1fr 1fr 1fr;
  grid-gap: 20px;
  grid-auto-rows: minmax(100px, auto);
}
```

Rows which contain content that is shorter than 100 pixels will be 100 pixels tall. Rows with more content than can fit in 100 pixels will be taller as they go to `auto`. When you design a layout to be built using Grid, you can think about this kind of functionality and be more precise in your layouts, knowing that in the situation where the content might overflow, Grid can help you deal with it.

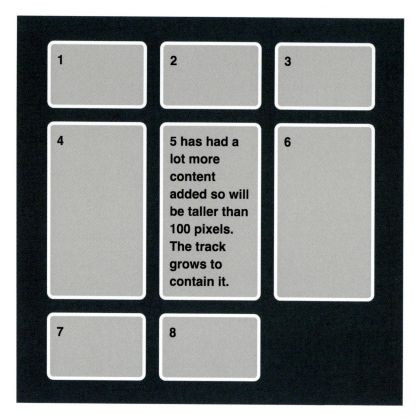

Rows created using minmax() *can be a fixed height, but still grow if there is more content added.*

It is important to remember the two-dimensional nature of grid. One cell's growth to contain content will cause the *entire row to grow*. Content in the other cells needs to be able to cope with this expansion too.

Repeating

There is another use of `minmax()` that means you can specify a track listing that will create as many tracks as will fit, with a specified minimum. To do this, you need to use `repeat` notation when declaring your grid.

By using `repeat` you can duplicate an entire track listing or section of a track listing. To get four `1fr` tracks, for example, you would create the following track listing using `repeat`:

```
.grid {
  display: grid;
  grid-template-columns: repeat(4, 1fr);
}
```

You can replace the number of times to repeat (`4` in the example above) with one of two keywords: `auto-fill` or `auto-fit`. You will then need to use a length unit as the value to repeat, and Grid will create as many column tracks of that length as will fit into the container.

```
.grid {
  display: grid;
  grid-template-columns: repeat(auto-fill, 200px);
}
```

We can't use `1fr` as the value to get as many columns as will fit, because `1fr` will stretch to take up all available space: the number of `1fr` tracks you can have auto-filled in a container is one. However, we can use `1fr` as a maximum with `minmax`.

```
.grid {
  display: grid;
  grid-template-columns: repeat(auto-fill, minmax(200px,1fr));
}
```

With this statement as our track definition, the browser will fill as many 200-pixel-wide columns as will fit. It is likely, then, that there will be a little bit left over; with the maximum set to `1fr`, that bit left over will be distributed evenly to all tracks. Therefore, we end up with as many flexible tracks as will fit, with a minimum size of 200 pixels.

The `auto-fill` and `auto-fit` keywords work in the same way as each other *unless* you do not have enough grid items to fill the container. In that case, if you use `auto-fill`, any completely empty tracks will still have space reserved for them – there would be a space at the end. With `auto-fit`, after laying out the items any completely empty tracks are collapsed to zero, and the space redistributed to the tracks that contain grid items.

As you can see, you have a range of solutions to draw on when sizing tracks. When you develop components for your sites, keep in mind these different options. Use them in combination with one another and you will probably find that you need to resort to media queries far less, and are able to create more reusable components.

Box Alignment

We frequently look at grid layout examples where elements on the grid are stretched over the entire grid area they have been placed into. The default behavior of an element without an intrinsic aspect ratio is to stretch in both directions.

```
.grid {
  height: 80vh;
  display: grid;
  grid-template-columns: 1fr 1fr 1fr;
  grid-gap: 20px;
}
```

```
.grid :first-child {
  grid-row: 1 / 3;
  grid-column: 1 / 3;
}
```

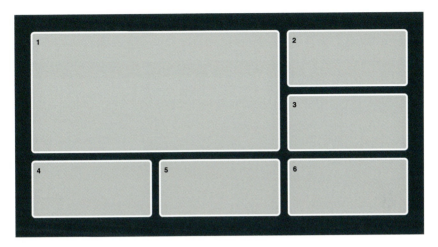

By default, items stretch to fill their grid area.

This behavior matches setting the value of `align-items` and `justify-items` to `stretch`. You can play around with alignment of grid items, and in doing so can create the impression of breaking a strict grid.

Using `align-items` on the grid container will change the alignment of all the grid items in the *block direction*. Block direction is the direction in which blocks (a paragraph, for example) display down the page. The items will be aligned within their defined grid area. Using the same grid as in the example above, I can set `align-items: start` and all of the items now display at the start of the block axis within each area of the grid.

```
.grid {
  height: 80vh;
  display: grid;
  grid-template-columns: 1fr 1fr 1fr;
  grid-gap: 20px;
  align-items: start;
}
```

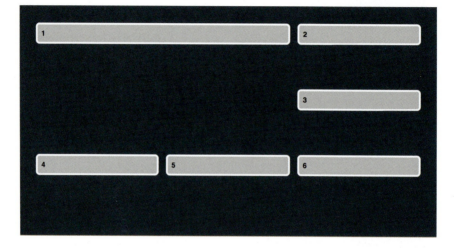

Aligning items to start *in the block direction.*

Using justify-items changes alignment to the *inline direction*. Inline direction is the direction that text in a sentence runs on your page. Once again, the content is aligned inside each defined grid area.

```
.grid {
  height: 80vh;
  display: grid;
  grid-template-columns: 1fr 1fr 1fr;
  grid-gap: 20px;
  align-items: start;
  justify-items: start;
}
```

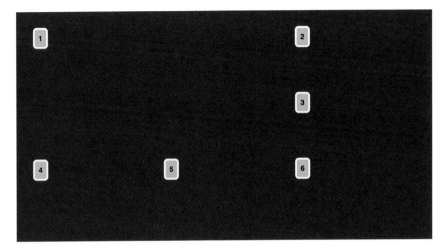

Items are aligned to start on both axes.

It's much easier to see what is happening when you align and justify items if you use Firefox's Grid Inspector. You'll then be able to see the extent of each grid area and the alignment of the item inside it.

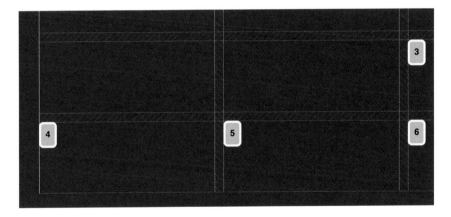

Highlighting areas with Firefox's Grid Inspector.

The available values for `align-items` and `justify-items` are as follows:

- `auto`
- `normal`
- `start`
- `end`
- `center`
- `stretch`
- `baseline`
- `first baseline`
- `last baseline`

> *Note:* Specifying `baseline` as the value will align items with the first baseline in the alignment group – this will be the same as specifying `first baseline`. The value `last baseline` aligns the items with the last baseline of the group. All Grid-supporting browsers support `baseline`. At the time of writing, only Firefox supports `first baseline` and `last baseline`. Check the page on MDN for up-to-date support information and examples.[4]

Applying the `align-items` and `justify-items` properties to the grid container will change the alignment of all of the items as a group. However, you can target individual items with `align-self` and `justify-self` in the CSS rules of the relevant grid item.

4   http://smashed.by/alignitems

```css
.grid :nth-child(2) {
  align-self: end;
}
.grid :nth-child(3) {
  justify-self: center;
}
```

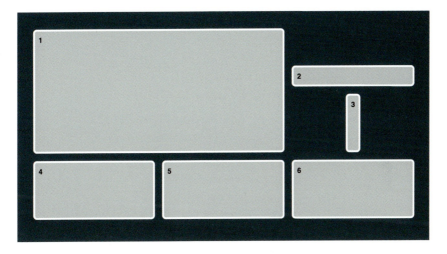

Aligning individual items with `align-self` *and* `justify-self`

Note that the default stretching behavior only applies to items without an intrinsic aspect ratio. Anything with an aspect ratio, such as an image, will be aligned to start on both axes. This is to prevent an image being pulled out of shape. (If that is what you actually want, then use `align-self: stretch` and `justify-self: stretch` on the item concerned.)

Aligning the Grid Tracks

The properties we have looked at so far deal with shifting content around inside a grid area. You can also align grid tracks when your grid container has more space than is needed to display the tracks.

In the following code, I'm creating three grid column tracks, each 100px wide, and three row tracks that are 100 pixels tall. The grid container is 500 pixels wide and 500 pixels tall. This means we have more space in both dimensions than is needed to display the tracks.

```
.grid {
  height: 500px;
  width: 500px;
  border: 2px dotted #fff;
  display: grid;
  grid-template-columns: 100px 100px 100px;
  grid-template-rows: 100px 100px 100px;
  grid-gap: 20px;
}
.grid :first-child {
  grid-column: 1 / 3;
  grid-row: 1 / 3;
}
```

The properties used to align and justify tracks are `align-content` and `justify-content`. If you do not provide a value, they default to `start`, which is why our grid tracks line up at the start of the grid container for both rows and columns.

> *Note:* Remember that `start` is only `top-left` because I am working in English, a `left-to-right` and `top-to-bottom` language. If I were working in Arabic, written `right-to-left` then `start` would align the tracks to the top and right of the grid container.

You can use any of the values of `align-content` and `justify-content` to align the tracks.

- `normal`
- `start`

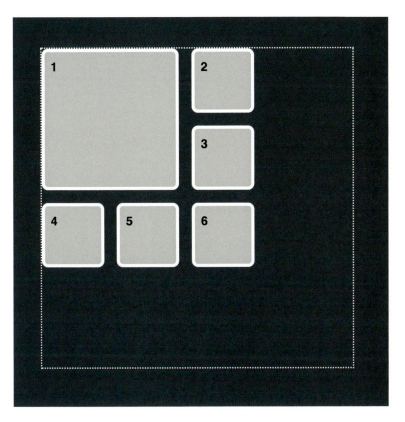

With more space in the container than needed for the tracks, items line up at the start.

- `end`
- `stretch`
- `space-around`
- `space-between`
- `space-evenly`
- `baseline`
- `first baseline`
- `last baseline`

There are no `-self` values of `align-content` and `justify-content` because these properties work by distributing space between the entire group of items.

Note that any items spanning more than one grid cell will need to absorb the extra space created if you use values such as `space-between`, `space-around` or `space-evenly`.

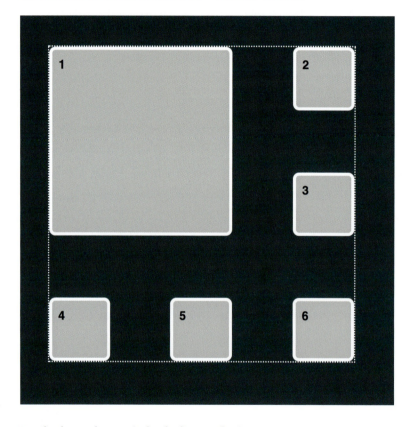

Box 1 has become larger as it absorbs the space that it spans.

```
.grid {
  height: 500px;
  width: 500px;
  border: 2px dotted #fff;
  display: grid;
  grid-template-columns: 100px 100px 100px;
  grid-template-rows: 100px 100px 100px;
  grid-gap: 20px;
  justify-content: space-between;
  align-content: space-between;
}
```

GRID GUTTERS AND ALIGNMENT

In previous versions of the Grid specification were included the properties `grid-column-gap` and `grid-row-gap`, along with their shorthand `grid-gap`. These properties allowed us to specify a gutter or alley between grid tracks.

In 2017, these properties were moved into the Box Alignment specification, to sit alongside the alignment properties. At this point they were also renamed to make them generic properties that can be used in other specifications, not just Grid. The renamed properties are `column-gap`, `row-gap` and a shorthand of `gap`. Currently you need to use the `grid-*` prefixed properties; browsers will be aliasing these to the new properties, so should maintain support. To be bulletproof, you could add both properties, in the same way we add the real property name after vendor-prefixed properties.

```
.grid {
  display: grid;
  grid-gap: 10px;
  gap: 10px;
}
```

If you combine grid gutters and alignment of tracks with `align-content` and `justify-content`, you should be aware that this can make the gutters larger than expected, as seen in the previous example.

Responsive Design

Grid has been designed to be responsive by default, and because of this we generally find we can use far fewer media queries and breakpoints in our work. For example, we don't need to work out percentages, as the fr unit means we can let the computer do that work. We can display as many columns as will fit, with a minimum size being assigned.

It's definitely worth considering if there is a Grid method to do what you need to without adding a media query – quite often there is. That said, media queries remain very useful, particularly when used for larger components, and for full page design you may need to use media queries to change your layout at different breakpoints. You essentially have two choices when adding a media query, and you can choose either or both in your design:

1. Redefine the grid by changing the `grid-template-columns` and `grid-template-rows` values.
2. Redefine the grid areas by changing how many tracks an element spans.

The second approach is very similar to how existing grid systems work in frameworks like Bootstrap. You always have a twelve-column grid, but at narrower breakpoints items span more tracks of the grid. With a simple grid layout, laying out three boxes, we could have the following code:

```css
.grid {
  display: grid;
  grid-template-columns: repeat(12, minmax(0,1fr));
  grid-gap: 20px;
}
.col1, .col2, .col3 {
  grid-column: 1 / -1;
}
@media (min-width: 500px) {
  .col2 {
    grid-column: 1 / 7;
  }
  .col3 {
    grid-column: 7 / 13;
  }
}
@media (min-width: 700px) {
  .col1 {
    grid-column: 1 / 5;
  }
  .col2 {
    grid-column: 5 / 9;
  }
  .col3 {
    grid-column: 9 / 13;
  }
}
```

This sets up a twelve-column grid. At very narrow breakpoints, items are displayed one below the other. I have spanned the item from column line 1 (the start line) to column line -1 (the end line).

At the narrowest breakpoint, items span all twelve columns.

Once we reach 500 pixels, I change the second and third box to display as a split layout of half the number of columns each.

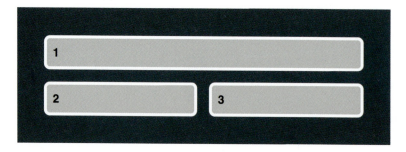

A medium breakpoint: the bottom two items each span six columns.

With more screen real estate, I have a one-row layout of three equal-width boxes. In this way, we keep our twelve-column grid; where the columns are narrower, we span more of them.

At the widest breakpoint there are three items each spanning four columns.

An alternate approach to redefining the grid can work well if you are relying on auto-placement to lay out your items.

```
.grid {
  display: grid;
  grid-template-columns: 1fr;
  grid-gap: 20px;
}
@media (min-width: 500px) {
  .grid {
    grid-template-columns: 1fr 2fr;
  }
}
@media (min-width: 700px) {
  .grid {
    grid-template-columns: 1fr 2fr 1fr;
  }
}
```

In this example I am using auto-placement to lay out my items, and then using media queries to redefine the grid definition itself.

At the narrowest breakpoint the items display in a single `1fr` column.

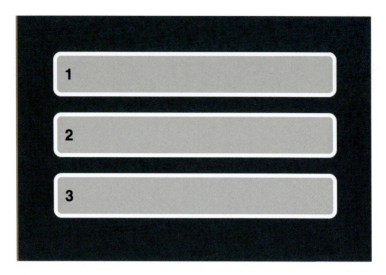

The narrow view.

We get slightly wider and have two columns of 1fr and 2fr.

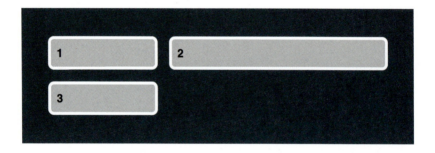

The middle breakpoint.

The widest breakpoint has three columns. In this case, then, we have different numbers of column tracks at the different breakpoints. You can, of course, combine both approaches and redefine the grid, as well as where items sit on the grid.

The widest breakpoint.

In general, you should find your use of media queries reduces – but don't be afraid to experiment. Sometimes adding a breakpoint is what the design needs to provide the best experience.

Browser Support and Fallbacks

Before deciding how to support browsers that don't recognize Grid, it is worth working out what you mean by support. Support might mean that the site has to look absolutely identical in all the browsers on your list. It might mean that you are happy for some finishing touches not to be available in all browsers. Or that you are testing these browsers but are happy for them to receive a much simplified experience. This is a discussion you should have with your client or the project owner, to make sure that everyone understands what the aim is.

At the time of writing, Edge, Chrome, Firefox, Opera, Safari, and iOS Safari all support Grid Layout. IE10 and IE11 have support for the original spec with an `-ms` prefix. *Older* browsers you might consider include:

- Internet Explorer 9 (or IE 11 and below if only considering the new spec)
- Edge 15 and below
- Firefox older than version 52

- Safari and iOS Safari older than version 10.1
- Chrome older than version 57
- Samsung Internet older than version 6.2

These popular desktop and mobile browsers are joined by browsers more commonly used in emerging markets, some of which haven't yet adopted Grid. If we take a worldwide view, UC Browser comes in at 8.1% of traffic – the third most popular browser in the world. Yet you may never have heard of it if you live in the US or Europe. Therefore, considering the site's goals and reach is important too.

Can We Polyfill Grid?

Grid does things that are impossible with older layout methods. To replicate Grid in browsers that don't support it, you would need to do a lot of work in JavaScript. Even on a well-resourced computer with a fast rendering engine, you are likely to have something of a janky experience as heights are calculated and items positioned. As we already know, the browsers that don't support grid are older and slower, or most often found on lower-powered devices in emerging markets. Why would you force a bunch of JavaScript onto those devices?

Instead of searching for a polyfill, consider how using Grid Layout can actually provide a better experience to people whose browsers don't support it. Grid allows you to create complex layout experiences for supporting browsers with minimal CSS, while still offering a good experience to those without support. Yes, it will be a little more work than just throwing a polyfill at the problem, but by doing so you are ensuring that support means providing a good experience, rather than making the most important goal getting the site to look the same.

It turns out that CSS itself has evolved to a point where you can provide that good experience just by writing CSS, and you can do so in a way that doesn't involve completely replicating your code.

Browsers Ignore CSS They Don't Understand

The first part of the picture is the fact that browsers ignore CSS they don't understand. If a browser that doesn't support CSS Grid comes across the `grid-template-columns` property, it doesn't know what it is and so discards that line and continues. Nothing breaks, we just don't get any column tracks.

This means that you can use some old CSS, like floats or `display: table-cell` to provide a Grid-type layout for older browsers, just as you would in the past. The browsers that do not support Grid will use this layout and ignore all the grid instructions. Browsers supporting Grid Layout will continue, discover the grid instructions and apply those. So we need to consider what happens if an item using another layout method becomes a grid item.

New Layout Knows About Old Layout

Defined in the specification is exactly how Grid behaves if you have elements in your page positioned by other layout methods. The methods you are likely to want to use are:

- floats
- `display: inline-block`
- `display: table`

- the `vertical-align` property, along with `display: inline-block` or the `table-*` values
- Flexbox
- multi-column layout

Floated items or those that use the `clear` property, and which then become a grid item, no longer exhibit any floating or clearing behavior, as though they were never applied. This means that in the example below, if the browser does not support Grid Layout, the user will see the floated layout. If the browser supports Grid they get the grid layout without any float behavior intruding.

```
.grid {
  display: grid;
  grid-template-columns: 1fr 1fr 1fr;
  grid-gap: 20px;
}
.grid > * {
  float: left;
}
```

The same is true for `inline-block`. The value `inline-block` can be applied to the child item, but as soon as the parent has `display: grid` the `inline-block` behavior will no longer be applied.

```
.grid {
  display: grid;
  grid-template-columns: 1fr 1fr 1fr;
  grid-gap: 20px;
}
.grid > * {
  display: inline-block;
}
```

I often use `display: table-cell` when I need to create a column layout and also align items in non-supporting browsers, since the `vertical-align` property works when you use `display: table-cell`.

```
.grid {
  display: grid;
  grid-template-columns: 1fr 1fr 1fr;
  grid-gap: 20px;
}
.grid > * {
  display: table-cell;
  vertical-align: top;
}
```

When you use `display: table-cell` to create columns, CSS will create what are known as *anonymous boxes*. These are the missing parts of the table: a table cell in a real HTML table will be inside a `<tr>` element, and that will be inside a `<table>` element. The anonymous boxes essentially fix these missing parents. If your table-cell item becomes a grid item, however, this happens *before* the boxes are generated, and so once again the item will act as if the CSS tables display had never happened.

The `vertical-align` property does not apply once in Grid Layout either, so if you use it in a CSS tables layout or with `inline-block` you can safely ignore that and use Box Alignment for Grid Layout.

You can also use Flexbox as a fallback. If you have used the `flex` property or individual `flex-grow`, `flex-shrink` or `flex-basis` properties on the item, these will be ignored once it becomes a grid item.

```
.grid {
  display: flex;
  display: grid;
  grid-template-columns: 1fr 1fr 1fr;
  grid-gap: 20px;
```

```
}
.grid > * {
  flex: 1 1 auto;
}
```

Finally, don't forget that Multi-column Layout can be used in some cases as a fallback; for example, when laying out a list of card components or images. Items will be displayed in columns rather than across the row, but in some circumstances this can be useful. Apply `column-count` or `column-width` on the container to make it a multi-column container. If you then apply `display: grid` the `column-*` behavior will be ignored.

The example below will display a three-column multi-column layout if Grid Layout is not supported, and a three-column grid layout if Grid is supported. The difference is that in multi-column layout, the boxes will display by column, rather than by row.

```
.grid {
  column-count: 3;
  display: grid;
  grid-template-columns: 1fr 1fr 1fr;
  column-gap: 20px;
  grid-gap: 20px;
}
```

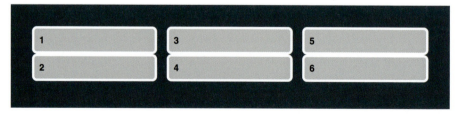

In Multi-column Layout, the boxes display down each column.

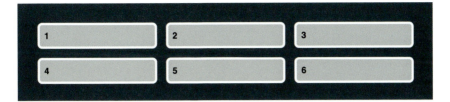

In the Grid version, the boxes display by row.

Feature Queries

Because you can simply overwrite one layout method with another means that, in many cases, you won't need to fork your code and can provide two different ways of creating the layout: a simple one using old methods enhanced with your more complex design. There are certain situations, however, where things you need to create your layout method for non-Grid browsers will also be interpreted by Grid-supporting browsers. A key situation like this is when you have applied widths to items.

As discussed earlier, older layout methods rely greatly on adding widths to items and then lining the items up so they look like they are in a grid. However, If you have applied a percentage width to a floated item, and then turn it into a grid item, the width will still be applied – even though the float is not. The item will become a percentage of the grid area it has been placed in, which is probably not what you want.

```
.grid {
  display: grid;
  grid-template-columns: 1fr 1fr 1fr;
  grid-gap: 20px;
}
.grid > * {
  float: left;
  width: 33%;
}
```

The items are now one-third of the width of each grid area.

In this situation we need a way to tell the browser that if it supports Grid Layout, it should not use the width, as the size of the item will now be controlled by the grid area it is in. This is where CSS feature queries are useful. Feature queries (using `@supports`) act very much like media queries, but instead of querying the size of the viewport or device orientation, we check whether the browser has support for a certain feature. If it does, we can do things like override the width, setting it back to `auto`.

```
.grid > * {
  float: left;
  width: 33%;
}
@supports (display: grid) {
  .grid > * {
    width: auto;
  }
}
```

It is possible to check whether a browser *doesn't* support a certain feature, though this is currently less useful. Should the browser support neither Grid nor media queries, the code will never run. Instead, continue by doing what you need to for non-supporting browsers, then overwriting it for browsers with support – with or without an accompanying feature query.

Grid Layout in IE10 and IE11

While Edge has now updated to modern Grid Layout, IE10 and 11 have support only for the early version first shipped with an `-ms` prefix in those browsers. The Grid specification we know today came originally from Microsoft. Far from being unhappy about this old implementation, we should be glad they kickstarted the process and gave us Grid in the first place. You can read more about the story in the article "The Story of CSS Grid, from Its Creators."[5]

You might decide to offer IE10 and 11 a fallback experience based on a floated or other layout type as described above. This will work well, as will using feature queries, which are not supported in IE10 and 11. As long as you use these to overwrite your older methods, checking for support then creating the version for supporting browsers, IE10 and 11 will continue to use the older method.

You could make use of the `-ms-grid` version to create a fallback method. However, this prefixed version is not the same as modern Grid Layout; it was the first – and experimental – version. Things have changed in the five years or so since it shipped. This means you can't just use Autoprefixer[6] to add the prefixes. That approach will probably leave IE10 and 11 users with a worse experience than if you do nothing at all. Instead, you need to create a layout using this different and more limited spec.

---

5   http://smashed.by/cssgridstory
6   http://smashed.by/autoprefixer

The key points to note are as follows:

1. There is no auto-placement. You need to place each item on the grid using line-based positioning.
2. The `grid-template-areas` ASCII-art method of positioning is not part of the implementation.
3. There are no grid gap properties.
4. Instead of specifying start and end lines, you specify a start line and the number of tracks to span.

You can find a full breakdown of all of these properties in my blog post, "Should I try to use the IE implementation of Grid Layout?"[7]

If you have a high number of users with these browsers, you may find that this old spec is helpful. It is definitely worth knowing it exists, even if you only use it to solve a couple of small issues that are real showstoppers for you.

How to Add Grid Components to an Existing Site

If you are working on an existing project it is very unlikely that you will throw everything away and replace it with a grid layout. But Grid has been designed to coexist very happily with older layout methods in CSS. You can start to use Grid for new components that are being introduced into your pages, and benefit from being able to take a more creative approach, or simply having far less CSS to deal with.

---

7   http://smashed.by/iecssgrid

An Image Gallery Panel

Let's say I need to add an image gallery to an existing site that uses Bootstrap. Grid would be ideal as I can avoid using media queries to work out how many columns of images I can display. I can use the `auto-fill` method to create as many flexible columns as will fit in the container for the gallery.

Some larger images span two tracks, and I am using `grid-auto-flow: dense` to backfill the gaps left in the grid. These are benefits of Grid Layout that aren't available with any other layout method, making it worth using Grid for this component – I gain advantages if I do so, and the Grid code to achieve all of this is tiny.

```
<ul class="gallery">
  <li class="landscape"><img src="myimage.jpg" alt="alt text"></li>
  <li class="portrait"><img src="myimage.jpg" alt="alt text"></li>
</ul>
img {
  max-width: 100%;
  display: block;
}
.gallery {
  list-style: none;
  margin: 0;
  display: grid;
  grid-gap: 2px;
  grid-template-columns: repeat(auto-fill,minmax(200px, 1fr));
  grid-auto-flow: dense;
}
.gallery img {
  object-fit: cover;
  height: 100%;
  width: 100%;
}
.landscape {
  grid-column: auto / span 2;
}
```

Gallery component.

In a browser that does not support Grid Layout the images will display in regular block flow, one after another.

I can then make a decision about how to display these images for other browsers. Maybe I simply leave it alone: images displaying one after another isn't a terrible experience. It is likely, though, that you will feel there are enough non-Grid browsers visiting your site to want to do a bit more than that.

Which layout method I choose will depend on the browsers I know are visiting my site. With an existing site you have this knowledge, which can be pretty helpful! If I know that most browsers have Flexbox, then my fallback could be Flexbox.

With Flexbox, I won't have the spanning of tracks and backfilling possibilities, or grid gap. The items won't stay in a strict grid either, but I can get a nice layout. As we've already discovered, once a flex item becomes a grid item, the flex properties no longer apply, so we can safely implement Flexbox and then add Grid.

```css
.gallery {
  list-style: none;
  margin: 0;
  display: flex;
  flex-wrap: wrap;
  display: grid;
  grid-gap: 2px;
  grid-template-columns: repeat(auto-fill,minmax(200px, 1fr));
  grid-auto-flow: dense;
}
.gallery > * {
  flex: 1 1 200px;
}
.gallery img {
  object-fit: cover;
  height: 100%;
  width: 100%;
}
.landscape {
  flex: 1 1 400px;
  grid-column: auto / span 2;
}
```

The Flexbox version of the layout. The fallback requires six extra lines of code.

In this case, if a browser does not support Grid or Flexbox they will still see the images displayed one after another in block layout. This isn't a disaster and is better than a completely broken layout.

If I know some very old browsers visit the site, I might decide to add as my fallback a method supported by pretty much everything. So I am picking an `inline-block` layout. This will never be as neat as the Grid, or even Flexbox, version of the layout, but with a small amount of code we can make a reasonable fallback, and as soon as those items become flex or grid items, all `inline-block` behavior is removed.

For this layout, I also need to add a CSS feature query, with `@supports`, to remove the width applied to items once we are in Grid Layout.

```css
.gallery {
  list-style: none;
  margin: 0;
  display: flex;
  flex-wrap: wrap;
  display: grid;
  grid-gap: 2px;
  grid-template-columns: repeat(auto-fill,minmax(200px, 1fr));
  grid-auto-flow: dense;
}
.gallery > * {
  display: inline-block;
  vertical-align: top;
  width: 33%;
  flex: 1 1 200px;
}
@supports (display: flex) or (display: grid) {
  .gallery > * {
    width: auto;
  }
}
.gallery img {
  object-fit: cover;
  height: 100%;
  width: 100%;
}
.landscape {
  flex: 1 1 400px;
  grid-column: auto / span 2;
}
```

A few more lines of code provide an `inline-block` *fallback.*

As a demonstration of how this component can sit happily within an existing layout, I have taken a standard Bootstrap 3, floated two-column layout and dropped my panel into it. The gallery panel works well and is responsive owing to the `auto-fill` columns, and it coexists happily with the Bootstrap layout.

Our component in the Bootstrap layout.

Grid Alongside Other Tools and Techniques

I've shown you how Grid Layout can work as a component of an existing site. But existing sites also are likely to be using tools such as Sass or PostCSS plug-ins.

In general, the developers of commonly used tools have been quick to adopt Grid Layout. If your site was built prior to Grid landing in browsers, then you should check you are using up-to-date versions of any tool you use. If you are using the named lines syntax, you should ensure that Sass has a version greater than 3.5, as support for bracketed lists was added in this version.[8]

Having learned there is an older version of Grid Layout in IE10 and IE11, with an `-ms` prefix, you might wonder if using that old version of Grid is as simple as running Autoprefixer. The team at Autoprefixer have made efforts to get this to work, and if you have very simple grid layouts it may well do. However, as detailed earlier in this chapter, new Grid Layout is fundamentally different to old Grid Layout. Test the result of using Autoprefixer, if you try it, as it could well be that the experience is worse than it would be if you served IE10 and 11 the same fallbacks as used for other browsers. You always have the option of disabling Grid in Autoprefixer if you find it makes a mess of your layouts, by setting `grid: false`.

Is Grid Really Ready for Us to Use Now?

A final thought to leave you with as I close this chapter: I've heard the thought voiced that Grid is "too new" and will be poorly implemented in browsers with huge numbers of bugs. This isn't the case. Grid was developed in browsers for over five years, but behind an experimental flag so most people didn't know about it. The implementations and the specification are at an advanced stage, and you will be surprised to discover how few issues remain.

If you want to track the bugs we know about, you can keep an eye on my GridBugs site.[9] Everyone wants the Grid implementations to be as bug-free as possible, so things are being fixed very quickly as they are found.

8   http://smashed.by/sassrelease
9   http://smashed.by/gridbugs

Learning Grid Layout: Tutorials and References

With Grid Layout being new, there are a huge number of resources being created and updated all the time. If Grid is completely new to you, I have a set of free video tutorials explaining the various concepts.[10]

There is also a comprehensive set of guides on the MDN website.[11] On Smashing Magazine we have some extensive guides and articles on Grid Layout,[12] and I keep an up-to-date set of resources as they are published.[13]

About The Author

Rachel Andrew is a front and back-end web developer, author, speaker, and Editor-in-Chief of Smashing. She has written several web development books, most recently "CSS Grid Layout." She also the founder of edgeofmyseat.com, the company behind Perch CMS.

---

10 http://smashed.by/gridbyexample
11 http://smashed.by/mdncssgrid
12 http://smashed.by/smashingcss
13 http://smashed.by/gridbyexample2

CHAPTER 4

A Strategy Guide to CSS Custom Properties

Mike Riethmuller

A Strategy Guide to CSS Custom Properties by Mike Riethmuller

CSS custom properties (also known as CSS variables) are now supported in all modern browsers, and people are starting to use them in production – great! But they're different from variables in preprocessors, and I've already seen many examples of people using them without considering what advantages they offer.

Custom properties have huge potential to change how we write and structure CSS and, to a lesser extent, how we use JavaScript to interact with UI components.

Getting to Know Custom Properties

Custom properties are a little bit like variables in preprocessors, but have some important differences. The first and most obvious difference is the syntax.

BASIC SYNTAX

With SCSS we use a dollar symbol to denote a variable:

```
$smashing-red: #d33a2c;
```

In Less we use an @ symbol:

```
@smashing-red: #d33a2c;
```

Custom properties follow a similar convention and use a `--` prefix:

```
:root { --smashing-red: #d33a2c; }
.smashing-text {
  color: var(--smashing-red);
}
```

One important difference between custom properties and variables in preprocessors is that custom properties have a different syntax for assigning a value and retrieving that value. When retrieving the value of a custom property, we use the `var()` function.

We can give the `var()` function a second value to use as a fallback for when the custom property is not defined:

```
.smashing-text {
  color: var(--smashing-red, #d33a2c);
}
```

This fallback value is only used when the custom property `--smashing-red` is not defined. If the browser does not support custom properties, `color` will have an invalid value and will be ignored, like other invalid properties in CSS.

WHERE TO USE CUSTOM PROPERTIES

Another difference between custom properties and preprocessor variables is in the name. They are called 'custom properties' because they really are CSS properties. In preprocessors, you can declare and use variables almost anywhere, including outside declaration blocks, in media rules, or even as part of a selector.

```
$breakpoint: 800px;
$smashing-red: #d33a2c;
$smashing-things: ".smashing-text, .cats";
@media screen and (min-width: $breakpoint) {
  #{$smashing-things} {
    color: $smashing-red;
  }
}
```

Most of the examples above would be invalid using custom properties.

Custom properties have the same rules about where they are valid as normal CSS properties. In fact, it's far better to think of them as *dynamic properties* rather than variables. Custom properties can only be used *inside* a declaration block. That means custom properties are tied to a selector. This can be the `:root` pseudo-class selector, or any other valid selector.

```
:root { --smashing-red: #d33a2c; }
@media screen and (min-width: 800px) {
  .smashing-text, .cats {
    --margin-left:  1em;
  }
}
```

You can retrieve the value of a custom property anywhere you would otherwise assign a value to a CSS property. This means they can be used as a single value, as part of a shorthand statement, or even inside `calc()` equations.

```
.smashing-text, .cats {
  color: var(--smashing-red);
  margin: 0 var(--margin-horizontal);
  padding: 0 calc(var(--margin-horizontal) / 2);
}
```

Remember the `var()` function only works when assigning values to CSS properties. In other words, they *can't* be used inside media queries, or selectors including `:nth-child`. The following examples are *not* valid:

```
/* You cannot use the var() function in a media query */
@media screen and (min-width: var(--min-width) ) {
  /* You cannot use the var() function in a selector */
  li:nth-child(var(--custom-property)) {
    border-bottom: solid 1px;
  }
}
```

VALID VALUES

Almost any string can form a valid custom property value. There are a few small exceptions to this, all of which you are unlikely to encounter. (Examples include strings containing unmatched closing brackets or an exclamation mark anywhere other than at the end of a property, where it will be ignored.)

Custom property values are made of one or more *tokens* that describe to the browser how the custom property should be interpreted. These tokens can comprise numbers, units, color functions, and `calc()` statements, as well as values from other custom properties.

All of the following examples are valid custom property values:

```
.example {
  --one: 5;
  --two: var(--one, 2);
  --three: calc(var(--two) * 2);
  --color: hsl(var(--three), 50%, 50%);
  --gradient: linear-gradient(to top, var(--color), tomato);
}
```

Custom properties are parsed and determined to be valid, but their values are not computed until runtime. Therefore, changing the value of the custom property `--one` in the example above will change the value of all other custom properties.

Custom properties can become invalid at runtime. Changing the value of --one to anything other than a number would cause the --color and --gradient values to become invalid.

Converting Custom Properties to Units with calc()

Because custom property values are so permissive, it is possible to convert them from numbers to units at runtime using `calc()`. For example, we can convert a custom property with a number value of 50 to a percentage value like this:

```css
.example {
  --example-width: 50;
  width: calc(var(--example-width) * 1%);
}
```

This will resolve to `calc(50 * 1%)` and a final used value of 50%. We can do the same with almost any unit type. This can be useful for converting values from JavaScript to CSS units, or where we want to add values together, such as:

```css
:root {
  --animation-speed: 0.75;
}
.my-animation {
  --seconds: 3;
  animation-duration: calc(var(--seconds) * var(--animation-speed) * 1s);
}
```

This will result in `calc(3 * 0.75 * 1s)` which will resolve to `2.25s`. Techniques like this can be especially useful for theming and applying user settings, particularly in combination with color functions and CSS transitions.

Dynamic and Static Variables

Cosmetic differences aside, the most significant difference between variables in preprocessors and CSS custom properties is how they are scoped. We can refer to variables as being either statically or dynamically scoped. Variables in preprocessors are static, whereas custom properties are dynamic.

PREPROCESSORS ARE STATIC

For preprocessing in CSS, static means you can update the value of a variable at different points in the compilation process, but this cannot change the value of code that came before it.

```
$background: blue;
.blue {
  background: $background;
}
$background: red;
.red {
  background: $background;
}
```

results in:

```
.blue {
  background: blue;
}
.red {
  background: red;
}
```

Once rendered to CSS, the variables are gone. We could potentially read an entire *.scss* file and determine all of its output without knowing anything about the HTML, browser, or other inputs; this is not the case with custom properties.

Preprocessors have a kind of "block scope", where variables can be temporarily changed inside a selector, function, or mixin. This changes the value of a variable inside the block, but it's still static: it's tied to the block, not the selector. In the example below, the variable `$background` is changed inside the `.example` block, but it changes back to the initial value outside the block, even if the same selector and variable name are used.

```
$background: red;
.example {
  $background: blue;
  background: $background;
}
.example {
  background: $background;
}
```

results in:

```
.example {
  background: blue;
}
.example {
  background: red;
}
```

CUSTOM PROPERTIES ARE DYNAMIC

Custom properties work differently. Being dynamically scoped means they are subject to inheritance and the cascade. A property is tied to a selector, and if its value changes, this affects all matching DOM elements, just like any other CSS property.

This feature allows you to change the value of a custom property inside a media query, with a pseudo-class selector, such as `:hover`, or even with JavaScript.

```
a {
  --link-color: black;
}
a:hover,
a:focus {
  --link-color: tomato;
}
@media screen and (min-width: 600px) {
  a {
    --link-color: blue;
  }
}
a {
  color: var(--link-color);
}
```

We don't have to change which custom property is used – we change the value of the custom property within a selector. Using the same custom property, we can have different values in different places on the same page.

Global and Local Variables

In addition to being static or dynamic, variables can also be either global or local. If you write JavaScript you will be familiar with this. Variables can either be applied to everything inside an application, or their scope can be limited to specific functions or blocks of code.

CSS is similar, we have some things that global, and some things that are local. Brand colours, vertical spacing, and typography are all things you want applied globally and consistently across your website or application. CSS also has local things. A button component might have small and large variants, and you wouldn't want the sizes from these buttons being applied to all input elements, or even every element on the page.

This is something we are familiar with in CSS. We've developed design systems, naming conventions, and JavaScript libraries, all to help isolate local components and global design elements. Custom properties provide new options for dealing with this old problem.

By default, CSS custom properties are locally scoped to the specific selectors we apply them to, making them a little like local variables. However, custom properties are also inherited, so in many situations they behave like global variables, especially when applied to the `:root` selector. We need to be thoughtful about how to use them.

Many examples show custom properties being applied to `:root`. Although this fine for a demo, it can result in a messy global scope and unintended inheritance issues. Luckily we've already learnt many good practices for structuring CSS and working with inheritance and the cascade. We can apply these lessons to custom properties as well.

GLOBAL VARIABLES TEND TO BE STATIC

There are a few exceptions, but generally speaking, most global things in CSS are also static.

Global characteristics like brand colors, typography, and spacing don't tend to change much from one component to the next. Alterations tends to stem from a global rebranding or some other significant change that rarely happens with a mature product. It still makes still sense for these things to be coded as variables: they are used in many places, and variables help with consistency. But it doesn't make sense for them to be dynamic. The value of these variables does not change in any dynamic way.

For this reason, **I strongly recommend using a preprocessor for global (static) variables.** This not only ensures that they remain static, but it visually denotes them within the code. This can make CSS a lot more readable and easier to maintain.

LOCAL STATIC VARIABLES ARE OK (SOMETIMES)

Given my strong stance on global variables being static, you might suspect all local variables need to be dynamic. While it's true that local variables tend to be dynamic, this is nowhere near as strong as the tendency for global variables to be static.

Local static variables are perfectly OK in many situations. I use preprocessor variables in component files, mostly as a developer convenience.

Consider the classic example of a button component with multiple size variations.

Multiple size variations for a button component.

My SCSS might look something like this:

```scss
$button-sml: 1em;
$button-med: 1.5em;
$button-lrg: 2em;
.btn {
  // Visual styles
}
.btn-sml {
  font-size: $button-sml;
}
.btn-med {
  font-size: $button-med;
}
.btn-lrg {
  font-size: $button-lrg;
}
```

Obviously, this example would make more sense if I was using the variables multiple times, or deriving margin and padding values from the size variables. But the ability to quickly prototype different sizes might be sufficient reason to use them.

Because most static variables are global, I like to differentiate static variables used only inside a component. You can prefix such variables with the component name, or another prefix, such as `c-variable-name` for component, or `l-variable-name` for local. Use any prefix you want, or prefix global variables. Whatever you choose, it's helpful to differentiate, especially if converting an existing codebase to use custom properties.

When to Use Custom Properties

Since it's alright to use static variables inside components, when should we use custom properties? Converting existing preprocessor variables to custom properties usually makes little sense. After all, the purpose of custom properties is completely different. Custom properties make sense when we have CSS properties that change relative to a condition in the DOM – especially a dynamic condition, such as `:focus`, `:hover`, media queries, or changes with JavaScript.

I suspect we will always use some form of static variable, although we might need fewer in future, as CSS offers new ways to organize logic and code. Until then, in most situations we'll work with a combination of preprocessor variables and custom properties.

It's helpful to know we can assign static variables to custom properties. Whether they are global or local, it often makes sense to convert static variables to locally dynamic custom properties.

> *Note:* Did you know that `$var` is a valid value for a custom property? Recent versions of Sass recognize this, and therefore we need to interpolate variables assigned to custom properties, like this: `#{$var}`. This tells Sass you want to output the value of the variable, rather than just `$var` in the style sheet. This is only needed for situations like custom properties, where variable names can also be valid CSS.

If we take the button example above, and decide all buttons should use the small variation on mobile devices, regardless of the class applied in the HTML, this is now a more dynamic situation. For this, we should use custom properties.

```
$button-sml: 1em;
$button-med: 1.5em;
$button-lrg: 2em;
.btn {
  --button-size: #{$button-sml};
}
@media screen and (min-width: 600px) {
  .btn-med {
    --button-size: #{$button-med};
  }
  .btn-lrg {
    --button-size: #{$button-lrg};
  }
}
.btn {
  font-size: var(--button-size);
}
```

Here I create a single custom property: `--button-size`. This custom property is initially scoped to all button elements using the `.btn` class. I then change the value of `--button-size` above 600px for the classes `.btn-med` and `.btn-lrg`. Finally, I apply this custom property to all elements in one place.

Don't Be Too Clever

When preprocessors gained wide adoption, many of us created libraries with clever abstractions using mixins and custom functions. In rare cases, examples like this are still useful today, but I've found that the longer I work with preprocessors, the fewer features I use. Today, I use preprocessors almost exclusively for static variables.

Bill Sourour wrote an excellent article on this topic called *"Don't do it at runtime do it at design time."* [1]

In the article, Bill gives this example:

```
var letters = [];
for (let i = 65; i <= 90; i++) {
  letters.push(String.fromCharCode(i))
}
```

This example creates an array containing letters of the alphabet by looping over character codes. It's clever, concise, and obviously faster than writing out all the characters by hand. But I agree with the author: the letters of the alphabet are not going to change any time soon. And because we read code much more often than we write it, I'd rather see all the letters written in long form into the array.

The dynamic nature of custom properties also allows us to create some clever and complicated abstractions.

Just like the JavaScript example, custom properties work at runtime, so complexity that might have been borderline acceptable with preprocessors, might not be a good idea with custom properties.

One example that illustrates this is:

```
:root {
  --font-scale: 1.2;
  --font-size-1: 1rem;
  --font-size-2: calc(var(--font-scale) * var(--font-size-1));
  --font-size-3: calc(var(--font-scale) * var(--font-size-2));
  --font-size-4: calc(var(--font-scale) * var(--font-size-3));
}
```

[1] http://smashed.by/designtime

The code above generates a modular scale: a series of numbers that relate to one another through a ratio. They are often used in web design to set font sizes and spacing.

The interesting part here is that each custom property is determined using `calc()`. By taking the value of the previous custom property and multiplying it by the ratio, we get the next number in the scale.

The font-sizes are calculated at runtime, and you can change them by updating only the value of the `--font-scale` property. For example:

```css
@media screen and (min-width: 800px) {
  :root {
    --font-scale: 1.33;
  }
}
```

This is clever, concise, and much quicker than calculating all the values again should you want to change the scale. It's also something I would **not** do in production code. Although useful for prototyping, in production I'd much prefer to see something like this:

```css
:root {
  --font-size-1: 1rem;
  --font-size-2: 1.2rem;
  --font-size-3: 1.44rem;
  --font-size-4: 1.728rem;
}
@media screen and (min-width: 800px) {
  :root {
    --font-size-1: 1rem;
    --font-size-2: 1.333rem;
    --font-size-3: 1.777rem;
    --font-size-4: 2.369rem;
  }
}
```

I find it helpful to see what the actual values are, and global values such as font scales don't change frequently in production.

The example above is still not perfect. It violates the principle I mentioned earlier, that **global values should be static**. I'd much prefer to use a preprocessor for these variables and convert them to locally dynamic custom properties using the techniques demonstrated in the section: "When to Use Custom Properties".

It is also important to avoid changing from using one custom property to a different custom property. Which can happen when we name properties like this.

Change the Value, Not the Variable

Change the value, not the variable is one of the most important strategies for using custom properties effectively.

As a general rule, you should never change which custom property is used for any single purpose. It's easy to do because this is exactly how we do things with preprocessors, but it makes little sense with custom properties.

In the next example we apply two custom properties to a component. I switch from using the value of `--font-size-small` to `--font-size-large` depending on the screen size.

```css
:root {
  --font-size-small: 1.2rem;
  --font-size-large: 2rem;
}
.example {
  font-size: var(--font-size-small);
}
@media screen and (min-width: 800px) {
  .example {
    font-size: var(--font-size-large);
  }
}
```

A better way would be to define a single custom property scoped to the component. Then, using a media query, or any other selector, change its value.

```css
.example {
  --example-font-size: 1.2rem;
}
@media screen and (min-width: 800px) {
  .example {
    --example-font-size: 2rem;
  }
}
```

Finally, in a single place, retrieve the value of this custom property and assign it to font-size:

```css
.example {
  font-size: var(--example-font-size);
}
```

So far in this chapter, media queries have only been used to change the value of custom properties. You might also notice there is only one place where the `var()` statement is used and regular CSS properties are applied. This separation of variable declarations from property declarations is intentional. There are many reasons for this, but the benefits are most obvious when thinking about responsive design.

Strategies for Responsive Design

One of the difficulties with responsive design that relies heavily on media queries is that no matter how you organize your CSS, styles relating to a particular component become fragmented across the style sheet. It can be very difficult to know what CSS properties are going to change.

CSS custom properties can help us organise some of this logic related to responsive design and make working with media queries a lot easier.

IF IT CHANGES, IT'S A VARIABLE

Properties that change using media queries are inherently dynamic, and custom properties provide the means to express dynamic values in CSS. If you are using a media query to change any CSS property, you should consider placing this value in a custom property. You can then move this, along with all the media rules, hover states, or any dynamic selectors that define how the value changes, to the top of the document.

SEPARATE LOGIC FROM DESIGN

When done correctly, this results in a separation of logic and design that means **media queries are only used for changing the value of custom properties** and nothing else. All the logic related to responsive design will be at the top of the document, and wherever we see a `var()` statement in our CSS, we immediately know that this property changes. With traditional methods of writing CSS, there was no way of knowing this at a glance.

Many of us became very good at reading and interpreting CSS quickly, while tracking in our heads which properties changed in different situations. I'm tired of this and I don't want to do it anymore! Custom properties now provide a link between the logic and its implementation, so we don't need to keep track of changing CSS properties, and that is incredibly useful.

THE LOGIC FOLD

Declaring variables at the top of a document or function is not a new idea. It's something we do in most programming languages, and now we can do it in CSS as well. Writing CSS in this way creates a clear visual distinction between CSS at the top of the document and CSS below. I describe this differentiation with a metaphor: the *logic fold*.

Above the fold are all the preprocessor variables and custom properties. This includes all the different values a custom property can have, making it easy to trace how it changes.

CSS below the fold is straightforward, highly declarative and easy to read. It feels like CSS was before media queries and the other necessary complexities of modern CSS.

Take a look at a really simple example of a six-column flexbox grid system. The above the fold might look like this:

```
.row {
  --row-display: block;
}
@media screen and (min-width: 800px) {
  .row {
    --row-display: flex;
  }
}
```

```css
.col-1 { --col-basis: 16.66%; }
.col-2 { --col-basis: 33.33%; }
.col-3 { --col-basis: 50%; }
.col-4 { --col-basis: 66.66%; }
.col-5 { --col-basis: 83.33%; }
.col-6 { --col-basis: 100%; }
```

Below the fold we might find:

```css
.row {
  display: var(--row-display);
  flex-direction: row;
  flex-wrap: nowrap;
}
.col-1, .col-2, .col-3,
.col-4, .col-5, .col-6 {
  flex-grow: 0;
  flex-shrink: 0;
  flex-basis: var(--col-basis);
}
```

Because they are custom properties, we immediately know `--row-display` and `--col-basis` are values that change. We can look above the fold and trace the logic. Initially `--row-display` is set to `block`. Then, above 800px, the display mode is changed to `flex`, causing all the `--col-basis` custom properties to come into effect.

What's interesting here is that the `--col-basis` custom property is applied in only one place but has a different value depending on the classname used in the HTML. Writing CSS in this way can help trace the logic of values that change in responsive design and can also make the CSS less verbose.

This example is fairly simple, but you could try expanding it to include a flexible-width column that fills the remaining space. To do this, it's likely the `flex-grow` and `flex-shrink` values would need to be converted to custom properties.

Strategies for Theming

In this chapter I've mostly argued against using custom properties for global dynamic variables and, I hope, implied that attaching custom properties to the `:root` selector is in many cases considered harmful. But every rule has an exception – for custom properties, it's theming. Limited use of global custom properties can make theming a whole lot easier.

Theming typically refers to letting users customize the UI in some way. These changes may be aesthetic such as choosing colors and background images. But can also include, light and dark modes for reading, or layout changes that improve accessibility and the user experience. For example *Gmail*, has options for "Default", "Comfortable" and "Compact" display modes, that change the layout of the inbox.

Gmail display modes.

Theme changes can also be more localized, such as choosing the color of a note in the *Google Keep* application.

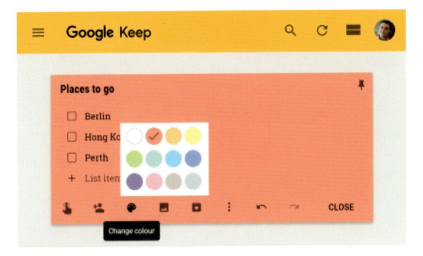

Google Keep application.

Theming usually involves compiling separate style sheets to override default values with different themes, or compiling a different style sheet for each user. Both of these can be difficult and have an impact on performance.

Custom properties allow us to avoid compiling a different style sheet; we only need to update the value of custom properties according to user preferences. Since custom properties are inherited values, if we attach them to the `:root` selector, they can be used anywhere in our application.

CAPITALIZE GLOBAL DYNAMIC PROPERTIES

Custom properties are case-sensitive. Since most custom properties will be local, it can make sense to capitalize global dynamic properties. For example:

```
:root {
  --THEME-COLOR: #d33a2c;
}
```

Capitalizing variables like this often signifies global constants. For us, it signifies that the property is set elsewhere in the application, and we should probably not change it locally.

Custom properties accept a fallback value. It's useful to avoid directly overwriting the value of global custom properties and keep user values separate. We can use the fallback value to do this.

```
:root {
  --THEME-COLOR: var(--user-theme-color, #d33a2c);
}
```

The example above sets the value of `--THEME-COLOR` to the value of `--user-theme-color` (if it exists). If `--user-theme-color` is not set, the value of `#d33a2c` will be used. This way, we don't need to provide a fallback every time we use `--THEME-COLOR`.

DON'T OVERRIDE THEME PROPERTIES DIRECTLY

Rather than override `--THEME-COLOR` directly, we should set the value of `--user-theme-color`.

In the next example, you might expect that the `background` will be `green`. However, the value of `--user-theme-color` is set on the `body` rather than the `:root` selector, and since we are inheriting `--THEME-COLOR` from `:root`, its value has not changed.

```
:root {
  --THEME-COLOR: var(--user-theme-color, #d33a2c);
}
body {
  --user-theme-color: green;
  background: var(--THEME-COLOR);
}
```

If `--user-theme-color` is set on `:root`, the background would be green. Indirectly setting global theme properties like this protects them from being overwritten locally, and ensures user settings are always inherited from the root element. This is a useful convention to safeguard your theme values and avoid unintended inheritance, such as this case, where we don't want different theme colors for the same user.

If we do want to expose specific theme properties to inheritance, we can replace the `:root` selector with a `*` selector:

```
* {
  --THEME-COLOR: var(--user-theme-color, #d33a2c);
}
body {
  --user-theme-color: green;
  background: var(--THEME-COLOR);
}
```

Now the value of `--THEME-COLOR` is recalculated for every element and, therefore, the local value of `--user-theme-color` can be used. In other words, the background color in this example will green. This can be useful when we need localised theming, such as in the example of allowing a user to select the color of a note in a note-keeping application.

You can see some more detailed examples of this pattern in the section "Manipulating Color with Custom Properties."

UPDATING CUSTOM PROPERTIES WITH JAVASCRIPT

If you want to set custom properties using JavaScript, there is a fairly simple API and it looks like this:

```
const elm = document.documentElement;
elm.style.setProperty('--user-theme-color', 'tomato');
```

Here I'm setting the value of `--user-theme-color` on the document element in JavaScript, which is equivalent to the `html` element, or the `:root` selector in CSS. Here, the value will be inherited by all elements in the DOM.

This is not a new API: it's the same JavaScript method for updating styles on any element. These are inline styles, so they will have a higher specificity than regular CSS. This means it's easy to apply local customizations:

```
.note {
  --note-color: #eaeaea;
}
.note {
  background-color: var(--note-color);
}
```

Here I set a default value for `--note-color` and scope this to the `.note` component. I keep the variable declaration separate from the property declaration, even in this simple example.

```
const elm = document.querySelector('#note-uid');
elm.style.setProperty('--note-color', 'yellow');
```

I then target a specific instance of a `.note` element in the HTML and change the value of the `--note-color` custom property for that element only. This will have higher specificity than the default value and the background color will change.

USE CUSTOM PROPERTIES IN STYLE ATTRIBUTES

If you are retrieving values from a database, or if you are using a static site generator, or templating language, it can be handy to know you can set the value of a custom property in a `style` attribute and, because of specificity, this will override any other value in the CSS.

```
<div class="note" style="--user-theme-color: yellow;">...</div>
```

Not only can we set custom properties in `style` attributes, we can also retrieve the value of custom properties using the `var()` function in any HTML attribute.

You might have seen a similar examples where `currentColor` is used as a variable in inline SVG elements.

```
<svg>
  <path fill="currentColor" ... />
</svg>
```

This means they can have the same stroke or fill as the surrounding text. If you use `currentColor` like this you can make the CSS `color` property to change the fill of an SVG.

The Smashing Cat image is an inline SVG that always has the same fill color as the surrounding text color.

This technique is great for single color icons, but what if we want to use more colors? That's where custom properties can help.

```
<svg>
  <path fill="var(--svg-color-1)" ... />
  <path stroke="var(--svg-stroke)" fill="var(--svg-color-2)" ... />
</svg>
```

This means we can use the same inline SVG and set different color variations with HTML and CSS. This is great for icons, logos, and other UI elements that use SVG.

```
.smashing-logo-1 {
  --svg-color: #000;
  --svg-background: #888;
}
.smashing-logo-2 {
  --svg-color: #bc3428;
  --svg-background: #27aae1;
}
.smashing-logo-3 {
  --svg-color: #264a9c;
  --svg-background: #c95d5ac3;
}
```

The Smashing Cat image is an inline SVG with fill colors inherited from custom properties.

MANIPULATING COLOR WITH CUSTOM PROPERTIES

In addition to hex values and named colors, CSS has color functions such as `rgb()` and `hsl()`. These allow us to specify individual components of a color, such as the hue, saturation and lightness. Custom properties can be used to set individual parts of a color function.

```
:root {
  --hue: 25;
}
body {
  background: hsl(var(--hue), 80%, 50%);
}
```

This is useful, but some of the most widely used features of preprocessors are color functions that allow us to modify a base color using functions like `lighten`, `darken` or `desaturate`. For example:

```
darken($base-color, 10%);
lighten($base-color, 10%);
desaturate($base-color, 20%);
```

It would be useful to have some of these features in browsers and luckily the `color-mod()` function is coming to CSS soon, but until we have this, custom properties can fill some of that gap.

We've seen that custom properties can be used inside existing color functions like `rgb()` and `hsl()` and that they can be used in `calc()`. This means we can convert a real number to a percentage by multiplying it; for instance, `calc(50 * 1%) = 50%`.

```
:root {
  --lightness: 50;
}
body {
  background: hsl(25, 80%, calc(var(--lightness) * 1%));
}
```

The reason to store the lightness value as a real number, rather than a unit, is to manipulate it with `calc()` before converting it to a percentage. For example, if I want to darken a color by 20%, I can multiply its lightness by 0.8. We can make this a little easier to read by separating the lightness calculation into a locally scoped custom property named `--l`:

```
:root {
  --lightness: 50;
}
body {
  --l: calc(var(--lightness) * 0.8);
  background: hsl(25, 80%, calc(var(--l) * 1%));
}
```

We *could* even abstract away more of the calculations and create something like color modification functions in CSS using custom properties.

```css
:root {
  --HUE: 0;
  --SATURATION: 80;
  --LIGHTNESS: 50;
}
* {
  --color: hsl(
    calc(var(--HUE) + var(--hue-rotate, 0)),
    calc(var(--SATURATION) * (1 - var(--desaturate, 0)) * 1%),
    calc(var(--LIGHTNESS) * (1 - var(--darken, 0)) * 1%)
  );
}
```

By exposing the `--color` custom property with the `*` selector, we are able to pick up local values for `--hue-rotate`, `--desaturate`, and `--darken` that modify the global *constants* that define the base color.

This allows us to create our own set of custom properties that modify global values locally. Although the initial setup is a bit complex, it results in highly semantic CSS that clearly describes the color modifications:

```css
.complementary {
  --hue-rotate: -180;
  background: var(--color);
}
.dark-split {
  --hue-rotate: -150;
  --darken: 0.2;
  background: var(--color);
}
.dark-split-2 {
  --hue-rotate: 150;
  --darken: 0.2;
  background: var(--color);
}
```

This example is probably too complex for most practical cases of theming. You should only use something like this if you really need it. In his article "*Dark Theme in a Day,*"[2] Marcin Wichary says:

> *I considered going even further, expressing some colours as variations on others. But that felt like overkill here. The slightly inelegant way CSS expresses variables, combined with the need for calc() would make this CSS much less readable.*

Be sure to read this article if you are considering using custom properties for theming or color modifications in any way.

Strategies for Refactoring

Let's put some of this theory into practice and look at refactoring some Sass variables to use custom properties.

Imagine a simple note-keeping application that has the following HTML:

```
<div class="notes">
  <div class="note"> - Get Milk </div>
  <div class="note"></div>
  ...
</div>
```

It might look something like this:

[2] http://smashed.by/darktheme

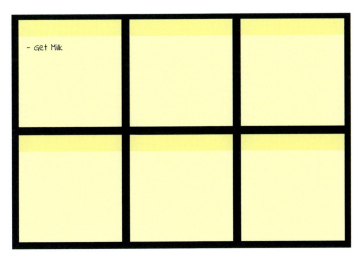

An example note-keeping application built with HTML and CSS.

The CSS has some Sass variables to control the background color and the color of the notes in the application:

```
$background-color: #263238;
$note-color: #FFF9C4;
body {
  background: $background-color;
}
.note {
  border-top: solid 40px darken($note-color, 10%);
  background: $note-color;
}
```

The layout is controlled using CSS Grid and media queries. The application will have between one and four evenly spaced columns, depending on the viewport width.

```
.notes {
  display: grid;
  grid-template-columns: 1fr;
  grid-gap: 20px;
  max-width: 1200px;
  margin: 0 auto;
}
@media screen and (min-width: 600px) {
  .notes {
    grid-template-columns: 1fr 1fr;
  }
}
@media screen and (min-width: 800px) {
  .notes {
    grid-template-columns: 1fr 1fr 1fr;
  }
}
@media screen and (min-width: 1000px) {
  .notes {
    grid-template-columns: 1fr 1fr 1fr 1fr;
  }
}
```

If we want to refactor this code to use custom properties, we should:

1. Look at the existing variables and determine if they are static or dynamic
2. Look for dynamic logic in the CSS that should be in a custom property
3. Separate logic from design and ensure media queries only change the value of custom properties

As tempting as it is, I would not immediately convert the Sass variables to custom properties. It would be better to simplify the logic related to the media queries changing number of grid columns.

Let's do this and move all the logic to the top of the document:

```
$note-color: #FFF9C4;
$background-color: #263238;
.notes {
  --notes-grid-col-layout: 1fr;
}
@media screen and (min-width: 600px) {
  .notes {
    --notes-grid-col-layout: 1fr 1fr;
  }
}
@media screen and (min-width: 800px) {
  .notes {
    --notes-grid-col-layout: 1fr 1fr 1fr;
  }
}
@media screen and (min-width: 1000px) {
  .notes {
    --notes-grid-col-layout: 1fr 1fr 1fr 1fr;
  }
}
```

Now, below the fold, `grid-template-columns` has a single custom property value that varies depending on the viewport with. This small change has separated logic from the implementation of design.

```
.notes {
  display: grid;
  grid-template-columns: var(--notes-grid-col-layout);
}
```

At this point, our Sass variables have remained the same. They are static, and there is no reason to convert them to custom properties. However, if we want to extend this application to allow notes with custom colors (local theming), we need to convert `$note-color` to a custom property.

We keep the global Sass variable, as this will now be the default color. Then within the `.note` selector, we convert the static variables to two custom properties: `--note-color` and `--note-border-color`.

```
.note {
  --note-color: #{$note-color};
  --note-border-color: #{darken($note-color, 10%)};
}
.note {
  border-color: var(--note-border-color);
  background: var(--note-color);
}
```

We can then change the value of these custom properties for individual notes. We can do this with CSS, inline styles, or JavaScript:

```
#note-3 {
  --note-color: #FFCCBC;
  --note-border-color: #ffa589;
}
```

```
<div class="note" style="--note-color: #E3F2FD; --note-border-color: #b3dcfa;"></div>
```

```
note.style.setProperty('--note-color', '#DCEDC8');
note.style.setProperty('--note-border-color', '#c4e0a2');
```

So far, we have dealt with examples of local theming. If we want to allow users to change the background color, this is a global theme change. To do this, we remove the Sass variable `$background` and replace it with a global custom property: `--THEME-COLOR`.

We assign this custom property a value of `--user-theme-color` and a fallback value that will be the default background. We then apply this to the `body`:

```css
:root {
  --THEME-COLOR: var(--user-theme-color, #263238);
}
body {
  background: var(--THEME-COLOR);
}
```

To allow the theme color to change, we need to update the value of `--user-theme-color` on the root (HTML) element. Once again, we can do this with CSS, inline styles or JavaScript.

```
:root {
  --user-theme-color: #ddd;
}
<html style="--user-theme-color: #ddd;">
const elm = document.documentElement;
elm.style.setProperty('--user-theme-color', '#ddd');
```

Strategies for Accessibility

HIGH CONTRAST SETTINGS

According to the World Health Organisation, about 4% of the world's population are visually impaired. Many of those impairments reduce sensitivity to contrast, and in some cases the ability to distinguish colors.

Allowing users to switch to a high-contrast theme can be of particular benefit to low-vision users, but a well-crafted high-contrast theme can also provide an better reading experience for everyone. High-contrast themes assist in poor light conditions, and some color schemes may help reduce eye strain when reading at night.

Search engine DuckDuckGo implements dark and light themes.

The specific conditions and experience users with low vision have varies, so it's best to provide options. Custom properties make this far less challenging.

For Windows users, there are built-in high-contrast options that can be enabled via the user settings menu.

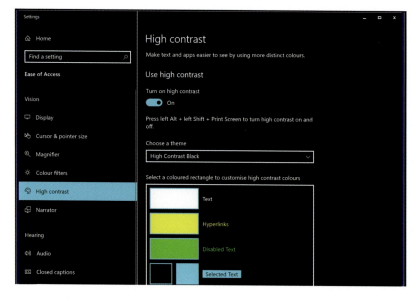

High contrast theme in Windows 10.

These settings can be detected with media queries but unfortunately, at the time of writing, this feature is only supported in Microsoft Edge. Nonetheless, when available, you can use this to enable high-contrast themes automatically.

You can detect whether any high-contrast theme is active, or if the user has selected a preference for a black-on-white or white-on-black theme.

```
@media (-ms-high-contrast:active) {...}
@media (-ms-high-contrast:black-on-white) {...}
@media (-ms-high-contrast:white-on-black) {...}
```

Note that these settings also change the default user-agent style sheet, so always test them in the Edge browser.

For other browsers, it's necessary for users to set these preferences within the application. When a user has selected these options you can add a classname to the HTML element. For example:

```
<html class="high-contrast">
...
</html>
/* Default */
:root {
  --text-color: #555;
  --body-color: #ddd;
}
/* Windows\Edge detect high-contrast preference */
@media screen and (-ms-high-contrast:active) {
  :root {
    --text-color: #000;
    --body-color: #fff;
  }
}
/* User preference */
.high-contrast {
  --text-color: #000;
```

```
  --body-color: #fff;
}
body {
  background: var(--body-color);
  color: var(--text-color);
}
```

REDUCED MOTION

Some people are particularly sensitive to certain types of movement and animation on the web. It can make them feel dizzy or nauseous, or simply give them a headache. People with certain types of vestibular disorders (issues that affect balance) can have more immediate and severe reactions.

Other people just don't like animations. They may have performance issues on older devices, can be battery-draining and resource intensive.

Despite this, good animation can be an important part of the user experience. Providing options that allow users to set preferences related to animation is easier than ever with custom properties.

To start with, we set a global custom property `--ANIMATION-DURATION` to the value of `--user-duration` and give it a fallback value of 1.

```
:root {
  --ANIMATION-DURATION: var(--user-duration, 1);
}
```

Since the user preference has not been set, the value of `--ANIMATION-DURATION` will be 1. We can then apply this value to our transitions with `calc()`:

```
.fade-out {
  transition: opacity calc(var(--ANIMATION-DURATION) * 1s) ease-out;
}
```

The result of `calc(1 * 1s)` will be `1s`, so the duration of the animation remains unchanged.

To apply user preferences to this, we can use the `prefers-reduced-motion` media query to update the `--user-duration` on the `:root` selector.

```
@media screen and (prefers-reduced-motion: reduce) {
  :root {
    --user-duration: 0;
  }
}
```

Once again, this feature is only supported by a limited number of browsers, at this time Safari and iOS. Also, once again, we can provide custom options for reduced-motion within our application or website. We could add the classname `prefers-reduced-motion` to the HTML element when the user has selected this option. And we add the following CSS:

```
.prefers-reduced-motion {
  --user-duration: 0;
}
```

This selector must target the `<html>` element because the global `--ANIMATION-DURATION` is looking for this value on the `:root` selector.

Now that we have set this value to `0`, the `calc()` equation will be `calc(0 * 1s)`, which results in `0s` and therefore, the transition will be instant. Any value between 0 and 1 could be used to reduce animation durations.

Strategies for Using Custom Properties Today

Even if you're supporting IE10 and 11, you can start using custom properties today. Most of the examples in this chapter are about how we write and structure CSS. The benefits are significant in terms of maintainability; yet most of the examples only reduce what could otherwise be done with more complex code.

I use a tool called *postcss-css-variables*[3] to convert most of the features of custom properties into a static representation of the same code. Other similar tools ignore custom properties inside media queries or complex selectors, treating custom properties more like preprocessor variables.

What these tools cannot do is emulate the runtime features of custom properties. This means no dynamic features like theming, or changing properties with JavaScript. This might be OK in many situations. UI customization might be considered a progressive enhancement, and the default theme could be perfectly acceptable for older browsers.

If you really need to support dynamic theming in old browsers, you may need a different approach. Traditional methods of compiling user style sheets on the server might be a good option.

Although tempting, emulating the runtime features of custom properties with JavaScript is probably not a good idea. Dealing with custom properties in a broad and general way is a complex problem. Any polyfill that needs to parse and rewrite CSS will require a lot of expensive JavaScript that is intended to run on the slowest browsers and devices.

3   http://smashed.by/postcssvar

A better option might be to write some custom JavaScript to deal with a limited number of specific requirements, such as toggling a light and dark theme.

LOADING STYLE SHEETS

There are many ways you can use PostCSS.[4] I use a gulp process to compile separate style sheet s for newer and older browsers. A simplified version of my gulp task looks like this:

```
import gulp from "gulp";
import sass from "gulp-sass";
import postcss from "gulp-postcss";
import rename from "gulp-rename";
import cssvariables from "postcss-css-variables";
gulp.task("css-no-vars", () =>
  gulp
    .src("./src/css/*.scss")
    .pipe(sass().on("error", sass.logError))
    .pipe(postcss([cssvariables()]))
    .pipe(rename({ extname: ".no-vars.css" }))
    .pipe(gulp.dest("./dist/css"))
);
gulp.task("css", () =>
  gulp
    .src("./src/css/*.scss")
    .pipe(sass().on("error", sass.logError))
    .pipe(rename({ extname: ".css" }))
    .pipe(gulp.dest("./dist/css"))
);
```

This results in two CSS files: a regular one with custom properties (*styles.css*); and one for older browsers (*styles.no-vars.css*). I want IE10 and 11 to be served *styles.no-vars.css*, and other browsers to get the regular CSS file.

4   https://postcss.org/

Normally, I'd advocate using feature queries, but IE11 doesn't support *feature queries*[5] and we've used custom properties so extensively that serving a different style sheet makes sense in this case.

Intelligently serving a different style sheet and avoiding a flash of unstyled content is not a simple task. If you don't need the dynamic features of custom properties, you could consider serving all browser *styles.no-vars.css* and using custom properties simply as a development tool.

If you want to take full advantage of all the dynamic features of custom properties I suggest using a critical CSS technique.[6] Following these techniques, the main style sheet is loaded asynchronously, while the critical CSS is rendered inline. Your page header might look something like this:

```
<head>
  <style> /* inlined critical CSS */ </style>
  <script> loadCSS('non-critical.css'); </script>
</head>
```

We can extend this to load either *styles.css* or *styles.no-vars.css* depending on whether the browser supports custom properties. We can detect support like this:

```
if ( window.CSS && CSS.supports('color', 'var(--test)') ) {
  loadCSS('styles.css');
} else {
  loadCSS('styles.no-vars.css');
}
```

5   http://smashed.by/supports
6   http://smashed.by/criticalcss

STRATEGIES FOR WORKING WITH CUSTOM PROPERTIES EFFECTIVELY

If you've been struggling to organize CSS efficiently, have difficulty with responsive components, want to implement client-side theming, or just want to start off on the right foot with custom properties, this guide should tell you everything you need to know.

It comes down to understanding the difference between dynamic and static variables in CSS, as well as a few simple principles:

1. Global variables are usually static.
2. Separate logic from design.
3. If a CSS property changes, consider using a custom property.
4. Change the value of custom properties, not which custom property is used.
5. Don't override theme properties directly.

If you follow these conventions, you will find working with custom properties is a whole lot easier. This might even change how you approach CSS in general.

About The Author

Mike Riethmuller has worked on some of Australia's largest websites as well as some of the smallest community sites. When he's not building websites or writing about it, he likes to experiment with code. When he's not exploring the digital landscape, he likes to explore the world and is currently trying to find a way to do both those things at the same time

CHAPTER 5

Building an Advanced Service Worker

Lyza Gardner

Building an Advanced Service Worker

by Lyza D. Gardner

Oh, yes! Service workers! They can make sites and apps work offline. They're an integral part of progressive web apps (PWAs). They're big boons for network performance. You'll need service workers if you want to get at some of the nifty new web APIs like Web Notifications or Web Background Synchronization.

Yep: they enable a wide array of great features and are beginning to feel like a lynchpin of the modern web. Yet even folks who've cooked up a few service workers of their own can be hard-pressed to explain exactly what a service worker *is*.

Let's start here: a service worker consists of a script – its behavior is defined by a JavaScript file. The JavaScript in that file is executed in the background within a browser, on a separate thread from the pages loaded in the browser's windows or tabs. A service worker, then, has a different *context* from a web page, and it is able to access some features and APIs you can't get at otherwise.

The canonical use case for a service worker is as a *proxy*, intercepting network requests for resources within its scope and deciding how to handle them. That's vague, so let's break it down. A service worker sits between your site or app and the network, and can decide what to do whenever a resource (like an HTML page or an image) is requested by the browser.

For any given request, the service worker can opt to go to the network and fetch fresh content from a server, or it might retrieve a resource from a cache (where the service worker has previously stashed the resource).

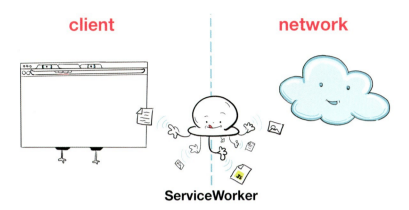

A service worker acts as a proxy, sitting between the client – your site or app's web page JavaScript – and the network.

A service worker is only able to intercept requests that fall within its *scope*: a range of URLs within the service worker's control.

In addition, a service worker has a bunch of special goodies available in its global context: references to the aforementioned Notifications and Background Sync APIs, for example. You can't get to some of these APIs from *web-page-loaded-in-a-browser*[1] JavaScript.

Fetch handling – responding to requests for resources that fall within its scope – is a fundamental functionality of service workers. However, if you read the Service Worker spec[2] (I highly encourage this, by the way; it's fairly short and concise), you'll see it doesn't define how `fetch` works. That's because `fetch`, though critical even to the simplest service worker, is its own separate standard, and is not part of Service Worker itself.

---

1 That, if you can believe it, is not the scientific term. JavaScript in a web page executes in a browsing context (global object: window), while service workers have a different context, specifically `ServiceWorkerGlobalScope`.
2 W3C Service Workers 1 Working Draft (http://smashed.by/serviceworkersw3)

Note: The Service Worker API makes heavy use of JavaScript Promises. If you're new or rusty with Promises, do a Google or two and read up a bit. The Mozilla Developer Network's (MDN) coverage[3] is clear and readable.

Browser support for service worker functionality continues to strengthen. At the time of writing, some level of support is available in every major browser – Chrome, Firefox, Opera, Safari and Microsoft Edge. Not all Service Worker features are supported in every browser. Google is a major driver of these technologies – unsurprisingly, some of the newer Service-Worker-related APIs and features are supported only in Chrome.[4]

Service workers are not too hard to work with. There are two hard-and-fast rules, however:

- The code in a service worker needs to be responsive and non-blocking. A browser has the right to terminate any service worker that is taking too long to do its thing. That means that web APIs that are inherently slow and block the execution thread (like `LocalStorage` or synchronous XHR) are no-nos in service workers.

- Service workers are only able to mediate communication for pages served over HTTPS. There is a handy exception to this for development purposes: resources served from `localhost` do not have this HTTPS requirement.

---

3 http://smashed.by/mdnpromise
4 See Jake Archibald's "Is service worker ready?" for the latest details of who supports what: http://smashed.by/isserviceworkerready/.

The Life of a Service Worker

A service worker doesn't go away when you close a tab, navigate to another site, or shut down the browser. It has its own life, related to but definitely distinct from the pages it controls. It executes in a different context from a web page and is event-driven, relying on an assortment of relevant events to get its job done.

UNDERSTANDING CONTEXT

To understand a bit more about how service workers tick and how their lives work, let's talk about their API parentage. Service workers are a kind of *web worker*. Service workers inherit from web workers the trait of running in the background, on a different thread from the pages displayed in a browser's tabs or windows.

A service worker executes within a `ServiceWorkerGlobalScope`, which extends `WorkerGlobalScope` (the global scope for any web worker) with a few things that service workers need to be, well, service workers.

A web page in a browser tab or window, on the other hand, executes in a *browsing context*, represented at a global level by the `window` object. A browsing context is, as the HTML spec explains, "an environment in which Document objects are presented to the user."[5] There's some additional nuance, but for the purposes of our explorations we can say that each open window or tab in your browser corresponds to a browsing context.[6]

---

5   http://smashed.by/browsingcontext
6   `iframe` elements also get their own browsing contexts.

As such, a web page and its controlling service worker are in separate bubbles. They can't manipulate each other directly,[7] and each context has different stuff in its global scope.

A `ServiceWorkerGlobalScope` has no `window` object or DOM – that wouldn't make sense, as the service worker is always invisible and in the background.

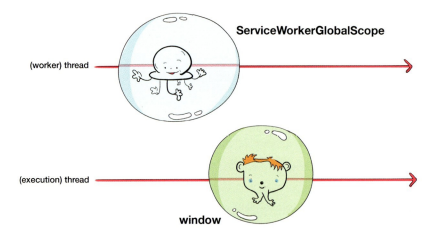

Web workers, including service workers, execute on a different thread and in a different context than the clients (web pages) they control.

SERVICE WORKER LIFE CYCLE

From the moment it's created until it's done and retired, a service worker's capabilities change in predictable ways. That is, a service worker has a *life cycle*, and its position in its overall life cycle at any given moment is indicated its by its `state` attribute. `state` has one of the following values:

---

[7] They can, however, absolutely communicate – see the "Channel Messaging API" section later in this chapter.

- parsed
- installing
- installed
- activating
- activated
- redundant

All service workers start out as parsed. Subsequently, they move through an installation phase and eventually, if everything goes right, get activated. Though they sound similar, those two life cycle phases – installation and activation – have distinct meanings and purposes.

The installation phase is used to get the service worker ready, typically by stuffing some things into a cache that it'll need to access later (such as core, application shell resources). The activation phase is for housecleaning, providing an opportunity to clean up after old service worker versions and caches (like deleting crufty cache entries).

SERVICE WORKER SCOPE

A service worker applies to a specific *scope*: a range of URLs it can control. A service worker is unable to respond to anything happening that relates to resources at URLs outside of its scope.

A browser that implements the Service Worker API is required to keep track of registered service workers, mapping between service workers and the scope that each covers,[8] so it can figure out which to select for a given URL. There can be only one *active* service worker for a given URL at one time.

---

8 Technically, browsers map `ServiceWorkerRegistration` objects to scopes, not `ServiceWorker` objects directly.

Just because a service worker registration is maintained in the browser doesn't mean the associated service worker is always *running*. Service workers are event-driven: if a given service worker doesn't have anything to do – there's no event to handle at the moment – a browser can opt to terminate it.[9]

It can be confusing: the word *scope* has two different meanings! There's scope as it pertains to execution context: all JavaScript executing in the browser has a scope; in Service Worker's case this is represented by `ServiceWorkerGlobalScope`. But service workers are also associated with a scope: a range of URLs they can control.

Because of the browser's prerogative to shut down inactive service workers, you should never rely on persisting something in global scope (keeping track of something by incrementing a global variable, for example).

SERVICE WORKER AND EVENTS

Events are what make service workers *go*. A service worker's functionality resides primarily in handling several key events: two *life cycle events* (`install` and `activate`), as well the functional event `fetch`:

- `install` is dispatched after the service worker moves into the installing state.
- `activate` is dispatched after the service worker moves into the activating state.
- `fetch` is dispatched whenever the browser wishes to fetch a resource that falls within the given service worker's scope.

---

[9] Browsers will likely shut down a service worker if it hasn't done anything for about thirty seconds.

`install`, `activate` and `fetch` are the key Service-Worker-related events, but they are not the only ones a service worker might choose to listen for. Other useful events include, but are not limited to: `message` (Channel Messaging API), `push` (Push API) and `sync` (Background Sync API).

Anatomy of a Basic Service Worker

There are two real-world pieces to a service worker: the service worker script file itself and a bit of code that goes in your site or app's web page(s) to *register* that service worker against a scope.

REGISTERING A SERVICE WORKER

Something has to tell the browser to register a service worker and where to find it. Otherwise, how would it know what to do? This job is handled by a bit of JavaScript you can put in your site's web pages. This registration code looks like this:

```
<script>
  navigator.serviceWorker.register('service-worker.js', './');
</script>
```

Browsers that support Service Worker expose `serviceWorker` on the global `navigator` object.[10] In browsers that don't support Service Worker, `navigator.serviceWorker` will be undefined. To keep those browsers from choking,[11] you can wrap the registration call in a simple feature test:

---

10 Specifically, `navigator.serviceWorker` returns a `ServiceWorkerContainer` object, which contains methods for registering and unregistering service workers.
11 Trying to invoke `navigator.serviceWorker.register` in a browser with no exposed `navigator.serviceWorker` will throw a `TypeError`.

```
<script>
if ('serviceWorker' in navigator) { // make sure navigator.serviceWorker
exists
  navigator.serviceWorker.register('service-worker.js', './');
}
</script>
```

The register method takes two arguments: a script URL and an optional options object. The following three statements are functionally identical:

```
// Service Workers 1 defines only one recognized option property: scope
navigator.serviceWorker.register('service-worker.js', { scope: './' });
// Shorthand is supported: pass `scope` as a string instead
navigator.serviceWorker.register('service-worker.js', './');
// Default scope is './' when the argument is not present
navigator.serviceWorker.register('service-worker.js');
```

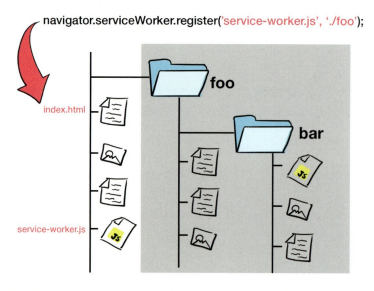

In index.html, a service worker at service-worker.js is registered against the scope './foo'. Once activated and in control, that service worker can respond to fetches for resources in the shaded area – within the foo directory – but could not respond to fetches outside of that range of URLs.

Note: Scope is relative to the service worker script's location, not the registering web page.

A service worker's highest allowed scope is the location of its script file. If this proves problematic, there's an Service-Worker-Allowed HTTP header you can take advantage of.[12]

YOUR FIRST (USELESS) SERVICE WORKER

The other piece of the puzzle is, of course, the service worker script itself. Let's start with something very simple inside of *service-worker.js*:[13]

```
self.addEventListener('fetch', event => {});
```

Recall that a fetch event is dispatched whenever the browser wants to fetch a resource that falls within the service worker's scope.

Within a fetch handler function we can opt to respond to a fetch, satisfying the browser's needs by determining what kind of response to use and where to retrieve it from (a great example of a service worker acting as a proxy between the browser and the network). Of course, our stub of a fetch handler doesn't do anything (yet).

There are several ways to respond to a fetch, but the most common techniques are:

---

12 Appendix B: Extended HTTP headers, Service Workers 1 Working Draft: http://smashed.by/httpheaders
13 You can name your service worker file anything you like, of course, but I'll use *service-worker.js* throughout this chapter.

- using the fetch API to retrieve a resource from the network
- using the caches API to retrieve a previously-cached resource (avoiding the network)
- generating our own Response object

Let's start by learning about fetch.

In web-page JavaScript, the window object provides a reference to the global object. In Service Worker JavaScript, it is conventional to use the reference self when accessing methods or properties on the global object (e.g. `self.addEventListener`). These references will certainly work without the self notation (i.e. addEventListener will work by itself) but can feel "magical." Being explicit about scope, by using self when applicable, can make your code more readable and easier to maintain.

Not all browsers support arrow functions (`() => {} notation`), but every browser that supports Service Worker does. So you can use that syntax with impunity within service workers. The same goes for the `const` keyword and other modern JavaScript features used in examples here.

Fetch API

The Fetch API lets you go out and get resources from the network asynchronously. It's not too different from `XMLHttpRequest` but it does more things and is certainly easier to pronounce.

Fetch's bread and butter are Request and Response objects. You feed `fetch()` a `Request` object and it returns a `Promise` which – if everything goes OK and the network is available – resolves to a `Response` object. Requests in, Responses out:

```
var aResponseIHope = fetch(someRequest);
```

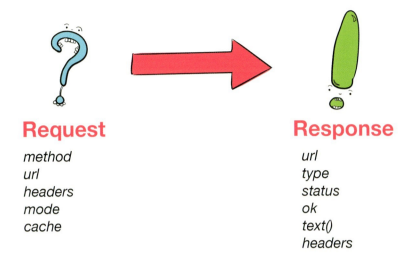

Request
method
url
headers
mode
cache

Response
url
type
status
ok
text()
headers

Conceptually, Request *objects are fed to* fetch *and* Response *objects result.*

FETCHEVENT OBJECTS

A Request defining what the browser is trying to obtain is available to fetch handlers within the FetchEvent passed to the function.

We've already created an (empty) event handler for fetch events inside of our service worker:

```
self.addEventListener('fetch', event => { });
```

The argument passed to a fetch event handler – the event parameter in our code snippet – is a FetchEvent.

FetchEvent objects have a request property – aha! That's the Request object representing what the browser is looking for in this fetch.

If you crack open a `FetchEvent` object, you'll find, among other things, a relevant Request and a vital method, `respondWith`.

If we want the service worker to intercept this particular fetch and supply its own Response, we need to be explicit by using the `FetchEvent`'s `respondWith` method.[14] Like so:

```
self.addEventListener('fetch', event => {
  // FetchEvent.respondWith takes a Response or a Promise
  // that will ultimately resolve to a Response
  event.respondWith(
    fetch(event.request)
  );
});
```

This explicitly fetches the given Request from the network, using the Fetch API, and returns the result (a Promise which we hope will resolve to a Response).

---

14 If you neglect to invoke `FetchEvent.respondWith`, whatever Response you cook up or return will not get used by the browser, so don't forget to use it!

Guess what? Still functionally useless. All we've done is what the browser would do by default anyway: fetch things from the network. Don't worry: it's not always pointless to use the Fetch API. We'll encounter some good reasons to use it within fetch handlers as we continue on our journey.

A fetch handler is by no means expected to *respond* to every fetch it handles. If `FetchEvent.respondWith` is not invoked during a fetch-handler invocation, that's fine: the browser will carry on and go to the network to try to find the resource it needs.

Working with Caches

One of a fetch handler's greatest superpowers is to avoid trips to the network at all, instead responding to certain requests with responses from cache. This can be a great boon to performance.

A service worker can create, add items to, and remove items from an arbitrary number of caches. A Cache object is, in a nutshell, a map: it relates Request objects to Response objects.

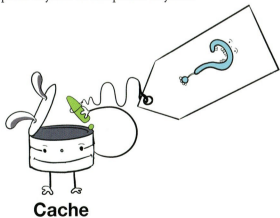

A Cache object is a collection of Responses keyed by Requests. It behaves similarly to a JavaScript Map object. `Request-Response` *pairs are added to a Cache so they can be available for use later.*

CACHE OBJECTS AND THE CACHESTORAGE INTERFACE

All access to and manipulation of Cache objects is handled through the CacheStorage interface, available globally in service workers as caches. CacheStorage is a kind of directory, a file drawer full of all of the caches available to you.

CacheStorage

All of the available Cache objects are accessed through the CacheStorage interface. Cache objects are keyed by the names you give them.

You create and manage your own caches – these Cache objects are completely distinct from the browser's built-in caching mechanism. They are entirely under your control.

Cache access is origin-based. That means you'll have access to the same set of caches, via CacheStorage, from any service worker running on the same origin.

To add to or retrieve items from a Cache, you first need to get a hold of it by asking the CacheStorage interface to open it:

```
const myCacheIHope = caches.open('my-cache-name');
```

Opening a Cache you've previously created and creating a new Cache looks identical: if a Cache with the key given to `CacheStorage.open` doesn't correspond to an existing Cache, a new, empty Cache will be created and returned.

The value of a Cache object's key (name) is up to you: any string will do.

`myCache` is a Promise that will resolve to a Cache object representing the cache you've asked for. Once the Promise resolves, you can work with the cache you've opened:

```
myCacheIHope.then(cache => {
  // Do something with this cache!
});
```

Remember, Cache objects that you manipulate in service workers are completely distinct from a browser's built-in caching.

PUTTING THINGS IN CACHES

To be able to get things out of caches when responding to fetch events, a service worker needs to put things in them in the first place. Remember, caches are entirely controlled by the logic in the service worker – nothing happens automatically. There are three useful methods on Cache objects for putting stuff inside of them. We'll try out each of these in subsequent recipe examples:

- `Cache.put(request, response)`: puts a `Request-Response` pair into the cache.
- `Cache.add(RequestOrURL)`: retrieves the Request or URL and stores the Response in the cache.
- `Cache.addAll([urls])`: Takes an array of URL strings and retrieves each, adding their Responses to the cache.

The behavior of `Cache.put` is a little different from `Cache.add` and `Cache.addAll`. `Cache.put` takes both a Request and a Response, allowing you to pair any Request with any Response – this gives you the most fine-grained control over what goes into a cache. `Cache.add` and `Cache.addAll` go to the network to retrieve the corresponding Responses that get stored.

CAUTION: `Cache.put`, `Cache.add` and `Cache.addAll` all return a Promise (which resolves to undefined). When that Promise resolves is in flux at present: early supporting browsers resolve it when the Response is fully written to storage, but there is a push underway to make the Promise resolve earlier for better performance.

GETTING STUFF OUT OF CACHES

Of course, you'll also need to be able to look for something in cache when you need it (likely in a fetch handler). Once again, there are three ways you can do this (all three return Promises):

- `Cache.match(request)`: look for a match for the given Request inside of a specific Cache.

- `Cache.matchAll([requests])`: look for matches for an array of Requests in a specific Cache (the returned Promise will resolve to an array of all matching entries).

- `caches.match(request)`: look for a match to a given Request across all caches you have access to.

Given that `Caches.match` doesn't require you to first open a specific Cache, it can be convenient; but there are times when the specificity of `Cache.match` is useful (for example, to rule out duplicate requests in other caches).

THE INSTALL LIFE CYCLE PHASE

Looking at Cache object management in the abstract, you may reasonably wonder when exactly you're supposed to stick stuff into caches for later retrieval from within fetch handlers.

The way to do this is to take advantage of the `install` life cycle event, stashing resources you know you'll need later into cache. This is a technique used in a common service worker recipe for pre-caching application shell files (images, styles, scripts, and so on, used on all or most pages of your site or app).

You can add an `install` handler in your service worker:

```
self.addEventListener('install', event => {
  // Take care of install concerns like pre-caching
});
```

EXTENDABLEEVENT OBJECTS

Opening up a cache and putting items in it are asynchronous operations. You can run into problems if you do something like this:

```
self.addEventListener(`install`, event => {
  // psssst: don't do this:
  caches.open('some-cache').then(cache => cache.addAll(arrayOfURLs);
});
```

The reason that this is potentially problematic is that the service worker may keep marching along through its life cycle; installation may complete before this handler has successfully added the items to cache.

Fortunately, ServiceWorker life cycle events – install and activate – are a kind of `ExtendableEvent`. `ExtendableEvent.waitUntil()` gives you the ability to say, "Hey! Wait until I'm done doing some stuff before you move on!", stretching out the lifetime of the event.

```
self.addEventListener('install', event => {
  event.waitUntil(caches.open('some-cache').then(cache => cache.
addAll(arrayOfURLs)));
});
```

Altering the code to read like the above will cause the install phase to hang on, to wait *until* the `Promise` given to `event.waitUntil` resolves before moving on.

Generating Custom Responses

In fetch handlers, we can respond to the request in any way we like, as long as we're satisfying the browser's need for a Response object. Using the fetch API or retrieving a Response from cache are typical ways of doing this, but there's nothing stopping us from rolling our own Response objects:

```
self.addEventListener('fetch', event => {
  // Remember, FetchEvent.respondWith is looking for a Response
  event.respondWith(new Response('<p>Service Worker has taken over</p>', {
    headers: { 'Content-Type': 'text/html' }
  }));
});
```

Let's talk about what this does. For every fetch that occurs within the service worker's scope, it will respond with a Response that looks like a web page.[15]

---

15   The first argument to the Response constructor is the body of the Response – here an HTML paragraph. Setting a Content-Type header to text/html in the second, options argument makes the Response look like a web page to browsers.

Intercepting fetches for HTML pages – so-called *navigation requests* – and responding with this bogus little web page is silly enough, but it gets even goofier when you consider that *all* fetches are being intercepted and responded to in this manner – including those for images, CSS, scripts, and so on. Obviously, you wouldn't want to respond with a (lame) web page when the browser is really looking for a PNG or a JavaScript file. But you *could*. That's the power of service workers!

Classic Service Worker Recipes

All right: that's some high-level overview of some key APIs involved in service workers: fetch, caches and their allies. Now let's see how these work together in the real world to do real things.

Inspect and debug tools for developing service workers are getting more mature and fully featured. The service worker features in Chrome's Developer Tools[16] are especially powerful. Some key service-worker-related tips:

- You can simulate offline behavior by toggling the **Offline** checkbox, which can be found both on the **Network** tab and in the **Service Workers** section of the **Application** tab (they function identically).

- The **Application** tab has a **Service Workers** section, which shows details about all service workers for the current origin.

- You'll also find a **Cache Storage** section in the **Application** tab, which allows you to see (and manipulate) all of the entries in available caches.

---

16 As I write this, I'm using Chrome 68. By the time you're reading this, that will probably seem laughably obsolete.

Application→Service Workers tab in Chrome Developer Tools. Firefox provides an about:serviceworkers page that can be handy, too.

PROVIDING AN OFFLINE MESSAGE

We've seen how we can use the Fetch API and Response objects to respond to fetch events in useless or even ridiculous ways, but let's now look at a simple example that combines both in a way that could potentially be beneficial: providing an offline message. Let's say we want to display a simple web page that lets users know when they are offline. This is what we want to do:

```
self.addEventListener('fetch', event => {
  // 1. Try to satisfy the fetch by using the fetch API and retrieving
  from the network
  // 2. if that doesn't work - the network is unavailable - respond with
  an offline message
});
```

We can detect that a fetch didn't work out – the network is unavailable – because the Promise returned by fetch will reject instead of resolving. We can provide a handler for that by chaining a `catch` onto the Promise:

```
self.addEventListener('fetch', event => {
  event.respondWith(
    // 1. use the fetch API and try retrieving from the network
    fetch(event.request)
    // 2. on failure, return offline message
      .catch(error => {
        return new Response('<p>Oh, dear! You are currently offline.</p>',
          { headers: { 'Content-Type': 'text/html' } });
      })
  );
});
```

This is close to being sensible, with one wrinkle: it will respond to *all* failed fetches with an HTML page. Let's dial this back so it only does so if the request is a *navigation* request; that is, a request for a full HTML document:

```
self.addEventListener('fetch', event => {
  if (event.request.mode === 'navigate') {
    event.respondWith(
      fetch(event.request).catch(error => {
        return new Response('<p>Oh, dear! You are currently offline!</p>',
          { headers: { 'Content-Type': 'text/html' } });
      })
    );
  }
});
```

`Request.mode` is a new-ish property that will return the string navigate if this is indeed a navigation request.

`Request.mode` support is missing in some browsers, but those browsers also happen to be browsers that don't support Service Worker anyway (at least, not yet). An equivalent fallback is:

```
if (event.request.method === 'GET' &&
    event.request.headers.get('accept').includes('text/html'))
```

PROVIDING AN OFFLINE PAGE

Creating a simple Response object that masquerades as an HTML page to provide an offline message is a starting point, but we can do better. Cobbling together a more complex Response body within the service worker code itself is unwieldy and hard to maintain. Instead, we can designate a real HTML page – in this case, a file called offline.html at the same directory level as the service worker – to use as an offline fallback page when navigation requests can't be satisfied.

It's necessary to pre-cache the offline page during the service worker's installation so that it will be available later, when needed. The following recipe pre-caches the offline page (`install` handler) and responds to failed navigation fetches with it (`fetch` handler):

```
self.addEventListener('install', event => {
  event.waitUntil(caches.open('offline-fallbacks')
    .then(cache => cache.add('offline.html'))
  );
});
self.addEventListener('fetch', event => {
  if (event.request.mode === 'navigate') {
    event.respondWith(fetch(event.request)
      .catch(error => {
        return caches.open('offline-fallbacks')
          .then(cache => cache.match('offline.html'));
      })
    );
  }
});
```

You're not limited to offline (HTML) pages. You can also handle failed requests for other resource types with a similar approach. Images are a good example – the next recipe responds to failed image requests with a custom offline image.

If your designated offline page has any subresources (like CSS or images), those will also need to be cached. See the Pre-Caching Application Shell Resources recipe for how to cache a collection of things at one time and retrieve them from cache in a fetch handler.

PROVIDING AN OFFLINE IMAGE

SVG is a good choice for a fallback image because it will scale to fit wherever it's needed. What's more, an SVG is defined by an XML-based markup language, meaning that its source can be included in the service worker itself. The following defines a simple SVG that displays the text "offline" – it can go at the top of the service worker file:

```
const offlineSVG = `<svg role="img" aria-labelledby="offline-title"
 viewBox="0 0 400 300" xmlns="http://www.w3.org/2000/svg">
<title id="offline-title">Offline</title>
<g fill="none" fill-rule="evenodd">
<path fill="#D8D8D8" d="M0 0h400v300H0z"/>
<text fill="#9B9B9B" font-family="Times New Roman,Times,serif"
 font-size="72" font-weight="bold">
<tspan x="93" y="172">offline</tspan></text></g></svg>
`;
```

Unlike with the *offline.html* page, the SVG here won't need to be pre-cached in the `install handler`, as the meat of the Response – the body – is all contained within that `offlineSVG` string, generating an image that looks something like this:

Next, expand the fetch handler. Detect image requests and respond with the SVG if the fetch `Promise` rejects. But don't do this for *every* request!

To identify image requests, you can look at the Request's `Accept` header – accessible via `Request.headers.get('Accept')`. An image request will have an `Accept` header value that matches the substring *'image'* (for example, `'image/jpg'`, `'image/png'`).

```
if (event.request.mode === 'navigate') {
  // ... as before if you want to keep the offline page fallback
} else if (event.request.headers.get('Accept').indexOf('image') !== -1) {
  event.respondWith(fetch(event.request)
    .catch(error => {
      return new Response(offlineSVG,
        { headers: { 'Content-Type': 'image/svg+xml'}});
    })
  );
}
```

This is a good example of when it's useful (and not just a parlor trick) to create your own Response object.

There are many variations on this theme: you could return a different kind of offline image for different types of image request, and you could create more fallbacks for more resource types – videos, for example.

PRE-CACHING APPLICATION SHELL RESOURCES

We've already encountered the basic building blocks needed to pre-cache application shell resources, those static assets that are used on most or all pages and define your site or app's frame or chrome. That corresponds to things like core icons, scripts, and CSS. The recipe needs to:

1. Define a set of URLs corresponding to those static application-shell assets.

2. In an `install` handler, pre-cache those identified assets using `Cache.addAll`.

3. In a `fetch` handler, when a request's URL matches any of the app-shell asset URLs, return it from cache instead of fetching from the network.

This is a double-whammy: your app's shell always shows up (even when offline, as those assets are cached); *and* it has better online performance, as those network requests are avoided even when the network *is* available.

Here's a starting point for this recipe:

```
const appShellURLs = [
  'thing1.jpg',
  'thing2.jpg',
  'thing3.jpg'
];
self.addEventListener('install', event => {
  event.waitUntil(caches.open('static-assets')
    .then(cache => cache.addAll(appShellURLs))
  );
});
self.addEventListener('fetch', event => {
  const url = new URL(event.request.url);
  if (appShellURLs.indexOf(url.pathname) !== -1) {
    // url.pathname is a string relative to the site's root, e.g.
    '/foo/img/bar.jpg'
    event.respondWith(caches.match(event.request));
  }
});
```

The above fetch handler behaves just fine if everything works as expected – if the app-shell resource requested is in cache as expected – but doesn't have any safety nets. We really can't ever be *sure* that something is where we left it in cache. A user might manually clear out caches (it's not typical, but it *could* happen), or the browser might decide to ditch stuff. There's no contract that guarantees that things you put in the cache will remain there.

The returned Promise from `caches.match` (and `Cache.match`) doesn't reject if there isn't a match in the cache(s) – instead it resolves to undefined(!). That means the code above could end up responding to the fetch with undefined if the resource is not in cache – that's nasty stuff and will cause an error because, remember, the browser always wants a Response object. Let's fix it!

```
self.addEventListener('fetch', event => {
  const url = new URL(event.request.url);
  if (appShellURLs.indexOf(url.pathname) !== -1) {
    event.respondWith(caches.match(event.request)
      .then(response => {
        if (!response) { // No match in caches: any falsy response is no good
          // This will cause the chained `catch` to be invoked
          // similar in effect to a rejected `Promise`
          throw new Error('${event.request} not found in cache');
        }
        return response; // DO return the response if it's OK
      })
      .catch(error => fetch(event.request)) // fetch from network if not in cache
    );
  }
});
```

When adding assets to cache in an `install handler`, the URLs used (which will be used in the keys for the cache entries) should be relative to the root of your website, even if your service worker's scope is constrained to a subdirectory. This also makes it easier to move your service around later without having to worry about breaking paths.

Let's say a service worker is located inside of /foo/bar. The following will appear to work:

```
const appShellURLs = ['thing.jpg']; // actual file location: /foo/bar/
thing.jpg
self.addEventListener('install', event => {
  event.waitUntil(caches.open('static-assets')
    .then(cache => cache.addAll(appShellURLs))
  );
});
```

In the `install handler`, thing.jpg will be successfully retrieved by `Cache.addAll` (relative to the service worker) and cached – this creates a valid cache entry with a key of 'thing.jpg'. But in later fetch handling, the url.pathname will always be the full path: /foo/bar/thing.jpg:

```
self.addEventListener('fetch', event => {
  const url = new URL(event.request.url);
  // uh oh
  // ['thing.jpg'].indexOf('/foo/bar/thing.jpg') = -1
  if (appShellURLs.indexOf(url.pathname) !== -1) { // nope
  }
});
```

Always use URLs relative to web root and you'll protect yourself:

```
const appShellURLs = ['/foo/bar/thing.jpg'];
```

Note: Don't cache the service worker script itself!

DEFINING NETWORK STRATEGIES

As with pre-caching application shell resources, *network strategies* are a service worker trick that can produce that double-whammy boost: improving both offline and online performance.

With network strategies, you can tune which types of requests should get the freshest content possible and which should try to get responses from cache. That helps improve online performance by avoiding unnecessary network round trips for static assets.

Implementing network strategies involves using a technique called *read-through caching*. With read-through caching, as you respond to fetches, you proactively stick responses from the network into cache where they can be retrieved later if needed. This is a great trick for keeping copies of stuff around for potential reuse if the user is subsequently offline.

A network strategy can be thought of as a sequence of priorities inside of a fetch handler: first try to respond to the fetch in this manner; if that doesn't work out, then try this; then this... and so on. You reorder those priorities based on the type of resource being requested or other criteria specific to your site's needs.

For the purpose of this recipe example, let's say we're working with a site that has significant text content (in HTML pages) that changes often, but has images that rarely change. In this case, a reasonable approach can be sketched out as:

```
self.addEventListener('fetch', event => {
  // For navigation requests (HTML/content fetches):
  // 1. Try fetching from the network - we want fresh content if possible
  // 1a. If successful, read-through cache a copy of the Response for later use
  // 2. If fetching rejects, try seeing if there is a match in cache
  // 3. If not in cache, respond with offline fallback page (optional)
  // For image requests
  // 1. Try finding a match in cache - prefer cached copy of images
  // 2. If not in cache, try to fetch from network
  // 2a. If fetch successful, stash image in cache for later use (read-through)
  // 3. If fetch fails, respond with fallback image (optional)
});
```

The priorities used for navigation requests – getting the freshest content possible – constitute a *network-first* strategy, while the cache-preferring priorities for images represent a *cache-first* strategy.

Because both network strategies defined here share some chunks of logic, let's encapsulate the operations of putting things in cache and retrieving items out of cache into functions for convenience: addToCache to add items to cache during read-through caching; findInCache to retrieve items out of cache; and fallbackImage as a convenience function for generating an offline SVG Response.

```
function addToCache (request, response) {
  if (response.ok) {
    const copy = response.clone();
    caches.open('content')
      .then(cache => cache.put(request, copy));
  }
  return response;
}
function findInCache (request) {
  return caches.match(request).then(response => {
    if (!response) {
      throw new Error(`${request} not found in cache`);
    }
```

```
      return response;
    });
}
function fallbackImage () {
  return new Response(offlineSVG,
    { headers: { 'Content-Type': 'image/svg+xml'}});
}
```

There are two things to note about `addToCache`:

- `response.ok:` `fetch` Promises will reject if there is a network error and a Response cannot be obtained, but will still resolve happily if the Response is problematic (a 404, for instance). However, the ok property on a Response will return a false value if the HTTP status is not in the 200 range. Checking that makes sure we're dealing with a Response that we actually *want* to cache.

- `response.clone()`: In read-through caching like this, the Response will be used twice in the same overall `fetch` life cycle: it will be added to a cache here and it will satisfy the current fetch (and get used immediately). A Response's body can only be read once, so we'll make a copy of the Response (`Response.clone`) and store the cloned copy.

We have to check `Response.ok` here because we're using `Cache.put`. Neither `Cache.add` nor `Cache.addAll` will cache a bad (non-200) Response.

And now, the network-strategy-enhanced fetch handler (this code assumes that offline.html has previously been cached):

```
self.addEventListener('fetch', event => {
  const req = event.request;
  if (req.mode === 'navigate') {
    event.respondWith(
      fetch(req)                                       // 1. network-first
        .then(res  => addToCache(req, res))            // 2. read-through
caching
        .catch(err => findInCache(req))                // 3. cache fallback
        .catch(err => findInCache('offline.html'))     // 4. offline fallback
    );
  } else if (req.headers.get('Accept').indexOf('image') !== -1) {
    event.respondWith(
      findInCache(req)                                 // 1. cache-first
        .catch(err => fetch(req))                      // 2. network fallback
        .then(res  => addToCache(req, res),            // 3. read-through
caching
             err  => fallbackImage())                  // 4. offline fallback
    );
  }
});
```

Maintaining and Versioning Service Workers

Over time, your service worker will evolve. You might have new application shell files you want to pre-cache. Network strategies may need tweaking. Mistakes may be found. You'll need to have a plan for versioning and maintaining your service worker.

Once a service worker is installed and active, the browser will, from time to time, check to see if the service worker file from the server is identical to the one it has already installed and activated. If there are any differences between the two files, the browser will download the new, updated service worker and install it.

Put another way, making changes to the service worker script file will prompt the browser to download and install the new version. The (new) service worker will go through its life cycle phases – `install` and `activate` event handlers – with any changes introduced – will get invoked.

USING VERSION STRINGS

A common tactic for managing changes to service workers is the use of a version string, assigned to a constant within the service worker file itself. For example:

```
// Really, this string could have any value; the important thing is that
// you change it every time you update your service worker script.
// Personally, I use the names of lesser-known Greek deities on my own site
// (recent versions include Corus, the spirit of surfeit and disdain; and
// Stheno, an immortal gorgon).
const SWVERSION='39b4893a9f';
```

Doing this may initially seem extraneous or pointless, given that any changes to the service worker file will cause the browser to download and install the new version, but there are a few reasons that having a version string is useful.

For one thing, there are some situations in which you might want browsers to download and install a service worker afresh – kicking off a new install-activate cycle – without making any changes to the service worker script itself. Bumping the version string will make browsers see the service worker as changed. We'll run into this with the "Listing Application Shell Assets in JSON" recipe.

Version strings also give you a handy, version-specific string for naming caches. By prefixing all cache names (keys) with the string, you can differentiate between caches created by different versions – and delete caches associated with old versions. In fact, there's a life cycle phase targeted at just this kind of task: the activation phase.

CLEANING UP OLD CACHES DURING THE ACTIVATION LIFE CYCLE PHASE

The activation life cycle phase is intended for cleanup of stale service worker assets. It is especially handy for cleaning out crufty caches. Its associated event is activate.

First, make sure that whenever you create or reference a cache in your service worker, you involve the version string:

```
// prefixing cache names with a version key
self.addEventListener('install', event => {
  event.waitUntil(caches.open(`${SWVERSION}-static-assets`)
    .then(cache => cache.addAll(appShellURLs))
  );
});
```

By doing this, you know that any cache name that does not begin with the current version string is old and crufty. It's good practice to clean up – delete – those old caches within an activate event handler. In the handler function:

1. CacheStorage.keys returns a Promise that resolves to an array of cache keys (names) for all of the caches it knows about.
2. Filter this list of keys down to isolate cache keys that do not start with the current version string: these caches should be deleted.
3. Delete each of the old caches using CacheStorage.delete.

All of these asynchronous steps should be completed during the activation phase, so take advantage of `ActivateEvent.waitUntil` – the `activate` event is also an `ExtendableEvent`.

```
self.addEventListener('activate', event => {
  event.waitUntil(
    caches.keys()
      .then(cacheKeys => {
        const oldKeys = cacheKeys.filter(key => key.indexOf(SWVERSION) !== 0);
        const deletePromises = oldKeys.map(oldKey => caches.delete(oldKey));
        // Don't proceed until ALL delete operations are complete:
        return Promise.all(deletePromises);
      })
  );
});
```

Both `CacheStorage` and Cache objects have a keys method. `CacheStorage.keys` resolves to a list of all cache names, while `Cache.keys` resolves to a list of all keys for entries within that cache.

INSTALL AND ACTIVATE CHRONOLOGY

The activation phase comes after the installation phase, but the timing of when those phases occur depends on a few things.

Once any service worker is downloaded and parsed, it immediately moves into the installation phase, and any registered `install` handlers are invoked.

If the service worker is new new – that is, there is no already active service worker for the current scope – it will move immediately from installation into activation (and any registered `activate` handlers will be invoked).

However, if there is already an installed service worker, activation won't occur until any open client (window or tab) using the old service worker is closed. There's a way around this, however! The `skipWaiting` method available on `ServiceWorkerGlobalContext` will allow activation to occur immediately. It's a useful thing to add to the end of `install` handlers to keep things moving along:

```
self.addEventListener('install', event => {
  event.waitUntil(caches.open(`${SWVERSION}-static-assets`)
    .then(cache => cache.addAll(appShellURLs))
    .then(() => self.skipWaiting()) // Go on to activation!
  );
});
```

After activation, the newly activated service worker won't immediately take control (that is, actually do things like respond to fetches, and so on) until any open clients are reloaded. Once again you can get around this. Invoking the `clients.claim` method at the end of the `activate` handler will cause the activated service worker to take control of its clients immediately:

```
self.addEventListener('activate', event => {
  event.waitUntil(
    caches.keys()
      .then(cacheKeys => {
        const oldKeys = cacheKeys.filter(key => key.indexOf(SWVERSION) !== 0);
        const deletePromises = oldKeys.map(oldKey => caches.delete(oldKey));
        return Promise.all(deletePromises);
      })
      .then(() => self.clients.claim())
  );
});
```

LISTING APPLICATION SHELL ASSETS IN A JSON FILE

It's fine to define an array of application shell file URLs to pre-cache within your service worker script, but you may find it more streamlined to maintain that list in an external JSON file. A JSON file could be integrated with automated build tools, updating itself when your site is built or deployed, for example, or even being generated dynamically on the server when it is requested. A build script could even update the version string in the service worker file automatically. Even if you don't do any sophisticated integration like that, a JSON file might simply feel cleaner, like a better separation of concerns.

The JSON file merely contains an array of URLs:

```
[
  "/aFile.html",
  "/anotherFile.html",
  "/images/someImage.png",
  "/css/essentialCss.css"
]
```

In an install handler function, fetch the JSON file (here called *cache-files.json*) and parse the Response body as JSON (Response.json()) to generate an array of file URLs to pre-cache:

```
self.addEventListener('install', event => {
  event.waitUntil(
    caches.open(`${SWVERSION}-static-assets`).then(cache => {
      return fetch('cache-files.json')
        .then(response => response.json())
        .then(paths => cache.addAll(paths));
    })
  );
});
```

Any time the contents of the JSON file change, you'll want browsers to update what's in the app-shell cache to the latest list of files – you'll need browsers to redownload and reinstall the service worker so its life cycle begins anew and the `install` handler is invoked again.

Remember: browsers will only download a new service worker and kick off the install-activation cycle if the service worker script file itself has changed – you can't just change the JSON file and be done with it. Updating a version string within the service worker script whenever the JSON contents change is a good tactic for addressing this.

The Channel Messaging API

A service worker can't manipulate a client directly or vice versa – they're running in different contexts – but there are ways that the two can exchange messages and data. Sending a one-way message from a client to a service worker is straightforward, and is part of the Service Worker specification. In web page code:

```
function sendMessage () {
  navigator.serviceWorker.controller.postMessage('Identify yourself!');
}
if ('serviceWorker' in navigator) {
  navigator.serviceWorker.register('service-worker.js')
    .then(function () {
      if (navigator.serviceWorker.controller) {
        postMessage();
      } else {
        navigator.serviceWorker.addEventListener('controllerchange', postMessage);
      }
    });
}
```

`navigator.serviceWorker.controller` returns a reference to the serviceWorker currently in control. controller can be null for a few reasons.

The `controllerchange` event will fire when a new service worker takes control of this client – this happens when a freshly activated service worker takes over. Otherwise, if the controller is already extant, we can message with impunity.

A view of **Developer Tools** → **Console** in Chrome shows the service worker logging from the message event handler.

In the service worker script, you can listen for message events:

```
self.addEventListener('message', event => {
  console.log(`Client just said: "${event.data}"`);
  console.log(`I am ${SWVERSION}`);
});
```

Logging out to the console is helpful for debugging – you're able to see the service worker's logging in the browser console if you have Developer Tools open – but this really is a one-way system so far; messages go from the client(s) to the service worker, not the other way around.[17] Two-way messaging is possible, however, via the Channel Messaging API.

---

17 It is technically possible in some cases for the service worker to initiate communication, but it's dependent on being able to derive the ID of the client in question, which isn't always available. It's easier (and more appropriate) to use the Channel Messaging API for exchanging two-way messages.

The `postMessage` function in the client can be enhanced to use channel messaging:

```
function postMessage () {
  const messageChannel = new MessageChannel();
  messageChannel.port1.onmessage = event => console.log(event.data);
  navigator.serviceWorker.controller.postMessage(
    {cmd: 'identify'},
    [messageChannel.port2]);
}
```

The `MessageChannel` object created by the client has two ports.

A MessageChannel object has two ports that can be used to communicate: `port1` and `port2`, which are connected to each other; that is, shouting into `port2` will cause stuff to come out of `port1`. The client end will listen to `port1` for a message coming from the service worker, while handing over `port2` for the service worker's use.

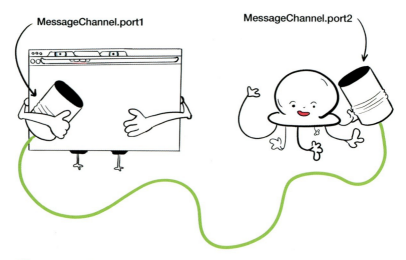

In `postMessage`, the client transfers MessageChannel.port2 ownership to the service worker. The service worker's message handler function has a reference to port2 through events.ports[0].

The first argument to `postMessage` – the data argument – can contain any value, not just a string. In this example, we're sending an object containing a fake-ish command (cmd) to the service worker, with the intent of making it tell us its current version string.

The second argument – `transferList` – is a sequence (an array, for example) of items whose ownership will get transferred to the recipient. We need to transfer `messageChannel.port2` to the service worker so it has a way to get back in touch with us.

In the service worker message event handler:[18]

---

[18] For brevity, this code assumes the existence of event.data.cmd, but you would want to be more careful, of course, in production code.

```
self.addEventListener('message', event => {
  if (event.data.cmd === 'identify') {
    event.ports[0].postMessage({ version: SWVERSION });
  }
});
```

The transferred `messageChannel.port2` from the client code becomes available at `MessageEvent.ports` – `event.ports[0]` is a reference to `port2` on the messaging channel created by the client. There's only one port available – the array only has one element because the other port (`port1`) is still owned by the client.

And the client is listening to `port1`, in the `postMessage` function:

```
messageChannel.port1.onmessage = event => console.log(event.data);
```

Chrome Developer Tools console showing the client's code logging of the message returned by the service worker. Of course, you could do more useful things with the event's data than logging it!

Web Push and Notifications

Push notifications are one of those killer, native-app-like features. Even though Push and Notifications like to go together in a single phrase, it's helpful to understand that they are two separate web APIs:

- *Web Push*: an API that allows a web worker to receive messages from a server, with an associated event, push, that the worker can handle.

- *Web Notification*: an API that allows a web worker to display a UI notification to the user.

You can have Notifications without Push, but it's rare (albeit possible) to use Push without Notifications. The two do tend to go hand-in-hand.

Setting up Web Push can be somewhat involved, but can be boiled down to these oversimplified steps:

1. Set up a *subscription* in client code via the `ServiceWorkerRegistration` interface.
2. Send that subscription's information to a remote server.
3. Respond to push events from the server in the service worker and show notifications.

STEP 1: SUBSCRIBING TO PUSH

Setting up a Push subscription occurs in client (web page) code. Now, before we get started, we need an *application key* we can give to the `PushManager.subscribe` method. This is intended to be a public key, part of a signing pair that is generated by an application server, and it needs to be a particular kind of `ArrayBuffer`.[19]

Generating a legit key pair is beyond the scope of this example, but you can cook up a fake local public key by cobbling together a `Uint8Array` that has the right kind of structure – this is ferociously hacky, but it will allow you to try out push notifications locally in the browser:[20]

---

19 More details about applicationServerKey can be found in the Push API spec: http://smashed.by/pushsub
20 If this grosses you out too much, you could instead use a public key generated by Google's Push Companion (https://web-push-codelab.glitch.me/), though you'll still need to convert it to a UInt8Array. You can find a utility function to do so in the Google Web Push Code Lab repository: http://smashed.by/mainjs

```
// ALERT! ONLY USE THIS TO TRY OUT PUSH API LOCALLY IN YOUR BROWSER!
ALERT!
function fakestKeyEver () {
  const fakeOutputArray = new Uint8Array(65);
  fakeOutputArray[0] = 0x04; // First octet must be 0x04
  return fakeOutputArray;
}
const appKey = fakestKeyEver(); // The kind of UInt8Array required by Push
```

Now we're ready to set up a subscription:

```
if ('serviceWorker' in navigator && 'PushManager' in window) {
  navigator.serviceWorker.register('service-worker.js')
    .then(subscribeUser);
}
function subscribeUser (swRegistration) {
  return swRegistration.pushManager.getSubscription()
    .then(sub => {
      if (sub === null && Notification.permission !== 'denied') {
        return swRegistration.pushManager.subscribe({
          userVisibleOnly    : true,
          applicationServerKey: appKey
        });
      }
    })
}
```

`navigator.serviceWorker.register` resolves to a `ServiceWorkerRegistration` when successful. That registration gets passed to `subscribeUser`, where it provides access to PushManager. Before invoking `PushManager.subscribe`, the code validates that a subscription doesn't already exist (it's null) and that the user has not denied permission previously.

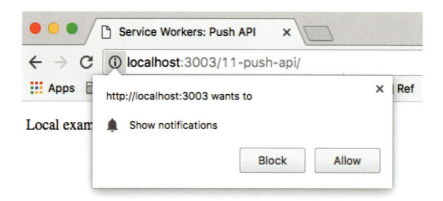

If you load a web page containing the code above, you'll see that the `PushManager.subscribe` *invocation causes a (notification) permission dialog to appear.*

Even though the Push API is responsible for the subscription here, the user permission is associated with the Notification API. The `userVisibleOnly` options property indicates that the intended purpose of this push subscription is to show notifications to the user for push events. Chrome requires this property to be present and only accepts the value of `true`. Thus, the `subscribe` here will cause a permission prompt for the user.

STEP 2: SEND SUBSCRIPTION INFO TO SERVER

The Promise returned by `PushManager.subscribe` resolves to a `PushSubscription` object when successful, and that object contains vital subscription details, including an endpoint (URL) for a push server. Push messages can be sent to that URL and they will reach the associated service worker. It's not hard to see that security is important here – that endpoint URL needs to be kept secret.

In real-life code, you'd need to send the `PushSubscription` object to an application server, using `XMLHttpRequest` or similar.[21]

STEP 3: HANDLE PUSH EVENTS IN THE SERVICE WORKER

The service worker's job is to respond to push events. In this example, a notification is displayed on every push event (we already have notification permissions via the subscription). Notifications have a `title` – first argument to `showNotification` – and some straightforward attributes:

```
self.addEventListener('push', event => {
  event.waitUntil(self.registration.showNotification('Check it out', {
    body : 'Well, hello there',
    icon : 'smashing.png',
    badge: 'smashing.png'
  }));
});
```

The service worker can also handle the notificationclick event, which is triggered when a user clicks on the notification UI itself:

```
self.addEventListener('notificationclick', event => {
  event.notification.close(); // Close the notification UI
  event.waitUntil( // open a window to Smashing Magazine's Site
    self.clients.openWindow('https://www.smashingmagazine.com/')
  );
});
```

---

[21] This very detailed post from JR Conlin at Mozilla digs deeper into generating key pairs and working with server-side pieces of Push: http://smashed.by/mdnpushnotes

In this view of the Chrome Developer Tools **Application** tab, the **Service Workers** section is active (left side channel), displaying information about service workers at this origin. Note the "Push" link at the far right.

You can try out this local Push example in Chrome: clicking on the Push link for this service worker in the Developer Tools → Application → Service Workers section will trigger a push event and show the notification.

A notification shown by the service worker's push event handler function.

Background Sync

The Background Sync API (supported in Chrome since spring 2016) allows you to put off doing things until a user's connectivity is assured or restored. Background Sync is not on the standards track at this time and is only supported by Chrome.

Background Sync has an uncomplicated API. You register for a sync in client code

```
if ('serviceWorker' in navigator && 'SyncManager' in window) {
  navigator.serviceWorker.ready.then(function(reg) {
    return reg.sync.register('my-tag');
  });
}
```

`ServiceWorkerRegistration.sync.register` takes a string tag, which you can use to identify your registered syncs. Service workers can listen for `sync` events:

```
self.addEventListener('sync', event => {
  console.log('I heard that!');
  // You might choose to do different things based on the sync's tag...
  console.log(event.tag);
  event.waitUntil( /** ... whatever needs to be done **/);
});
```

Note: As with Push, you can emulate `sync` events from within **Developer Tools → Application → Service Worker**. Try it out!

You may be wondering when `sync` events occur. If there is currently a network connection, the `sync` event will happen immediately; otherwise, sync will happen when the browser next detects a network connection. The idea is that you can register a sync for actions that require a network connection.

You can register a sync with the same tag multiple times; only one `sync` event for that tag will get fired. If you want multiple events, use multiple different tags.

The Future

There's a lot in the web standards pipeline related to service workers. Much targets performance, including changes to data streams in the browser and the navigation preload feature.

There is a potential performance hit when a browser navigates to a site or page whose service worker isn't currently running and needs to be started up. The delay while the service worker gets going ranges from about 50ms to as much as 500ms in problematic situations – enough to be a significant impact to page-load performance. Navigation preload allows the browser to get to work on the network fetch before the service worker is ready; that is, the fetching of the web page – the navigation request – won't be blocked by the service worker start-up process.

> *Note:* Navigation preload is currently behind a flag in Chrome (you have to go to *chrome://flags/* and enable the feature).

Advances in what you can do with streams on the web could make custom-built Responses more performance-friendly. Currently, if you respond to a fetch event with a Response from the network (via `fetch`) or from cache, those responses will stream without any effort on the developer's part. That's a good thing: the whole response body doesn't need to be present before the browser can start doing things with it. However, Response objects you construct yourself require some intervention – currently rather convoluted – to make them stream. API improvements here could make it a lot easier to cobble together streaming Responses.

The future for the service worker landscape seems to coalesce around two main themes: performance and stability improvements to Service Worker itself, as well as the rise of more APIs and features that require a service worker to access – like push notifications. As Service Worker gets more mature, your code can be simpler and more concise, and you can rely on it in a larger share of browsers. And the new APIs add more compelling, app-like functionality to the web platform. The combined advantages of performance *and* features make service workers an increasingly vital piece of the web puzzle.

About The Author

Lyza Danger Gardner is a developer and co-founder of Cloud Four. A 20-year veteran of the web, she is a generalist with an abiding commitment to making the web work everywhere. Lyza is a seasoned and spirited speaker, and is a writer for A List Apart, O'Reilly, net Magazine, Smashing Magazine and others.

CHAPTER 6

Loading Assets on the Web

Yoav Weiss

CHAPTER 6

Loading Assets on the Web

by Yoav Weiss

What does it take to deliver websites in the highest-performing way possible? What would it take for us to say that given certain bandwidth, latency, and CPU constraints, a website was delivered to the user at the best possible speed?

This is a question I've spent a lot of time on in the last few years, thinking about what ideal performance would take, on the browser side as well as on the server/content side.

Ideal performance would require many different conditions in order to happen:

- **Early delivery**: Content delivery needs to start as soon as possible.

- **Priorities**: Critical content is delivered before less-critical.

- **Full-bandwidth pipe**: The network bandwidth must be fully used at all times until no content delivery is required.

- **Full CPU use**: The CPU and the browser's main thread should be fully used, as long as processing is required to transform the delivered content into pixels on the screen, application behavior, and application logic.

- **No CPU blocking**: At the same time, the browser's main thread should not be blocked by long execution tasks at any point in the loading process, in order to remain responsive to user input.

- **Minimal content**: No unnecessary content should be sent to the user, and required content should be highly compressed.

- **Contention avoidance**: Bandwidth and CPU contention should be avoided between low-priority content and high-priority, as well as between same-priority resources, which need to be processed in their entirety.

- **Minimize latency impact**: Use a content delivery network (CDN) and improve content caching at the client.

- **Control**: Make sure that content – and in particular third-party content – does not get in the way of your user's experience.

- **Measurement**: Making sure that all the above conditions are in fact true and perform as expected.

This chapter will explore strategies for satisfying these conditions in order to avoid unnecessary delays when delivering assets on the web. These conditions may require changes in the way browsers load web content. However, they cannot rely solely on that. For some of these conditions to be met, web content must also be adjusted.

At the same time, due to limitations in size, this chapter won't be able to cover all the conditions above. Specifically, we'll focus on the ins and outs of resource loading, and leave aside CPU use, main thread blocking avoidance, and performance measurement.

But before we dive into the details of the different resource-loading phases and how they can be improved, let's take a short detour to examine browsers' resource-loading processes.

How Browsers Load Resources

A typical web page is built from multiple resource types and often many resources that make sure the user's visual experience is a pleasant one.

The HTML resource gives the browser the structure of the document; CSS styles the document; and JavaScript provides functionality and interactivity. Beyond those, fonts make sure the reading experience is optimal, and image, video, and audio resources provide visuals, as well as the audio often required to convey the full context of the page.

But all these resources are not declared in a single place when the browser initially fetches the HTML, when the user clicks on a link or types something into their address bar. All the browser has to go on at that point is the HTML itself, and only once fetched does it know of some of the other resources required for the full site experience.

So what happens when the browser navigates to a new page?

First, the browser starts the connection establishment process, using DNS to know which host to connect to, and then establishing TCP and TLS connections to that host. That process usually takes around four round-trip times. Then, it sends out a GET request for the HTML itself, and receives an initial buffer of the response from the server. The size of that response depends both on the HTML size and the initial congestion window of the server. A typical value for that is window is 10 packets of 1,460 bytes, or around 14 Kb of data.

HTML PROCESSING

One of the great things about HTML as a format is that it's progressive. It can be processed as it comes off the network, so even if the HTML the browser has is incomplete (as is often the case), the parts that have already arrived can be processed and acted on.

Now the browser needs to process that HTML to start building the DOM tree from it, and most importantly for our resource-loading interests, to figure out which resources are needed for it to fully construct and render the page. The HTML processing phase starts by the tokenization phase: the browser breaks apart the HTML string into tokens, where each token represents a tag start, tag end, or the text between the tags.

The tokens are a data structure representation of the HTML's text, bringing it one step closer to something that can be properly handled by the HTML parser. They might represent invalid HTML, as shown in the example below. That is expected, as it's not the tokenizer's role to enforce HTML parsing rules.

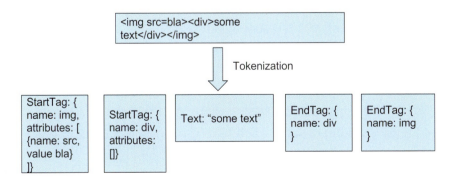

Invalid HTML gets tokenized: the `</img>` tag creates an "EndTag" token, despite it being invalid.

After the tokenization phase, the browser can start using those tokens to kick off resource loads. Since blocking scripts can cause the DOM creation, it's better not to wait to load resources until the DOM is ready. Instead, the browser uses its preloader[1] to scan through the tokens and figure out which resources are highly likely to be requested later on, and kick off those requests ahead of time.

After the preloader runs its course, the browser uses those same tokens and parses them according to HTML's parsing rules. The result is DOM nodes, interconnected as a DOM tree. Any tokens which represent invalid markup will be processed and used to create a perfectly valid DOM.

THE CRITICAL RENDERING PATH

We've seen how the browser discovers resources, but not all resources are created equal. In particular, there's a set of resources the browser requires to initially render the web page's content.

We talked about the creation of the DOM tree, and it is required for the browser to be able to render the page to screen, but unfortunately it is not sufficient. To render the page with its appropriate styling to the user (and avoiding a "flash of unstyled content"), the browser also needs to create the render tree and, in most cases, the CSS Object Model.

The CSS Object Model (CSSOM) is a set of APIs that enable scripts to examine the styles of various DOM nodes, as well as setting them to change their appearance.

---

[1] http://smashed.by/bigbadpreloader

To create both the CSSOM and the render tree, the browser needs to download all the external CSS resources and evaluate them. Then it processes those downloaded rules, along with any inline style tags and style attributes to calculate which styles (if any) are applied to each node in the DOM tree.

This is where blocking scripts come in. Blocking scripts (as their name suggests) block HTML parsing as soon as they are encountered, and HTML parsing does not continue until they finish being downloaded, parsed, and executed. Furthermore, in many cases at least, they cannot start executing until all CSS that preceded them has been downloaded and processed.

The reason is that those scripts can access the bits of the DOM that are already generated and query their CSSOM. If they do that, the CSSOM state must be stable and complete. Hence browsers must make sure this is the case, and they do that by downloading and processing all CSS before any CSSOM reads. The result can be a lot of delay to JavaScript execution, which in turn delays DOM creation. Sadness.

To top all that, this is applicable to external blocking scripts, as well as inline ones. Inline scripts can and will block your HTML processing if they are preceded by external style sheets.

Now, once the browser has built a sufficiently large DOM tree and calculated the styles for each DOM node, it can walk over the DOM and create the render tree, by creating an equivalent tree for each node that actually partakes in the page's rendering and is displayed on screen.

After that, the browser can proceed to laying out the different elements on the screen and eventually paint them.

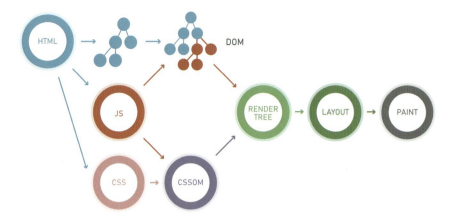

REQUEST DESTINATION AND CREDENTIALS MODE

One important thing to understand about loaded resources in the browser is that each request has its own destination as well as credentials mode.

Request Destination

The request's destination[2] indicates what type of resource we're expecting to receive from the server and how that resource will be used. Different destinations include "style," "script," "image," "font," and more. A request's destination has several implications for resource loading. As we'll discuss later, it determines the priority of the request. It is also used in various internal browser caches to make sure a previous response can be served to a current request only when their destinations match.

---

2   http://smashed.by/requestdest

Credentials Mode

A request's credentials mode[3] determines whether the request gets credentials information (cookies, in the typical case) sent along with it to the server. Possible values can be:

- include: a request will have credentials
- omit: it will not have credentials
- same origin: a request will have credentials only when sent to the same origin

Each resource type may have a different credentials mode by default. Resource fetches triggered by `<img>` and `<script>` will have a default credentials mode of "include" by default, while font fetches will have a "same origin" credentials mode. `fetch()` calls used to have a default "omit" mode, but recently changed to "same origin."

All that to say, as a performance-aware web developer, you need to pay close attention to the credentials mode of the resources you're loading.

In markup, developers can also change the credentials mode of the resources they load by including the `crossorigin`[4] attribute, which modifies the default for markup-based resource fetches:

- `anonymous` or an empty value indicates a `same origin` credentials mode.
- `use-credentials` indicates an `include` credentials mode.

3 http://smashed.by/credmode
4 http://smashed.by/crossorigin

Note that there's no current value which results in an "omit" credentials mode. But why does the credentials mode matter?

First of all, you may expect cookies on the server for a certain request, and understanding credentials mode will help you understand when they'd be there and when they would not be.

Otherwise, like the request destination, the credentials mode determines if a request and a response can be matched in the browser's internal caches. On top of that, some browsers (most notably Chrome) will use separate connections for requests of different credential modes. We'll expand later on the impact of that.

ALL SET?

With a better understanding of the way browsers load resources, let's now take a look at the different conditions required to make loading as fast as possible.

Early Delivery

When it comes to web performance, our goal is usually seemingly obvious: we want *meaningful* content to be accessible as quickly as possible. As part of that, we need resources on the critical path to be delivered early.

How early is early enough? Probably shortly after the browser sent out a request for it, typically after the user clicked on a link or typed something in their address bar. (Or even before that, if the application can have high enough confidence that they would; for example, when the user moves their mouse pointer within a certain proximity of a button.)

Protocol Overhead

Network protocols introduce overhead to network communication. That overhead is manifested in extra bytes – while most of our network traffic is content, some part of it is just protocol information enabling the delivery of that content. But the overhead is also manifested in time: establishing a connection or passing along critical information from client to server or vice versa can take multiple round-trip times (RTTs), resulting in those parts of the delivery being highly influenced by the network's latency.

The consequence is a delay until the point where the browser starts receiving the response from the server (also known as time to first byte, TTFB). Recent advances in the underlying protocols make that less of an issue, and can reduce TTFB significantly.

0-RTT

In their non-cutting-edge versions, the DNS, TCP, and TLS protocols require a large number of RTTs before the server is able to start delivering useful data.

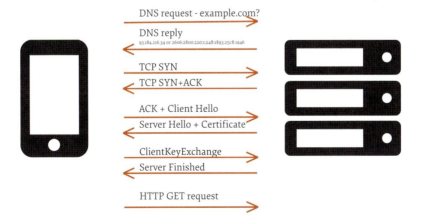

Protocol advancements such as Quick UDP Internet Connection (QUIC) on the one hand, and TCP Fast Open (TFO) and TLS 1.3 on the other, made most of that obsolete. These protocols rely on previously established connections to keep cryptographic "cookies" that remember past sessions, and allow previous sessions to be recreated instantaneously. There are still many caveats and many scenarios where the connection will take more than a single RTT to be established, but generally, using those cutting-edge protocols will mean there are very few RTTs to get in the way of delivering content to our users.

QUIC: Quick UDP Internet Connection

HTTP/2 brought many necessary improvements to resource delivery over HTTP. HTTP/1 had a severe head-of-line blocking issue, where the browser could send in practice only one request at a time on a connection. That created a linear relationship between the number of requests a page had and the number of RTTs it took for the page's resources to be downloaded. As a result, browsers settled on opening multiple connections per host (typically six connections for modern browsers) to reduce the latency by a fixed factor.

HTTP/2 fixed that head-of-line blocking issue by enabling multiplexing of multiple request and responses over a single connection, without incurring extra latency costs per request. As a result, browsers only use a single connection per host with HTTP/2. But a side effect of that is that HTTP/2 delivery is more sensitive to packet losses than HTTP/1, as each packet loss affects *all* the resources, rather than just one of them.

As a result, in highly lossy environments, there are scenarios where HTTP/2 ends up being slower than HTTP/1, making the switch to HTTP/2 tricky for sites that have large chunks of their audiences coming in from poor networking environments.

To resolve that, the Google Chrome team started exploring ways to make the transport layer more aware of HTTP/2's request–response streams. Since TCP is widely deployed and inspected by intermediary network components, it's practically impossible to significantly change the protocol without some of those network components breaking that traffic in the process. Reimplementing a reliable transport layer over a different transport protocol – the User Datagram Protocol (UDP) – was a simpler option.

The result is QUIC - a new protocol combining the transport, encryption, and application layers into a single, coordinated processing model.

This new protocol has several shiny new improvements over the protocols of yore:

- **0-RTT**: Combining layers means the protocol needs to establish a connection only once (for both transport and encryption layers). On top of that, once a user has established a connection to a server, the client can remember those encryption credentials and resume that same connection in the future with 0-RTTs (sending those past credentials along with the request).

- **Stream-aware loss handling**: Another major advantage of merging the layers is in handling packet losses. Both TCP and QUIC offer reliable transport, which means when a packet is lost, it has to be successfully retransmitted before the subsequent packets can be delivered to higher layers. However, TCP guarantees reliable delivery for the entire connection, while QUIC guarantees reliable delivery *per request–response stream*. That means a packet loss in QUIC will only delay the affected resources, while one in HTTP/2 over TCP will delay *all resources*.

- Tighter prioritization: Because QUIC is implemented over UDP, the transport layer logic and queues are all in the server's full control, where with TCP that logic is implemented as part of the operating system. As a result, it's easier for the server to have tighter controls over the priorities of the resources currently in the sending queues. One of the problems with the HTTP/2-over-TCP model is that the TCP queues are outside of the server's control. When the server sends down a mix of resources of different priorities, there can be situations where the TCP queues already contain not-yet-sent lower-priority resources, which will then delay the high-priority resource from being sent. With QUIC, a server implementation can have tighter control over the queues and make sure that lower-priority resources don't get in the way.

QUIC is not yet a standard protocol. It is only implemented as part of the Chromium project's network stack, and used as a library by Chromium and Android apps, as well as servers. At the same time, there are significant efforts at the Internet Engineering Task Force (IETF) to create a standard version of the protocol, so it can be implemented independently in an interoperable way across multiple browsers and servers.

PRECONNECT

While 0-RTT protocols enable us to forgo the four typical RTTs it takes the browser to establish a connection, preconnect enables us to get them out of the browser's critical path. Preconnect is a markup hint which indicates to the browser that resources would be downloaded from a certain origin, so the browser would do well to resolve that host's address, and create TCP and TLS connections to it ahead of time, before the resource is actually needed.

Preconnect is expressed as a `rel` attribute on a `<link>` element. For example, `<link rel=preconnect href="https://www.example.com">` tells the browser to create a connection to the host *www.example.com* even if it hasn't encountered any resources on that host just yet.

ADAPTIVE CONGESTION WINDOW

When the server starts sending data to the user, it doesn't know how much bandwidth it will have for that purpose. It can't be sure what amount of data will overwhelm the network and cause congestion. Since the implications of congestion can be severe, a mechanism called *slow start* was developed to make sure it does not happen. It enables the server to gradually discover the connection's limits, by starting to send a small amount of packets, and increasing that exponentially. But owing to its nature, slow start also limits the amount of data that we can initially send on a new connection.

Congestion Collapse

The reason slow start is needed is to avoid congestion collapse.

Let's imagine a situation where the server is sending down significantly more packets than the network can effectively deliver or buffer. Many or even most of these packets will get dropped. And what do reliable protocols do when packets are dropped? They retransmit them!

So now the server is trying to send all the retransmits for the dropped packets, but they are *still* more than the network can handle, so they get dropped.

What does the helpful transport layer do? You guessed it, retransmit *again*.

That process happens over and over, and we end up with a network passing along mostly retransmits and very little useful information.

This is the reason it pays off to be conservative. Start with a small number of packets and go up from there.

In the past, the recommended amount of packets for the initial congestion window – the initial amount of packets the server can send on a fresh connection – was somewhere between two and four, depending on their size.[5]

In 2013 a group of researchers at Google ran experiments all over the world with different congestion windows and reached the conclusion[6] that this value can be lifted to ten.

If you're familiar with the rule stating you should send all critical content in the first 14 KB of HTML, that's the rule's origin. Since the maximum ethernet packet size is 1,460 bytes of payload, 10 packets (or approximately 14 KB) can be delivered during that first initial congestion window. Those packets need to include both the headers and the critical content payload if you want your site to reach first paint without requiring extra round-trips.

However, in many cases the network can handle significantly more than that. The server may know that when the connection is over a network it has seen before.

5   http://smashed.by/tcpfourpackets
6   http://smashed.by/tcptenpackets

The browser itself can also, in many cases, take an educated guess regarding the quality of the network it's on. It can base that on the network radio type and signal strength, as well as past browsing sessions on that network.

Browsers already expose network information to JavaScript through the Network Information API,[7] and there's work underway to expose the same information using Client Hints. That will enable servers to modify their initial congestion window based on the effective connection type[8] and adapt it according to the browser's estimate. That would help to significantly minimize the time it takes the connection to converge on its final congestion window value.

The advent of *QUIC* as the transport protocol will also make this easier to implement on the server, as there's no easy way to increase the congestion window for an in-flight connection in TCP implementations today.

WHAT TO DO?

How can you make sure that you're minimizing your protocol overhead? That depends on your server's network stack. Moving to QUIC, TLS 1.3 or TFO may require upgrading your server's network stack, or turning on those capabilities in its configuration. Alternatively, you can use a CDN that supports those protocols, and have servers which sit between your users and your servers.

These protocol enhancements all relatively new, so support may not be widespread at the moment. QUIC, specifically, is still not standardized, so it can be hard to self-deploy, since that would require frequent

7 http://smashed.by/netinfoapi
8 http://smashed.by/connectype

updates as the Chrome implementation evolves. At the same time, keeping an eye on these protocols and taking advantage of them once they become available can be beneficial.

Alternatively, it is easier to turn on preconnect for your critical third-party hosts, by adding `<link rel=preconnect href=example.com>` to your markup. One caveat here is that preconnects are cheap, but not free. Some browsers have a limited number of DNS requests that can be up in the air (Chrome limits pending DNS requests to six, for instance).

Preconnecting to non-critical hosts can use up your quota and prevent connections to other hosts from taking place. Only preconnect to hosts your browser would need to preconnect to, and prefer to do that roughly in the same order as the browser would use those connections.

When using `preconnect`, you also need to pay close attention to the credentials mode of the resources will use that connection. Since Chrome uses different connections for different credential mode requests, you need to let the browser know which connection type it needs to preconnect to. You can do that with the `crossorigin` attribute on the `preconnect` `<link>` element.

And as far as the adaptive congestion window goes, that requires some more server-side smarts, but hopefully with the advent of network info in Client Hints and QUIC, we can imagine servers implementing that scheme.

Server-Side Processing

The other hurdle to overcome when it comes to early delivery is server-side processing. HTML content is often dynamic and, as such, generated on the server rather than simply delivered by it. The logic for its generation can be complex, might involve database access, and can also include different APIs from different services. That processing is also often done using interpreted languages such as Python and Ruby, which are not always the fastest choice, at least not by default.

As a result, generating the HTML once a request has hit our servers is a time-consuming activity, and one which wastes our users' time. Worse than that, it is time spent before the browser can do anything to advance the loading of the page.

EARLY FLUSH

One way to avoid forcing our users to wait for our potentially slow database responses is to flush the HTML's <head> early on. As part of the HTML generation process we can make sure that once the <head> is ready, it will be sent to the browser, enabling it to start processing it, issue the requests defined in it, and create the relevant DOM tree.

However, that is not always feasible in practice. Depending on your application logic, there are a few problematic aspects about flushing your HTML content early.

Committing an HTTP Response Code

When flushing HTML content early, you are committing to a certain HTTP response code, typically `200 OK`. But the eventual response may end up having a different status code, perhaps a `404` or a `500` error if the server failed to find the required information in the database. In such a case, you would have to redirect or modify the content using JavaScript, to show the error. But because that content was served with a `200` response code, search engines may not recognize it as error content, and that error content may find itself in search results. It also means we need to bake that eventual error logic into our client-side application logic, in order to make sure the negative user impact of that redirection is as unnoticeable as it can be.

Dynamic Response Header Logic

Any dynamic logic applied to the response headers must be applied ahead of time. Header-based cookies, Content Security Policy directives, and other header-based instructions have to be determined before the first content flush. In some cases that can delay early flushing of content; in others it can prevent it entirely (for example, if the cookie that is supposed to be set comes from a database).

Alternatively, you can try to build in application logic that converts these header-based browser instructions into content-based ones (like setting the cookies using JavaScript, or setting some headers using meta tags as part of the content itself).

Compression Buffering

Even if your application logic enables early flushing of your HTML's
<head>, misguided gzip or Brotli settings can result in undesired
buffering. When done wrong, they can nullify your attempts to send
content early to the browser. Gzip and Brotli have various settings to
control the trade-off between buffering content and compression ratio:
the more buffering, the better compression ratio these algorithms
can achieve, but at the cost of extra delays. When flushing early, you
should make sure that your server (and whatever other components
applying compression in your infrastructure) is set accordingly.

Gzip's[9] default buffering mode is Z_NO_FLUSH, which means it buffers data until it considers it has enough to create ideal compression output. Setting it to Z_SYNC_FLUSH can ensure that every input buffer creates an output buffer, trading off some compression ratio for speed.

If you're using on-the-fly Brotli to compress your content, there's a similar flag in the streaming Brotli encoder, called BROTLI_OPERATION_FLUSH,[10] you should use instead of the default.

SERVER PUSH

Another way to work around slow server-side processing is to use an HTTP/2 (or H2 for short) mechanism called *Server Push* to load critical resources while the HTML is generated.

That often means by the time the HTML is generated and starting to be sent to the browser, the browser already has all the critical resources in its cache. Furthermore, sending those critical resources starts the

---

9 http://smashed.by/gzip
10 http://smashed.by/brotliflush

TCP slow start process earlier and ramps up TCP's congestion window. When the HTML is finally ready, a significantly larger part of it can be sent down.

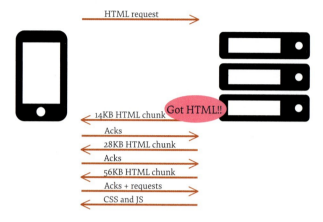

Loading process without Push: HTML download and slow start kick off only after HTML is generated.

Loading process with Push: critical resources and slow start kick off before HTML is generated, so once it is ready it can be sent down in a single RTT.

One of the biggest problems with Server Push today is that the server cannot see the browser's cache state, so when done naively the server is likely to send down resources that the browser already has. A recent proposal called Cache Digests[11] aims to solve that, by sending the server a condensed list of all the resources the browser has in its cache for that particular host, enabling the server to take that into consideration before pushing down resources.

In practice, because of the caching issues, you don't want to use Server Push naively. One easy way to implement Server Push is to make sure it's only in effect on your landing pages, and only working for first views. You can use a cookie to distinguish first views from repeat visits, and use the request's Accept headers to distinguish navigation requests from subresource ones.

Actually triggering Server Push varies per server: some servers use Link preload headers as a signal to push resources. The problem with that approach is it doesn't take advantage of the server's think time. Alternatively, configuring the server to issue pushes based on the arriving requests can prove more beneficial, as it triggers the push earlier.

If you want to go all in, there's also a service worker-based implementation of Cache Digests,[12] which can help you deliver Push on all your pages today, without waiting for Cache Digests to be standardized and implemented.

EARLY HINTS

Yet another alternative is a newly adopted HTTP standard header called *Early Hints*[13] (assigned with the response number 103). This header enables the server to send an initial set of headers that will be

---

11 http://smashed.by/cachedigest
12 http://smashed.by/swcachedigest
13 http://smashed.by/earlyhints

indications regarding the resources a browser should load, while still not locking down the final response code. That would enable servers to send down `Link preconnect` and preload headers in order to tell the browser as early as possible which hosts to connect to and which resources to start downloading.

The main downside here is that Early Hints is not yet implemented by any browser, and its implementation may not be trivial. Because the hints are received before the final HTTP response, the browser doesn't necessarily have in place the rendering engine process that will end up processing that document. So supporting Early Hints would require supporting a new kind of request that is not necessarily triggered by the rendering engine, and potentially a new kind of cache that will keep these resources around until the rendering engine is set up and has received the final headers and document.

PREFETCH

Finally, there's also the option of working around the server's think time by kicking it off significantly earlier, before the user has even expressed explicit interest in the page. Browsers use past user activity to predict where the user is likely to go next and prefetch those pages while they are typing in the address, or even before that.

`<link rel=prefetch>` is an explicit way in which developers can do the same and tell the browser to start fetching an HTML page or critical resources ahead of time, based on application knowledge.

Those fetches remain alive when the user actually navigates to the next page, and remain in the cache for a limited amount of time even if the resource is not cacheable.

If you make a reasonable guess of where your users will head next, prefetch can be a good way to make sure that when they do, the browser will be one step ahead of them.

Priorities

Since the download process of a web page comprises downloading dozens of resources (and sometimes more), properly managing the download priority of these resources is extremely important. We discussed the resource loading process earlier. Part of that process is determining each resource's priority.

REQUEST PRIORITIES

Once the browser detects a resource that it needs to load, it kicks off a request that will fetch that resource. We saw earlier that some requests may be more important than others. Resources that are in the critical path should ideally reach the browser before those that are not, and that are required at a later phase of the rendering process.

How do browsers make sure these critical requests get higher priority over less critical ones?

We'll talk about more sophisticated priority schemes later, but if we look at HTTP/1.X, the only method for browsers to control the priority of a specific request is by… not sending it up to the server in the first place. Browsers have a queue of requests that were discovered but should not yet be sent up to the server because there are more critical resources in flight, and we don't want the less critical ones to contend on bandwidth with them.

Different browsers use different schemes: some hold off all non-critical requests while critical ones are in progress, while others let through some non-critical requests to go out in parallel to critical ones, to improve image performance.

Browsers assign priorities to resources according to their type (strictly speaking, according to their `Request.destination`). In the priority queue model, they make sure that a request doesn't go out to the network before all higher-priority requests.

Typically, browsers will assign higher priorities to rendering-critical resources. In Chrome, that translates into the following order: HTML, CSS, fonts, JavaScript, in-viewport images, out-of-viewport images. Chrome also follows some further heuristics which go beyond what other browsers typically do:

- Blocking scripts at the bottom of the page are of lower priority than blocking scripts at the top of the page.

- Async and defer scripts are of even lower priority.

- Preloaded fonts get slightly lower priority than late-discovered fonts to prevent them contending with render blocking resources.

The purpose of these heuristics is to try to infer the developer's intent from various existing signals: the location of the resource on the page, whether it is a blocking resource, and so on. However, such an approach has its limits, and it's hard for developers to convey their real intent to the browser.

Which is why we need…

PRIORITY HINTS

We've seen before that browsers assign different priorities to different resource types based on various heuristics. But as much as these heuristics have done well over the years to optimize content download, they are not always accurate, and are based on indirect indications from the developer regarding which resources are most important for their site. The Priority Hints[14] proposal is an attempt to make those indications explicit, and let browsers take action based on them.

The proposal aims for developers to include new "importance" attributes to various resource-downloading HTML elements, which will indicate whether the resource's priority should be upgraded or downgraded.

That would clearly signal to browsers how to prioritize a resource against its counterparts, without binding them to direct developer instructions, which may not be accurate; for example, a blocking script with low importance attribute value is still blocking layout, and therefore should not have its priority downgraded.

At the time of writing, the proposal is to add an `importance` attribute on `<link>`, `<img>`, `<script>` and `<iframe>` elements, with possible values of `low` and `high`. The hints will enable developers to inform the browser about low-priority resources (such as non-critical JavaScript) as well as high-priority ones (like hero images).

A similar parameter will also be added to the `fetch()` API options, enabling setting the hint on dynamically generated requests.

14 http://smashed.by/priohints

STREAM INTERNAL PRIORITIES

One of the assumptions behind HTTP/2's prioritization scheme is that every resource has its priority. And that assumption works well for resources that have to be processed as a whole, such as CSS and JavaScript. Such resources are either critical or not, in their entirety.

However, for streaming resource types, such as HTML and images, that assumption doesn't necessarily hold.

If we consider HTML, its first few bytes, which contain the <head>, enable the document to be committed, and the critical resources to be requested are of the highest priority. At the same time, especially for long HTML files that go beyond the initial viewport, the last few bytes required to finish constructing the DOM, but not required for the initial rendering, are of lower priority.

Similarly, the first bytes of images, which contain the image's dimensions, are extremely important as they enable browsers to reserve space for the image and allow layout to stabilize. For progressive images, the byte range containing the first scan is significantly more important than the last bytes of the last scan. The former enable the browser to display the rough image (in low quality), while the latter provides small quality improvements.

So download schemes that would enable us to download the first scans of all in-viewport images provide a significantly better user experience than ones which download images one by one.

Currently, HTTP/2 priorities don't enable us to include such prioritization schemes in the protocol. And even if it did, there's currently no way for browsers to know the exact byte ranges of the various images before starting to download them. But that's potentially something we could improve in the future. In the meantime, smart servers could do it by overriding the priorities sent by the browser.

Delivering the Right Content at the Right Time

Since browsers discover content progressively, and content has different priorities, it is important to make sure the application including the content loads the right content at the right time, and critical and non-critical content are not mixed together.

CSS: CRITICAL AND NON-CRITICAL

Loading only the critical parts of your CSS up front, while lazy-loading the rest can be one of the highest impact optimizations you can apply to speed up your first paint and first meaningful paint-rendering metrics.

Your CSS can probably be divided into three parts:

- **Critical CSS**: CSS required to style elements present in the initial viewport.

- **Non-critical CSS**: CSS required to style elements outside of the initial viewport or in other parts of your site.

- **Unused CSS**: CSS rules not used anywhere on your site.

With the advent of front-end CSS frameworks, such as Bootstrap, many sites are downloading significantly more CSS than they actually use. More often than not, they are loading it up front, by simply adding `<link rel="stylesheet">` tags into their markup.

When the browser's preloader sees such tags, or when the equivalent elements get added to the browser's DOM tree, this CSS is downloaded at a high priority as it is considered critical.

Because of the cascade, before it can be processed to calculate the page's styles, the complete CSS code needs to be parsed and taken into account. That includes not just the CSS from a single file, but from all of your included CSS files – at least the ones in your document's `<head>`. The reason is that any CSS rule down at the bottom of your CSS can override any rule at the top of it, so to know which rules actually apply, all your CSS has to be processed.

Therefore it is highly recommended that you only deliver upfront your critical CSS: the CSS absolutely necessary for your page's initial render. All other CSS should be loaded asynchronously, in a way that doesn't block rendering.

Obviously, it's best to avoid sending down CSS you simply don't need.

HOW TO DELIVER CRITICAL CSS

What's the best way to send critical CSS to the browser?

The simplest option is to include a `<link rel="stylesheet">` tag in your markup and let the browser discover the CSS file and download it. While that works, it's not the fastest option. The browser has to tokenize the HTML to start that download, which means an extra RTT plus some processing time before it starts.

Another option is to inline critical CSS into your HTML so it will get delivered as part of the same resource, saving an RTT. That's a better option, especially if your critical CSS is fairly small. At the same time, your caching will suffer. Delivering the CSS inline means you'll be sending it for every repeat visit to every page on your site. If the CSS is small enough, it could be worth your while, but it's a trade-off you should be aware of.

A third option is to use H2 Push to deliver critical CSS before your HTML even hits the browser.

HOW TO DELIVER NON-CRITICAL CSS

We've seen that adding CSS to your HTML with `link rel="stylesheet">` causes browsers to think it is blocking and hold off rendering until it's fully downloaded and processed. How do we avoid that?

Using requestAnimationFrame as a First-Paint Proxy

One technique to make sure you don't load any non-critical CSS before the initial page render is to trigger the loading of that CSS only after the render happens. While there's no direct event that fires when the initial render happens, the first requestAnimationFrame event[15] of the page corresponds to it pretty well.

Loading CSS at that point will not block the page's initial rendering, so it will have no negative side effect.

```
var loadStyle = () => {
  var link = document.createElement("link");
  link.rel = "stylesheet";
  link.href = "non-critical.css";
  document.body.appendChild(link);
};
if (window.requestAnimationFrame) {
  window.requestAnimationFrame(() => {
    window.setTimeout(loadStyle, 0);
  }
} else {
  window.addEventListener("DOMContentLoaded", loadStyle);
}
```

Preload

An alternative technique to decouple CSS execution from loading is to use `<link rel="preload">` to trigger the CSS loading, and only process it and take its rules into account once it's loaded. To do that, we can take advantage of `HTMLLinkElement`'s `load` event.

```
<link rel="preload" as="style" href="async_style.css"
onload="this.rel='stylesheet'">
```

You can also combine the two methods above to trigger a download of the preload resource, only after the document has been painted. This avoids having it contend for bandwidth with more critical resources.

15 http://smashed.by/requestanimationframe

The downside of these two methods is that the resource will be downloaded with high priority, so it runs a real risk of competing with other resources on the page.

Inapplicable media Attribute

Another way to cause an early download of CSS without triggering its execution is to use the `media` attribute of `HTMLLinkElement` with the `stylesheet rel` attribute. Such resources are downloaded at a lower priority, yet not executed until the download has finished.

An example may look something like this:

```
<link rel="stylesheet" href="async_style.css" media="not all" onload="this.media='all'">
```

Progressive CSS Loading

The above methods all work but are not necessarily easy to use, as they require extra work to load your CSS in a performant way.

What if we could change the way CSS behaves to make it easier to progressively load, and have it only block the rendering of the contents below it?

That would let us load our CSS whenever we actually need it,[16] and browsers would just do the right thing.

Up until recently, that was (more or less) the way Firefox, Safari, and Edge loaded CSS, but not Chrome. Chrome and other Chromium-based browsers blocked the rendering of the entire page as soon as an exter-

16 http://smashed.by/progcss

nal CSS resource was discovered, even if it was in the `<body>`. That meant using this technique would have had a significant performance penalty in Chrome.

But starting from Chrome 69, Chrome aligned its behavior with other browsers. Developers can now include non-critical CSS, using `<link rel="stylesheet">` tags inside their content, without it having a negative impact.

One caveat is that Firefox doesn't always block rendering for in-`<body>` style sheets, which can result in a flash of unstyled content (or *FOUC*). A way to work around that is to include a non-empty `<script>` tag after the `<link>` tag, which forces Firefox to block rendering at that point until all styles have finished downloading.

An example of the above would be:

```html
<html>
  <head>
  <style>/* Critical styles */</style>
  </head>
  <body>
  <!-- Critical content -->
  <link rel="stylesheet" href="foo.css">
  <script> </script><!-- Note the space inside the script -->
  <!-- Content which is styled by foo.css -->
  </body>
</html>
```

A future improvement might be for browsers to adapt the CSS priority to its location, as it turns it from a render-blocking resource to a partial blocker.

Which One Should I Use?

We've discussed four different techniques to load CSS, but when should you use each one?

These techniques differ in the time in which requests are triggered, as well as in the request's priority. Also, some of them rely on script execution which, some argue, goes against the principles of progressive enhancement.

In the end, I believe the easiest and cleanest technique to load non-critical styles is to include them as `<link>` tags in the `<body>`, and have them block only the content that relies on them. If you have styles that are needed only for follow-up pages, you could use the inapplicable `media` technique, but arguably `<link rel="prefetch">` may be a better tool for the job.

JAVASCRIPT: CRITICAL AND NON-CRITICAL

Like CSS, blocking JavaScript also holds off rendering. Unlike CSS, JavaScript processing[17] is significantly more expensive than CSS and its render-blocking execution can be arbitrarily long.

On top of that, non-blocking async JavaScript can also block rendering in some cases, which we'll discuss further down.

At the same time, in many cases, JavaScript is responsible for engaging user experiences on the web, so we cannot wean ourselves off it completely.

17 http://smashed.by/costofjs

What's the middle ground? How can we enable performant JavaScript experiences? Advice here actually varies, depending on the role of JavaScript in your web app.

JAVASCRIPT-ENHANCED EXPERIENCE, AKA PROGRESSIVE ENHANCEMENT

Earlier we talked about the advantages of HTML as a streaming format. This might be considered an old-school opinion, but to create the highest-performing web experience, it is often better to build your application's foundations as HTML and (minimal) CSS, and then later enhance it with JavaScript for improved user experience.

You don't have to shy away from fancy JavaScript-based animations, or avoid dynamic updates to your content using JavaScript. But if you can make your initial loading experience not dependent on JavaScript, it is highly likely that it will be faster.

I'm not going to go into details regarding writing progressively enhanced web apps – this is well-documented elsewhere. I'm also not going to argue with the fact that, in some cases, JavaScript is mandatory and progressive enhancement makes little sense.

But if you're delivering content that the user then interacts with, it's likely better for you to deliver that content as HTML, and then enhance it with JavaScript.

How to Progressively Load JavaScript

If you follow the principles of progressive enhancement, you want to load your JavaScript in a non-blocking way, but still want enhancements to be there relatively early on. More often than not, the web platform's native mechanisms to load scripts will not be your friends. We talked at length about blocking scripts and why they're bad, so you can probably guess they are not the way to go. But what should you do?

Why Not async?

First, let's talk about what you shouldn't do. `async` is an attribute on the `<script>` element that enables it to be non-blocking, download in parallel to other resources, and run whenever it arrives at the browser.

While that sounds great in theory, in practice it can result in race conditions and have performance implications:

- `async` scripts run whenever they arrive. That means they can run out of order so must not have any dependencies on any other script in the page.

- Because they run whenever they arrive, they can run either before or after the page is first painted, depending on network conditions and network optimizations. This creates a paradox: optimizing your `async` scripts (better compress them or make sure they arrive earlier using Server Push or preload) can often result in performance regressions! Arriving sooner to the browser means their parsing and execution (which on mobile can be hefty) is now render-blocking,[18] even though their download was not.

For that reason, `async` is *not* a great download mechanism and should be avoided most of the time.

18 http://smashed.by/deferoverasync

One more thing: to even consider making certain scripts asynchronous, those scripts must avoid using APIs such as `document.write`, which require blocking the parser at the point in which the script is injected. They should also avoid assuming the DOM or the CSSOM are in a specific state when they run. (Avoid, for example, appending nodes to the bottom of the `<body>` element, or relying on certain styles to be applied)

defer

As far as native script mechanisms go, that leaves us with the `defer` attribute. `defer` has the following characteristics:

- A deferred script will download without blocking the rendering of the page.

- Deferred scripts run at a particular point in time: after the DOM tree is complete and before the `DOMContentLoaded` event fires. That means they run after all inline scripts, and can depend on them.

- Deferred scripts execute in the order they are included in the document, which makes it easier to have dependencies between them.

`defer` is a reasonable way to make sure scripts will *not* interfere with the page's first render, but those scripts will delay the browser's `DOMContentLoaded` event (which triggers JQuery's `ready()` callback). Depending on your app, that may be problematic if you rely on user visible functionality to hang off of that event.

In terms of priorities, in Chromium, both `async` and `defer` scripts are (at the time of writing) downloaded with low priority, similar to images. In other browsers, such as Safari and Firefox, that's not necessarily the case, and deferred and asynchronous scripts have the same priority as blocking scripts.

Similar limitations apply to deferred scripts as to asynchronous: they cannot include `document.write()` or rely on DOM/CSSOM state when they run – even though the latter is less restrictive, as there are guarantees that they'd run right before `DOMContentLoaded` and in order.

Using `<script defer>` only became a realistic option in the last few years. IE9 and earlier had a fatal issue with it, causing content that used `defer` to be broken under certain race conditions[19] if the scripts had interdependencies. Depending on the download order, deferred scripts that added HTML to the DOM (using `innerHTML`, for example) could have triggered the parser to start executing later scripts *before the first script had finished running*. That was a huge blocker for the adoption of `defer` scripts for many years.

But since the usage of IE9 and older is very low nowadays, unless your audience is very much old IE-centric, it is probably safe for you to use `defer` and ignore potential issues.

Why Not Use Blocking JavaScript at the Bottom?

Sending your non-essential scripts as blocking scripts at the bottom of the page used to be a popular mitigation technique to prevent blocking scripts from slowing down first render. It was born in an age where `defer` and `async` did not exist, and to be fair, was significantly better than the alternative: blocking scripts at the top of the page.

[19] http://smashed.by/deferbroken

That said, it's not necessarily the best option and has some downsides:

- While not as bad as blocking the HTML parser and DOM creation at the top of the document, blocking scripts at the bottom of the page still blocks them, which means `DOMContentLoaded` will be delayed.

- Blocking scripts at the bottom of the page are downloaded with medium priority in Chromium-based browsers, and with high priority elsewhere.

- Scripts at the bottom of the page are discovered late by browsers (after the entire HTML is downloaded and processed). Even in the advent of the browser's preloader, their download can start relatively late.

Dynamically Added, async False

Another method to dynamically load scripts is to insert them into the document using JavaScript, but make sure they are loaded in order, in case of dependencies between them.

According to the HTML spec, when scripts are dynamically added to the document, they are assumed to be asynchronous, so download starts immediately and they will execute whenever fully downloaded.

Setting the `async` attribute to false[20] on such scripts changes their behavior. They still don't block the HTML parser, and therefore do not block rendering. At the same time, they will be executed in order.

---

20 http://smashed.by/asynchfalse

The main advantage of this approach over previously mentioned ones, is that the scripts will execute in order, similar to `defer`, but will not wait till the DOM is fully constructed, right before `DOMContentLoaded` fires.

There are a few disadvantages, though: this method requires a script to load your scripts, which adds some cost. As a result of being script-based, these resources are not discoverable by the browser's preloader, so their requests tend to kick off a bit later. And if the page contains any blocking scripts above the loading scripts, they can be delayed significantly. The advantage of the approach can also become its disadvantage: the "execute once you download" approach can result in premature execution, which can stall more critical code or vital browser events (like first paint).

Using requestAnimationFrame as a First-Paint Proxy

Like we've seen for CSS, you can use `requestAnimationFrame` as a way to load non-critical scripts after the first render, ensuring they won't compete for bandwidth with critical CSS and JavaScript, but still kicking off their download as soon as possible.

Preload with Onload Handler

Similarly, we can use preload and its `onload` event handler to kick off script downloads and make sure they run once they finish downloading.

This is very similar to `async`, with some subtle differences:

- Priority of preloaded scripts is assumed to be identical to that of blocking scripts, while (at least in some browsers) `async` will get lower priority.

- Unlike async, with preload you can make sure the script doesn't run until some milestone is hit (for example, first paint happened)

A simple version of this, mixing both preload and rAF, might look something like this:

```
<script>
  var firstPaintHappened = false;
  var scriptPreloaded = false;
  var addScriptElement = () => {
    var script = document.createElement("script");
    script.src = "non-blocking.js";
    document.body.appendChild(script);
  };
  var preloadOnloadHandler = () => {
    scriptPreloaded = true;
    if (firstPaintHappened) {
      addScriptElement();
    }
  };
  if (window.requestAnimationFrame) {
    window.requestAnimationFrame(() => {
      firstPaintHappened = true;
      if (scriptPreloaded) {
        window.setTimeout(addScriptElement, 0);
      }
    })
  } else {
    window.addEventListener("DOMContentLoaded", addScriptElement);
  }
</script>
<link rel="preload" as="script" href="non-critical.js"
onload="preloadOnloadHandler">
```

Missing High-Level Feature

Similarly to CSS, preload gives us the platform primitives that enable us to load scripts decoupled from their execution. But for CSS, we can also now include styles in the `<body>`, and expect them to Just Work™ without affecting the portion of the document above them.

For scripts, we don't currently have such a high-level feature: an attribute on the `<script>` element that will enable us to simply load them without the script being blocking, while knowing that it will run, potentially in order, at a certain milestone (first paint, after `onload` completed, and so on).

This is a problem that's being worked on[21] in Chrome, where the problem is being defined and various solutions have been outlined. Once that work is done, the solution will hopefully be standardized and implemented in all other modern browsers.

JAVASCRIPT-RELIANT EXPERIENCE

Many websites today rely on JavaScript for their basic rendering, adding those scripts to the website's critical rendering path.

This significantly delays the initial rendering of the page, especially on mobile, as browsers need to download a hefty amount of scripts, parse them, and execute them before they can even start creating the real DOM. In such cases, early discovery of resources using the preloader is not really relevant, as the HTML tokens contain no interesting information about the resources that will be required.

---

21 http://smashed.by/scriptschedule

If you're starting out building a content site, I'd suggest avoiding building it in a way that relies on JavaScript for the basic rendering.

However, that doesn't necessarily mean that you can't develop your site using your favorite language and tools. Many frameworks today enable server-side rendering, where the first page the user sees is rendered with good old-fashioned HTML and CSS, and JavaScript kicks in later, enabling the single-page app experience from that point on.

Unfortunately, some popular JavaScript frameworks employ server-side rendering as a way to get the content to the user early, but then require a large amount of JavaScript execution to make that content interactive. Whenever possible, you should steer away from such frameworks, and look for alternatives where server-rendered content is functional on its own.

The best way to tell would be to test existing sites that use the frameworks you're considering for your project, and look at their interactivity metrics on mobile. If the page takes a large number of seconds to render on mobile, or if it renders quickly but then freezes for what seems like forever to the user, that's a big red flag warning you against that framework.

You can run such tests, on real devices, at webpagetest.org. You could also run a Lighthouse audit of those sites,[22] identifying the site's Time to Interactive (TTI) metrics, among others.

22 http://smashed.by/wptlighthouse

But I Already Rely on JavaScript. What Do I Do?

If you already rely on JavaScript for your existing site, look into server-side rendering (SSR) solutions. If they exist for your framework, they will help speed up your initial rendering. Unfortunately, SSR solutions can't always help improve your site's TTI metrics, if they weren't designed with that in mind. They often involve "hydrating" the DOM: attaching event listeners and binding data structures to it, which can require significant processing.

If there's no SSR solution for your case, `<link rel="preload">` can help you overcome the fact that your site is sidestepping the browser's preloader, and give your browser's network stack something to do while the user's CPU is churning away executing JavaScript. Because Priority Hints are not yet widely implemented, you need to make sure these preload links are either included in the HTML after more critical resources, or added to it dynamically after first paint.

You may be able to switch to a lighter version of your framework. Many popular frameworks have a lighter alternative, which is mostly compatible (so you could easily switch your content to it) while being faster.

There are, of course, some trade-offs, as that lighter weight may come at a cost to functionality you rely on. But often it just removes features you don't use, resulting in a faster experience at no particular cost.

Another way to make your JavaScript-reliant app faster is to use intelligent bundling solutions like *webpack*[23], *Rollup*[24] or *Parcel*[25] to code-split your application into route-specific bundles, and only load up front

---

23 http://smashed.by/webpack
24 http://smashed.by/rollupjs
25 http://smashed.by/parceljs

the code you need for your current route. Then you can use prefetch to download future routes as lower-priority resources.

Eventually, consider rewriting the major landing pages of your application, so that users can get them rendered and working relatively fast, and then use them to bootstrap the rest of your app.

LAZY LOADING IMAGES

Images often comprise a large chunk of the page's downloaded bytes. At the same time, many of the images on the web are downloaded, decoded, and rendered only never to be seen, as they were too far off the initial viewport and the user never scrolled that far.

Lazy loading out-of-viewport images is something that JavaScript libraries have been experimenting with for a while. There are many decent open source solutions for you to pick from, and they can significantly reduce the amount of data your users download by default, and make their experience faster.

A few things to note regarding lazy loading solutions:

- Lazy loading your in-viewport images is likely to make them *slower*, as they will be discovered by the browser later.

- The amount of in-viewport images may vary widely between different viewports, depending on your application.

- You need to make sure that the content is not relaid out when the images have downloaded, as that will introduce jank to the scrolling process.

The first two points are hard to get right, as to include the in-viewport images in markup and lazy-load the rest, you would need to automatically generate your HTML based on the device's viewport dimensions. The third requires you to pay particular attention to your markup and styles, and make sure your images' containers have well-defined widths and heights.

Recently browsers have started looking[26] into performing image lazy loading natively, but the same problems apply. Currently, browsers don't know which images will be in the viewport, nor what their dimensions are before at least some parts of the image are downloaded. I believe we will need to find a standard way for developers to communicate that information to the browser, so it can do the right thing. It will also be helpful to define a simple way for developers to define an element's aspect ratio, rather than rely on padding-top-based hacks.[27]

INTERSECTIONOBSERVER

JavaScript-based lazy loading has become significantly easier to implement in a performant way with the introduction of IntersectionObserver.[28] Traditionally, JavaScript-based lazy loading rested on listening to the browser's scroll events, and calculating the image's position relative to the viewport on each one of those events. That often resulted in a lot of main-thread jank, as it needed to perform these calculations as the user was scrolling.

IntersectionObserver enables developers to get a callback whenever a particular element is a certain distance from the viewport.

26 http://smashed.by/lazyloadbelowthefold
27 http://smashed.by/paddingtophack
28 http://smashed.by/intersectionobserver

Lazy-loading implementations achieve their goal, then, without spamming the main thread's event loop.

PLACEHOLDERS

You can also include a low-quality placeholder for your image until it gets loaded. This has a couple of advantages:

- If your users scrolled fast and the image has not yet loaded, a placeholder gives them a better experience.
- It will resolve re-layout issues without you having to define explicit image dimensions or CSS-based aspect ratios.

In its simplest form, you could create a thumbnail of your image and incorporate it in your markup as a data URI. You're probably better off doing that through a build-time automated solution than manually.

There are also more advanced techniques[29] available that can help you get a nicer blurred placeholder image, without paying more in bytes.

WHAT TO DO?

A few points worth looking into when picking an image lazy-loading solution:

- It should get bonus points for using `IntersectionObserver`, as it'll likely be less janky and more accurate.
- Avoid applying lazy loading for images in the viewport for most reasonable viewport sizes.

29 http://smashed.by/svgplaceholder

- Make sure your images' dimensions are well defined in markup or styles. Alternatively, include an inline placeholder, which will maintain the layout as well as present something to your users while they are waiting for the full image to load.

FONTS

When classifying resources as rendering-critical and non-critical, fonts sit somewhere in the middle. On the one hand, fonts do not block the page's layout, and therefore its rendering. On the other, they often do block the page's headers or text from becoming visible, preventing the user from seeing the content.

The default behavior for font loading varies between browsers: IE and Edge show the user a fallback font while they wait for the fonts to download; others prefer to block font rendering for three seconds, waiting for fonts to arrive, and only then render the fallback font. The default font-loading behavior of most browsers can be considered to be blocking, then, or at least "blocking for three seconds," which is not ideal.

What's the best way to control your font loading and make sure your users don't find themselves staring for seconds at a fully laid out page with no text to read?

There are various strategies[30] you can take to tackle this, but you have two major options.

---

30 http://smashed.by/webfontsloading

FONT-DISPLAY CSS RULE

The `font-display` CSS rules are fairly widely supported (all modern browsers except for Edge), and can enable you to control browser font-loading behavior and modify it to match your preferences:

- If you can live with the flash of unstyled text (FOUT), where the fallback fonts are rendered first and then replaced by the loaded fonts once they arrive, `font-display: swap` is probably the way to go.

- Alternatively, `font-display: fallback` left you make sure a switch from fallback font to loaded font won't happen too late during page load, and guarantees that if such a switch happens, it will only happen within the first three seconds of the font loading.

- If you can't live with FOUT, `font-display: optional` makes sure the loaded fonts are displayed only when they are immediately available to the browser (when they are cached from a previous session). Otherwise, only the fallback font is displayed.

Since Edge's default font-loading strategy is not very different from `swap`, the lack of support is probably not something you have to worry about too much.

One major caveat with CSS `font-display` is that different fonts may trigger the swap at different times; if you have multiple font files that represent different styles or weights, they may come in at different times, resulting in a potentially jarring experience to your users.

If this is your case, you *may* want to prefer the...

FONT LOADING API

The Font Loading API allows you to explicitly load fonts from JavaScript, and perform certain actions when they finish loading. If you have several font files that need to be rendered together, you can load programmatically and change the CSS rules to apply them (by adding a class on their container, for example, or adding the fonts dynamically) only once all of them have finished loading.

Full Bandwidth Pipe

Because web content comprises many smaller resources, traditionally it has been difficult to make sure the network's bandwidth is well used when delivering it. We've already discussed early delivery, but that's not the only piece of that puzzle. With HTTP/1, requests often incurred the overhead of starting their own connections, which introduced a delay between the time a resource was discovered and the time it was requested. That delay still exists, to a lesser extent, for HTTP/2 for third-party content: a separate connection still needs to be established.

Resource discovery itself is another tricky piece. Since web content is progressively discovered, it means network efficiency is often blocked by processing efficiency (the browser has to work on previously loaded resources to discover and request future ones). It also means that resource loading is latency-bound, as at least a full RTT has to be spent on downloading and processing each layer of the loading dependency tree, which is required to discover and download the next one.

EARLY DISCOVERY

What can we do to speed up this process and avoid it being latency- and processing-bound?

H2 Push, discussed earlier, is one way to make sure that by the time critical resources are discovered by the browser, they are already downloaded and are safely stowed in its cache.

PRELOAD

Another, slightly more flexible alternative is preload. We mentioned preload as a mechanism that decouples loading from execution, but it also enables us declaratively fetch resources ahead of time. For predictable late-discovered resources, we could include preload links for them in the document, and let browsers know about them and fetch them early on. Preloaded resources are downloaded using the right priorities for their resource type, which is defined using the `as` attribute.

Preload's `as` attribute lets browsers know what resource type is being fetched and therefore enables downloading with the right priority, while using the correct Accept headers.

Using it can be as simple as including `<link rel="preload" href="late_discovered_thing.js" as="script">` in your markup.

You can also use preload's `onload` event to create more sophisticated loading patterns, as we've seen previously.

One thing to note when using preload is the `crossorigin` attribute. The `HTMLLinkElement`'s default credentials mode is "include." Therefore, when preloading resources with a different credentials mode (such as fonts, as well as `fetch()`, `XMLHTTPRequest` and ES6 modules by default), you need to make sure the `crossorigin` attribute is properly set on your preload link, otherwise the resource may not be reused (since the internal caches will refuse to serve the preloaded response to the future request), which may result in double downloads.

PRELOADS JUMPING THE QUEUE

While preload was being developed, it was considered a panacea that would allow us to "PRELOAD ALL THE THINGS!" and solve the discovery problem in web content. However, it turned out things are not that simple. One concern with using preloads is that early discovery also means we rely more heavily on the server to prioritize the content according to HTTP/2 priorities, and avoid delaying high-priority resources in favour of low-priority ones. And since in HTTP/2 the browser has no request queue, discovered resources are immediately sent to the server with their appropriate HTTP/2 priority.

HTTP/2 priorities are fairly complex and not all servers fully respect them. Also, because HTTP/2 is built over TCP, prioritization is even trickier. It's possible that the server would start sending low-priority resources, then switch to high-priority ones, but have the low-priority resources fill up the TCP queues, blocking more critical content.

That means the order of requests in HTTP/2 matters as much as their priorities – if not sometimes more. As a result you should be careful that using preload does not result in low-priority resources being requested before high-priority ones. You can do that by incorporating the `<link>` elements in your markup below the critical path resources.

For Link headers, there's work underway[31] to resolve that in Chromium. There are also issues when preloaded content is delivered over separate connections: there is no server to correlate the requests according to their priorities. But we'll discuss that more when we talk about contention.

Minimal Content

We talked earlier about properly splitting and prioritizing critical and non-critical content, but it turns out on the web there's a third class of content: unneeded content.

DON'T DOWNLOAD UNUSED CONTENT

Owing to the use of CSS frameworks and large JavaScript libraries, as well as simple code churn, content on the web tends of contain a large percentage of unused code. There are many tools today that can help you spot such code as part of your build process and weed it out.

Puppeteer coverage API[32] enables you to detect such unused content and take action on it. It is very easy to use such tools to see how much unused CSS and JavaScript you have in your page. It may not be as trivial to take action on those unused parts and delete them automatically, and I'm not aware of any current tools that do that. But at the very least you should be able to monitor the amount of unused JavaScript in your application.

With that said, it's a bit tricky to distinguish unused code from code that will be used later on in some user scenario. That's probably the

---

31 http://smashed.by/linkheaders
32 http://smashed.by/classcoverage

part that requires developer intervention and understanding of your application. But once you detect such code, it would probably be better to lazy-load it when that scenario is likely to happen, rather than loading it up front and penalize users for no reason.

One caveat with tools that use headless Chrome for unused code detection: polyfills for features implemented in Chrome and not implemented elsewhere will be declared as unused code. While that is technically true, that code is likely to be needed in non-Chromium browsers. That is something worth keeping in mind when removing unused code.

As always, it's significantly easier to avoid unused code when you build a site from scratch than to weed out unused code from a legacy codebase. Finding out where each piece of code comes from and where it might be used can be a tiresome manual process. Make proper coverage checks part of your continuous integration and deployment process. That helps to make sure you don't add unneeded bloat whenever you incorporate a new library for that shiny new feature.

BUT THAT UNUSED CONTENT IS CACHED, SO THAT'S PERFECTLY FINE, RIGHT?

Well, not really. First of all, that content will not be cached for first-time visitors. That could be a large chunk of your users, depending on your audience, and as they say, you only get one chance to make a first impression. The content will also not be cached whenever you update it, which you should do fairly regularly to avoid any known security vulnerabilities[33] in popular libraries.

33 http://smashed.by/jslibvulnerability

On top of that, caches get evicted. Particularly on mobile devices (where it matters most), unless your site is the most popular one a user visits, your precious resources may have made room for others. Having bloated resources (which take up more cache space) actually increases the chances of that happening. And even if the resource is in the cache, larger resources are more likely to be stored over multiple blocks, which on spinning disk-based caches might mean longer retrieval times.

For JavaScript, extra code also means extra parsing costs. Some JavaScript engines cache their parsing products, making processing faster in repeat views. For example, V8 uses code caching to make sure JavaScript bytecode can be reused in repeat views, reducing parsing costs there. But that may not be true for all JavaScript engines and all JavaScript content (as some content may not be eligible for caching). There are also no guarantees that the cached parsing products won't get evicted before your content does.

Finally, unused CSS and JavaScript increases your site's memory footprint for no good reason, as the browser has to maintain the unused rules and code in memory for as long as your site is in memory. In low-memory environments like mobile, that could cause your site's tab to be kicked out of memory when the user is not looking.

COMPRESSION API

As mentioned above, the unused content on our sites is often due to including frameworks, where we don't use every bit of functionality. One solution could be to compress that data away.

If we look at framework data on the web, we'll notice a lot of it is shared across sites and can theoretically be very efficiently compressed if we were to use a static dictionary based on some older version of that framework.

Gzip has always had static compression dictionaries (albeit limited in size). Brotli recently joined it and defined shared Brotli[34] dictionaries.

At the same time, there have been proposals[35] to create a browser-native compression API, which will enable developers to use such dictionaries to decompress data.

Combining these two efforts will let us use compression to get rid of most of our unused code and not transport it to our users every time.

Two things are worth noting:

- Both These efforts are still in their early phases, so it may take a while before you can take advantage of them.

- Compressing the bytes over the network doesn't prevent us from paying up their parsing costs at runtime, as the parse time of JavaScript is related to its uncompressed size. So even if we could use it today, this should only be a fallback in cases where the removal of unused code is not feasible.

---

34 http://smashed.by/sharedbrotli
35 http://smashed.by/nativezipapi

WEB PACKAGING

Web Packaging[36] is a new standard proposal for a bundling format – a format that will allow us to send multiple different resources in a single, well, package.

The primary use case for that format is to be able to bundle pieces of content and enable users to pass them along between themselves (without going through a server), or enable content aggregators (such as Google Search) to serve such content from their servers, while the browser still considers the content provider's origin as the real origin (from a security perspective, as well as from a browser UI one).

But a secondary use for such a format could be to improve the web's bundling capabilities.

Historically, web developers used to concatenate their scripts and styles to reduce the number of requests, because with HTTP/1.1 each request incurred a cost. With the move to HTTP/2, the promise was that bundling and concatenation will no longer be necessary.

But in practice, developers soon found out[37] that bundling still has a role:

- HTTP/2 does not have cross-stream compression contexts (for security reasons), which means each resource is compressed on its own. But small files compress with a significantly lower ratio than large ones. So if you have many small JavaScript files in your application, you'll get much larger overall JavaScript payload over the network than if you bundle your small files into a single one.

36 http://smashed.by/webpackage
37 http://smashed.by/jspackaging

- Even though HTTP/2 has no extra cost per request over the network, that doesn't mean that requests have no extra overhead in the browser. In Chrome, at least, that overhead can make a difference when added up among hundreds of requests.

So, bundling still has a role and can improve overall performance if your site has many different JavaScript or CSS resources. But currently, bundling also has a cost. We've already discussed the fact that both JavaScript and CSS are resources that must be executed in their entirety. When we bundle resources together, we effectively tell browsers that they cannot be executed separately, and none of them starts executing until all of them have been downloaded and parsed.

Chrome 66 introduced a streaming parser[38] for JavaScript so it can be parsed on a background thread as it is being downloaded. That means, at least in some cases, the "all or nothing" approach to JavaScript is slightly mitigated; even though large bundles still have to be executed as a single unit, they may be parsed progressively. Other browsers don't yet have streamed parsing for JavaScript, but at least some of them are actively looking into it.

Another downside of bundling is the loss of caching granularity. When serving resources separately, if any are no longer fresh and need updating, they can be downloaded on their own, and the rest can be retrieved from cache. But once we've bundled resources, each small change in each one of the files means that all of them must be downloaded again. Even worse, for JavaScript, it means that whatever parsing products the browser created and cached for that file are no longer valid, and the browser has to create it again, expending precious user CPU time.

38 http://smashed.by/streamingparser

Current advice for developers is to find the right trade-off between these two approaches: bundle scripts, but avoid creating huge bundles that delay the scripts' execution and increase the probability of unnecessary cache invalidation.

But let's go back to Web Packaging and how it can help us. It can enable us to create a bundle comprising many smaller files, with each one of them maintaining its identity as an independent entity. Each one of them can be cached separately (based on its own caching lifetime directives) and processed separately. Therefore, we would no longer have to download the entire package to update a single resource within it, and we won't have to invalidate all of it if one resource has changed or needs revalidation. We also would be able to compress the entire bundle as a single resource, providing us the same compression benefits as today's bundling would.

This is all in its early days, and there's currently no concrete proposal for it, but almost all the building blocks are in place or in motion, so hopefully this will become a reality sooner rather than later.

Images

Images are another source of unnecessary content bytes. Too often, images are sent either oversized or under-compressed.

This subject is much too wide to be fully covered in this section. There's a chapter in *Smashing Book 5*[39] about it, as well as an entire book[40] dedicated to image optimization. But I'll do my best to give a brief summary.

39 http://smashed.by/sb5
40 http://smashed.by/hiperfimagesbook

RESPONSIVE IMAGES

The goal of responsive image solutions is to let developers serve appropriately sized images, no matter a user's device dimensions or how big the images are on that device. `srcset` and `sizes` in particular enable you to provide multiple alternative image sources, letting browsers pick the one that's most fitting for the user's device.

The `srcset` attribute declares several image alternatives to the browser, as well as their descriptors. `x` descriptors tell browsers about the image resource's density. `w` descriptors tell them about the image resource's width. Browsers then pick the right resource based on the device's screen density as well as its viewport dimensions.

Using `x` descriptors to serve a *fixed-width* image looks something like:

```
<img src="dec_500px.jpg" srcset="dec_750px.jpg 1.5x, dec_1000px.jpg 2x,
dec_1500px.jpg 3x" width="500" alt="The December wallpaper">
```

Using `w` descriptors to serve an image that can be in many different dimensions:

```
<img src="panda_fallback.jpg" srcset="panda_360.jpg 360w, panda_540.jpg
540w, panda_720.jpg 720w, panda_1080.jpg 1080w, panda_2160.jpg 2160w,
panda_3240.jpg 3240w" alt="A panda eating some bamboo.">
```

The `sizes` attribute can make the matching even tighter. When the browser requests the images, it isn't aware of their display dimensions (as layout may not have happened yet). `sizes` tells the browser the image display dimensions for different breakpoints of the design, so the browser can calculate the ideal resource provided by `srcset` and `w` descriptors.

The `sizes` value could be relatively simple, just stating a percentage of the viewport, such as:

```
<img src="tiger_500px.jpg" sizes="33vw" srcset="tiger_200px.jpg 200w,
tiger_500px.jpg 500w, tiger_800px.jpg 800w, tiger_1000px.jpg 1000w,
tiger_1500px.jpg 1500w, tiger_2000px.jpg 2000w" alt="Tiger">
```

It can also become a bit more complex in more involved designs:

```
<img src="thumb.jpg" sizes="(min-width: 1200px) 235px, (min-width: 641px)
24vw, (min-width: 470px) 235px, 50vw" srcset="thumb100.jpg 100w,
thumb200.jpg 200w, thumb235.jpg 235w, thumb300.jpg 300w,
thumb470.jpg 470w" alt="A rad animal.">
```

Client Hints

Client Hints is a content negotiation mechanism that can be also be used to serve responsive images, among other resource types.

In content negotiation the client provides the server various parameters about the resources it is interested in, and the server uses those to send the right resource.

With Client Hints, once the server has opted in (using Accept-CH and Accept-CH-Lifetime headers), the browser can start sending the server information using request Headers: *DPR* (device pixel ratio), indicates the screen density of the device. *Viewport-Width* indicates the width of the browser's viewport. *Width* gives the server the display width of the image (if the image has a `sizes` attribute). It can also indicate whether the user has opted in to data savings mode, using the Save-Data Client Hints header. The server can then serve the right resource to the client without requiring markup changes (or while requiring smaller ones).

IMAGE FORMATS

Another aspect of image optimization is proper compression. The gains we can get from image compression vary greatly based on the image format we pick.

Different browsers support different cutting-edge image formats, which means that serving the right image format in all cases requires some sophistication.

Serving different image formats to different browsers can be done in a couple of ways.

If you have control over your server, it's probably easier to use the image request Accept headers to detect if the browser supports WebP, JPEG-XR, or just the older (but reliable) JPEG and PNG. Then you can use your server-side logic to pick the ideal resource for that particular browser.

If you have no server-side control, you can use another variant of the responsive images markup to let the browser pick which format it supports.

```
<picture>
<source type="image/webp" srcset="president.webp">
<source type="image/vnd.ms-photo" srcset="president.jpxr">
<img src="president.jpg" alt="The president fistbumps someone.">
</picture>
```

Font Subsetting

Web fonts are another type of content where you can send your users excessive data. Fonts often contain full sets of characters outside the basic Latin Unicode block (typically used in non-English languages), which may or may not be relevant for your content. These extra characters add up, and if you're not using them, it might be best to drop them from the downloaded font entirely. At the same time, it's tricky to assume what you will and will not be using, as personal and location names may contain them. They can also be added to your site by content creators (or in user-generated content) after you have subsetted the fonts.

When you can make assumptions about the content at build time, there are tools (like subfont[41] or glyphhanger[42]) that can help you subset fonts to the minimal subset you need.

Contention Avoidance

We talked earlier about resource priorities and the way that browsers handle priorities in HTTP/2 by sending requests to the server and letting it send the high-priority resources first. However, there's one big problem with that scheme: on the web today *there is no single server*. Most sites are served from a multitude of servers, as different first-party resources are often served from different hosts (static files served from static hosting providers, images served from an image optimization service, and so on). On top of that, third-party resources are served from servers outside of the publisher's control.

---

41 http://smashed.by/subfont
42 http://smashed.by/glyphhanger

Each of these servers has no knowledge of the other resources downloaded from other hosts, and therefore cannot take them into account when considering resource priorities. It can only prioritize its own resources.

In practice, that often means every server handles only a handful of resources, in many cases of similar priority. So the server frequently finds itself with a low-priority resource at the top of the priority queue, and sends it to the user as it is the highest-priority resource on the connection!

That often leads to bandwidth contention between critical resources on the page and less-critical ones that are served from different hosts.

CONNECTION POOLS

Another source of contention is that at least some browsers open different connections for non-credentialed resources. That mostly impacts fonts, XHR and `fetch()`-based resources, but it means these resources are fetched on a separate connection where the same problem as above applies: these resources are fetched without taking into account most of the critical resources on the page's main connection – the credentialed connection. Firefox has changed that behavior[43] from Firefox 60, but Chrome still uses separate connection pools.

HTTP/2 CONNECTION COALESCING

HTTP/2 has a mechanism to get rid of some of these duplicate connections: if multiple hosts on your site all map to the same IP address and are all covered by a single certificate (so cross-origin hosts are covered

43 http://smashed.by/connectpools

by the navigation connection's certificate Server Alternate Name (SAN) extension), then the browser is able to coalesce all those connections together on a single host. While that is a great way to minimize the number of connections, it comes with some hurdles:

- A DNS request is still required (to verify that these hosts map to a single IP), adding some latency to the process.

- It's not always easy to convince your IT department to add multiple hosts as your certificate's SAN.

- DNS-based load balancing can mean it's tricky to make sure these hosts always map to the same IPs, and different browsers do different things when the hosts map to multiple IPs.

The fact that different browsers implement slightly different DNS requirements[44] makes using this mechanism even less reliable in practice.

SECONDARY CERTIFICATES

One solution to make connection coalescing easier is an upcoming proposal called Secondary Certs, which will enable some of those unrelated servers to share a single connection and properly prioritize the content on it. It enables the initial connection to declare its authoritativeness over the other connections used on the site.

A connection would prove authoritativeness over other hosts by letting the browser know that it holds the private keys for their certificates.

44 http://smashed.by/coalescing

That process is, in a sense, similar to a TLS handshake, but is performed on the same initial connection. After the server has proved it can handle requests for those other hosts, the browser can simply send those requests on that same connection, avoiding connection establishment and slow start overhead. Most of all, it can avoid bandwidth contention, as the server can handle the priorities of requests from different hosts on a single connection, and as part of a single priority queue.

DELAYED REQUESTS

Another potential solution to the bandwidth contention problem is to bring back client-side request queues to HTTP/2, and make sure that low-priority requests, which will go on a different connection from the main one, will get buffered on the client side until some point when we are certain they will not slow down the more critical resources.

While doing that mostly works for HTTP/1, for HTTP/2 it seems we can do better. Delaying the requests means they will hit the servers half an RTT after we decide it's OK to send them, because the risk of contention is gone (for example, the critical resources have downloaded). Also, by default, if we hold back the requests, no connection will be established. We could, then, implicitly preconnect to those hosts. That'd be better, but maybe still not perfect.

NET STACK ORCHESTRATION

A better alternative would be to be able to send those requests to the related servers, but use HTTP/2's session and stream flow controls to make sure the responses are not sent back (or don't take more than a certain amount of bandwidth) until the critical resources are well on their way.

If done well (with some heuristics, since we're not certain we know the size of the critical resources coming in), that can lead to perfect network stack-based orchestration of content coming in from multiple connections.

SAME-CONNECTION H2 CONTENTION

The previous section discussed contention in an H2 world where there are multiple connections, and resources on these separate connections contend with each other. But there are also scenarios in H2 where resources contend with same-priority resources on that same connection.

Consider a scenario where multiple JavaScript resources are being downloaded from a server, all at the same priority. The server can send those resources down in two different ways:

1. Interleave the resources, sending a buffer of each of them.
2. Send the resources one after the other.

Which of these approaches would be better?

When talking about JavaScript or CSS resources, the answer is obvious. Since these resources need to be processed in their entirety before they can be executed, sending the full files would mean we can execute each of those files earlier, resulting in faster overall experience.

Sending the full files one after the other means they can execute faster.

However, what if we're talking about resources that are processed in a streaming fashion, such as images? In that case, it's probably better to send down some data for each separate image, and provide the user with better visual feedback. That is particularly true for progressive JPEGs, where sending the first scan of each of the viewport images is enough to give the user the impression that the screen is full, even if the images are still of low quality.

Browsers can control the way that H2 servers send their resources and try to influence them, using H2's dependencies and weights. While weights represent the resource's priority, dependencies can tell the server to prefer to send a resource only after the entire resource it depends on was sent down. In practice, that translates to the server sending resources one-by-one, if it's possible.

The notion of in-stream H2 priority, discussed earlier, would enable browsers to indicate to servers that, for example, a certain resource's first few chunks are more important than its last.

WHAT CAN YOU DO ABOUT IT?

Unfortunately, most of the items listed above are things that browsers would need to improve in order for you to take advantage of them. But there are still a few things you can do to minimize the negative impact of third-party downloads on your main resources.

REWRITE STATIC THIRD-PARTY RESOURCES TO YOUR OWN DOMAIN

If at all possible, you'd be better off rewriting static third-party resources to point to your own domain, and rehost them there. From the browser's perspective, these resources become first-party, and can hitch a ride on the existing first-party H2 connection, and not contend for bandwidth with your own resources. Unfortunately, you have to be pretty sure these resources are public, static, and not personalized in any way.

From a security perspective, these resources can now be inspected by code running on your site, so you need to make sure these third-party resources are public, to avoid any security issues.

Another reason to make sure these resources are public is that if they depend on cookies in any way, the cookies will be lost when rewriting the URLs.

DELAY REQUESTING NON-CRITICAL THIRD PARTIES

Another alternative to avoid contention is to time-shift the non-critical third-party requests to a point in time when they will not contend with your main content. That may look very much like the lazy-loading of non-critical JavaScript content, but potentially delayed even further, to avoid contention with your own non-critical content.

USE CONNECTION COALESCING TO YOUR ADVANTAGE

We talked earlier about H2 connection coalescing and all of its caveats. But even with all those downsides, HTTP/2 connection coalescing is the only mechanism you can use today to reduce the proliferation of different connections competing with each other on your site. Connection coalescing is something you can take advantage of if you have your own "third-party" domains that you control, such as an images or a static resource domain.

If you do, you need to make sure that two conditions apply for the browser to coalesce those connections:

- The domain needs to be covered under the first-party domain's SAN.
- The domain needs to be DNS-resolved onto the same IP as the first-party domain.

Those are tricky conditions, and cannot always be satisfied (for IT/infosec reasons), but if you can make them work, you can enjoy connection coalescing today.

USE CREDENTIALED FETCHES WHEN POSSIBLE

We also mentioned that some browsers use different connection pools for non-credentialed resources, which means even some of your first-party resources can contend for bandwidth with your other resources. At least when it comes to `XMLHttpRequest` and `fetch()` requests, you can specify that these requests will be requested with credentials, and avoid them going out on a separate connection. Unfortunately, that's not possible for all CORS anonymous requests (there's no way to fetch fonts as no-cors, for instance).

The way you would do that for XHR would be something like:

```
var xhr = new XMLHttpRequest();
xhr.open("GET", "https://www.example.com/data.json");
xhr.withCredentials = true;
xhr.send(null);
```

For fetch(), you'd need to add the credentials parameter to the init JSON:

```
fetch("https://www.example.com/data.json", { credentials: 'include'
}).then((response) => {
  // Handle response
});
```

Minimizing Latency

One of the most important factors on resource loading performance is network latency. There are many aspects of loading that are affected by it: connection establishment, resource discovery, and the delivery itself. While we cannot reduce the latency of the physical network, there are various ways in which we can get around it.

PHYSICAL LOCATION

One way is to bring the content closer to the user. That can be done by hosting the content at various locations around the planet and serving users from the location closest to them. This will require you to synchronize the content between those different locations.

It turns out there are commercial services that will do that for you. Content delivery networks enable you to host your content at a single location, while their edge servers take care of distributing it all over the world. That enables significantly shorter latencies for both connection establishment and content delivery, assuming you set your content's caching headers correctly.

CACHING

Caching is an important part of of our fight against latency. Caching at the origin enables you to avoid spurious server-side processing, reducing both your server-side think time as well as your CPU requirements on the server. Caching at the edge enables you to offload content from your origin, again serving it faster and cheaper. Finally, caching at the browser enables repeat visitors to your site to download less content, and provides them with a significantly faster and cheaper experience.

There are a few essential caching policies you can employ.

IMMUTABLE

Any public content which you refer to from your pages and can change the reference to once the content changes, should be considered immutable. You can achieve that by having a content-addressable URL: a URL which contains either a hash or a version of the content itself, and which changes by your build system once the content changed. You would also need to annotate the content with something like the following headers:
`Cache-Control: public, immutable, max-age=315360000`.

That would tell the cache server or the browser that the content will never change (or tell them that the content will not change in the next ten years, if they don't support the immutable keyword). It would enable them to avoid content revalidation, and know that if it's in the cache and needed by the page, it can be served as is.

ALWAYS FRESH

Any content which users navigate to directly through links or from the address bar (usually your HTML pages) should have a permanent URL that does not change if the content does. Therefore, we cannot declare such resources to be immutable, as it will be impossible to modify them if we found an error in the page, a bug, or a typo.

You could argue that such content can be cacheable for relatively short times (probably hours). Unfortunately, that would make it very hard for you to change the content within that time window if you need to ship unpredicted changes. As such, the safest choice is to make sure the content gets revalidated with the server every single time. You can do that by using headers such as: `Cache-Control: no-cache`.

OFFLOAD

The problem with the previous approach is that it prevents origin and edge caches from offloading the content from your origin. If the cache gets hit with 1,000 requests per second, it needs to relay those 1,000 requests to the origin server, not providing much benefit as a cache to that type of content.

A different approach is to provide a very short caching lifetime to your public HTML content, giving just enough freshness to enable caches to offload your origin. That can be achieved with something like `Cache-Control: public, max-age=5`.

That will make sure your content is publicly cacheable for five seconds, and gets revalidated at the origin after that. So if your cache server gets hit with 1,000 requests per second, only one request in 5,000 will get revalidated at the origin, providing significant offload and time savings benefits.

Alternatively, you can use caching directives specific to shared caches, such as `s-maxage` to make sure the content is cached in shared caches for short periods of time, but will not be cached in the user's browser cache.

HOLD TILL TOLD

Another approach that is currently only feasible for origin or edge caches is "hold till told." In short, the origin indicates to the cache server that the resource is infinitely cacheable, but reserves the right to purge that content if a bug is found, a typo was corrected, or the wrong information was presented on that page and was then taken down.

The content is then present and valid in the cache for long periods of time, does not get revalidated at the origin, but gets evicted from the cache as soon as the origin explicitly indicates (through an API or other proprietary means) that it should be.

Unfortunately, that method has no standard alternative at the moment.

SERVICE WORKERS

Another great way to reduce the impact of latency and increase the power of caching in browsers is to use service workers.

A service worker is a JavaScript-based network proxy in the browser, enabling the developer to inspect outgoing requests and incoming responses and manipulate them. As such, service workers are extremely powerful, and enable developers to go beyond the regular browser HTTP cache in caching their resources. Lyza's chapter covers them in depth, so you probably already know that service workers enable a bunch of extremely interesting and beneficial use cases which weren't possible on the web before.

OFFLINE

The basic use case which service workers cover is offline support. Since they have access to requests and responses, as well as to the browser's cache API, they can use that to cache responses as they come in, and later use them if the user is offline. That enables sites to create a reliable offline experience, and serve their users even in shaky or missing connectivity conditions.

One of the patterns that has emerged is "offline first," where the previously cached content is served to the user before going to the network, providing them with a near-instant experience, while the resources fetched from the network are used to update the content displayed to the user once they arrive.

CONSTRUCTING STREAMED RESPONSES

The offline-first principle is easy to apply when your web application is a single-page app, but is not limited to that. You can achieve a similar impact by caching the static parts of your HTML content in your service worker's cache, and combine the cached content with content fetched from your server using the Streaming API.

That lets browsers start processing and displaying the static pieces of the HTML immediately, and fill in the gaps later with the content fetched from the server.

COMPRESSION DECODING

We mentioned the plans to include a compression API in the browser. Combining such an API with service workers can prove to be an extremely powerful tool. Right now, browsers have a monopoly on new compression schemes, and previous attempts to create custom dictionary compression on the web have failed owing to deployment hurdles. But a service worker-based compression API can give such schemes a second chance.

It can enable developers to create their own custom compression dictionaries and use them in service workers to achieve significantly better compression ratios.

HOLD TILL TOLD IN THE BROWSER

Another exciting aspect of service workers is that they enable in-browser hold-till-told caching semantics. The service worker cache can hold on to certain resources indefinitely, but purge them as soon as instructions from the server tell it to.

Such pages would need to build in some refresh mechanism to let them update themselves if they discover they have been purged after being served from the server. While not being ideal, that's the closest we can get to purge mechanisms on the web today.

Control Over Third Parties

An open secret in the web performance community is that improving your site's performance can make little difference if you introduce third-party resources to your page that will slow it down.

The web's ability to mash-up content from different sources and origins is what makes it a powerful, expressive platform. But it comes at a security and performance cost. Third parties on the web are often incentivized to maximize their engagement metrics, which don't always align with your users' performance and experience.

The Accelerated Mobile Pages (AMP) project was created, at least in part, as an effort to get those third parties in alignment with performance best practices, by eliminating most of them and allowing others controlled access to the page.

But if you're not using AMP, how can you make sure your third-party content doesn't cause too much damage to your user's experience?

LAZY LOADING

We talked earlier about lazy loading in the context of loading and contention avoidance, and it is very much applicable to third-party content. Because your third-party content will contend for bandwidth with yours, you should delay loading it for as long as you possibly can, while still allowing it to perform its function.

With third-party content, it's particularly important not to load it in a blocking manner; that is, not to load third-party scripts in blocking `<script>` tags. The reason is that if the third party is down for whatever reason, your site's parsing will halt until that third-party content is loaded, or until the browser gives up on loading it, which could take dozens of seconds, depending on the browser and the OS. That is usually referred to as a front-end single point of failure, or SPOF for short.

IFRAME YOUR THIRD PARTIES

Another useful way to get third-party content out of the way is to compartmentalize it in its own iframe. That is good for security (because it prevents it from accessing your page's DOM without your permission), as well as for CPU performance (as cross-origin iframes have their own main thread).

That's also the approach taken by AMP, where arbitrary third-party scripts can only run inside iframes.

Unfortunately, not all third parties are amenable to being iframed, and some require access to the main page's DOM to function properly. Past initiatives such as SafeFrame, which enabled controlled DOM access to iframed third parties, did not take off, and not many third parties support them.

CONTENT SECURITY POLICY

If you have to run your third-party scripts in the main page's context, you can restrict what content they can download and where they can download it from using Content Security Policy. Including CSP directives can help you make sure that, for example, image-based ads don't turn into video and audio ads without your permission. At the same time, you should note that CSP doesn't yet allow you to control what the iframes that load in your page are doing, so it cannot be used to enforce restrictions on ads loaded inside iframes, for instance.

SERVICE WORKERS TO AVOID SPOF

We talked about service workers in the context of caching and offline support, but they also enable you to enforce various rules on outgoing requests, if they are running in the context of the main page. For example, you can use service workers to make sure third-party content does not SPOF your page[45] if it doesn't load. Similarly, you can use service workers to delay loading your dynamically loaded third parties, and avoid them contending for bandwidth and CPU with your own resources.

45   http://smashed.by/subfont

FEATURE POLICY

Finally, one of the great promises of AMP is that it only enables the page and third parties a subset of the web's functionality. That doesn't seem like a great promise, but in practice it prevents both content as well as third-party developers from shooting themselves (and the user) in the foot.

One effort to bring the same type of enforcement to the web is the Feature Policy specification.[46] It allows developers to explicitly turn off features they know they won't need on their page, and prevent third parties from (ab)using those features. Features like video and audio autoplay, use of synchronous XMLHttpRequest, size of loaded images and their compression ratios, and more. Feature policies are inherited by iframes so the same restriction will apply to them as well. You can also define iframe-specific feature policies, so you can restrict your iframed third parties further than you restrict the main context.

In Summary

Loading resources on the web today is hard. At the very least, it's hard to do in an optimal way. But it's getting better. And browsers are investing heavily in improving it significantly, too.

WHAT TO DO?

We've covered many different subjects throughout the chapter, so it's easy to lose track of what is theoretical and what is actionable. Below is a checklist you can go over to refresh your memory, and find things to focus on to improve your site's performance.

46 http://smashed.by/featurepolicy

1. **Reduce protocol overhead**
   - *Preconnect*: Use preconnect to prevent connection establishment from blocking your critical path.
   - *TFO + TLS 1.3 or QUIC*: Use cutting-edge protocol stacks if you can to reduce protocol overhead.

2. **Early delivery and discovery**
   - *Server Push*: Use H2 Server Push to ensure early delivery of your critical resources on first views.
   - *Preload*: Make your resources discovered by the browser early.

3. **Load it when you need it**
   - *Progressive CSS* loading: Load styles for your out-of-viewport content at the point when they are needed.
   - *Non-blocking JavaScript loading*: Make sure your JavaScript is loaded in a non-blocking manner.
   Lazy-load images: Use one of the various lazy loading libraries (preferably one that uses `IntersectionObserver`) to lazy-load your out-of-viewport images.
   - Use smart font loading strategies: Prefer FOUT and use `font-display: swap` or the Font Loading API to achieve it.

4. **Load less**
   - Avoid sending *unused code*: Use code coverage tools to remove dead code from your JavaScript and CSS bundles.
   - Avoid JavaScript-reliant experience: Prefer your user's experience over your own and use a small amount of non-blocking JavaScript to avoid bogging down.
   - *Brotli*: Use Brotli compression to significantly reduce the size of your static JavaScript and CSS files.
   - Use *responsive images* and *Client Hints* to make sure you're not sending unnecessary image data.
   - *Subset your fonts* to avoid sending unused character data.

5. **Avoid bandwidth contention between your resources**
    - Rewrite static third-party files to your domain.
    - Dynamically delay requests for non-critical third parties.
    - Use credentialed fetches whenever possible.
    - Coalesce connections using the certificate's SAN and mapping hosts to the same IP address.
6. **Minimize latency**
    - Use caching headers to make sure your resources are properly cached in the browser and on intermediary caches.
    - Use a CDN to reduce latency between the user and the nearest server.
    - Service workers can make browser caching more predictable.
7. **Reduce impact of third-party resources**
    - iframe and lazy-load third parties whenever possible.

What's in the Future?

To wrap up the chapter with an optimistic view, here's where I want loading resources to be five years from now:

- The QUIC protocol will be standardized and universally deployed. It will resolve many of the underlying protocol issues that have plagued the web for a long while, and which HTTP/2 was the first stab at fixing. It will significantly reduce the protocol overhead and make transport significantly less sensitive to the network's latency.

- Third parties' impact on the network will be significantly limited, as browsers will avoid bandwidth contention between low-priority resources and high-priority ones, by delaying low-priority requests, and by orchestrating the different connections and streams based on their priority.

- Browsers will also avoid opening multiple connections to the same origin to prevent bandwidth contention. Secondary certificates will enable sites to easily coalesce their different domains onto the same connection for improved prioritization.

- The third-party ecosystem will be significantly more amenable to being iframed for increased performance and security.

- The framework ecosystem will make heavy use of workers, delegating more JavaScript work off the main thread.

- Feature Policy combined with iframed third parties will enable developers to take back control over their user's experience.

- Lazy-loading non-critical content will become significantly easier through new loading paradigms.

- Early delivery and resource discovery will be fixed using Server Push (with Cache Digests), preload and Priority Hints. Build tools will automatically create those instructions for developers at build time.

- JavaScript resources will be bundled using Web Packaging, enabling improved compression, caching granularity, and (combined with Cache Digests) avoiding sending resources already in the browser's cache.

- Common build processes will also help make sure completely unused JavaScript and CSS are never sent to browsers, and rarely or late used code is loaded later on.

- The combination of compression APIs and service workers will enable off-the-shelf delta compression solutions that will significantly reduce the amount of framework JavaScript and CSS users have to download.

- Client Hints with network quality estimations will simplify server-side implementations of adaptive congestion control algorithms. QUIC will make it simpler to change the congestion window after receiving the request with those hints.

- Web Packaging and packaged content will enable browsers to prefetch content as if it's coming from the origin without privacy implications and side effects.

- And finally, measurement APIs will enable us to keep track of all the above and make sure our users' experiences are as snappy as we want them to be.

These are all things that are currently being discussed and are in different phases of the standardization process. Some might not make it, and be replaced with more mature incarnations. But the aim is to solve all these problems in the next few years.

In aggregate, all these improvements would mean that loading resources in a performant way on the web would become easy, and the default way of creating content for the web. I believe that would make your lives as developers easier, and more importantly improve our users' default experience of the web.

About The Author

Yoav Weiss is a principal architect at Akamai, where he focuses on making the web platform faster by adding performance-related features to browsers as well as to Akamai's CDN. Yoav has been working on mobile web performance for longer than he cares to admit.

CHAPTER 7

On Designing Conversations

Adrian Zumbrunnen

On Designing Conversations

by Adrian Zumbrunnen

About two years ago I turned my website[1] into a chat between me and my visitors. What started as a small side project and experiment quickly turned into an insatiable interest in the topic and the two of us having this conversation right now.

In the pages ahead I'm going to share what I've learned from turning my website into a chat, and combine it with insights from working on the Google Assistant. The goal is to give you a bird's-eye view of the craft of conversational design, and outline a simple process you can follow to create your own conversational experiences. Let's get started.

...

Think about the last time you had an engaging conversation. When was it, and what made it engaging to begin with? We often have a hard time remembering why certain conversations made us feel the way they did. Since conversations typically happen spontaneously, and because they often evolve in unpredictable ways, we can't easily pinpoint their qualities to a few specific attributes. On top of that, we all value slightly different things when it comes to talking to people. Some of us appreciate conversations that help us feel connected, while others appreciate them for their unique ability to entertain and inform. No matter what our individual preferences, there are underlying rules and principles that affect whether we feel a conversation is effective or whether it's a waste of time. Take this interaction as an example:

1 https://azumbrunnen.me/

Waiter: *What can I get you today?*

Frank: *I'll do the spaghetti bolognese and a water with lemon.*

Waiter: *Sure! You got it!*

This is a typical everyday interaction that the average American engages in about four to five times a week.[2] It's so common, so habitual, that most of us would never question whether there was any other way to go about it. That changed when researcher Rick van Baaren and his colleagues decided to run an experiment. Instead of just using positive reinforcement like "OK," "Sure," or "Great," waiters were instructed to repeat what customers said, word for word:

Waiter: *That's spaghetti bolognese and a water with lemon. You got it!*

The result? This simple alteration turned out to significantly impact the waiters' monthly income, increasing their tips by up to 70%.[3]

Seemingly minor differences in communication can sometimes have a surprisingly big impact on what people get out of it. Customers clearly appreciated the additional reassurance of hearing their own words spoken back to them. But it goes far beyond that. Van Baaren's experiment was based on a psychological concept called mirroring.

---

[2] http://smashed.by/dining
[3] Rick van Baaren, Rob Holland, Brejge Steenart, Ad van Knippenberg: "Mimicry for money: Behavioral consequences of imitation" Journal of Experimental Social Psychology 39, no. 4:393-98 (July 2003)

In simple terms, we tend to feel more comfortable being around people who are similar to us. We subconsciously imitate body language, tone of voice, and facial expressions whenever we interact with someone.

This helps explain why the more time couples have spent together, the more they behave and look alike. It's why we can easily tell from a distance whether someone's date is going well. And it's why waiters get a bigger tip when they repeat a customer's order.

If we had to rephrase the findings of these studies we could argue that, above anything, people want to feel understood. And it doesn't have to be as psychologically involved as the concept of mirroring.

In his bestselling book How to Win Friends and Influence People, Dale Carnegie shares an insightful story of meeting a distinguished botanist at a dinner party in New York. Instead of talking to a wide range of attendants, Carnegie mostly focused on the botanist who was eagerly sharing his thoughts about his experiments with plants and indoor gardening. At the end of the night, as people started leaving, the botanist wouldn't stop praising Carnegie for being a great conversationalist. The interesting fact was that throughout the whole evening, Carnegie barely engaged in any talking. Instead, he just listened, kept asking questions, and was genuinely interested in the botanist's stories.

Contrary to popular belief, being a great conversationalist relies less on our ability to talk than our ability to listen. Listening can, therefore, be seen as one, if not the most critical building block of conversation. Without listening, conversation can't evolve and exchange of information becomes virtually impossible. When people don't listen, not only does the quality of conversation suffer, it's also widely considered to be inappropriate, or even worse: impolite.

According to Paul Grice, a British philosopher of language, the underlying expectation of any act of communication is the participants' willingness to cooperate. In what he called the cooperative principle and the maxims of conversation, Grice summarized some of the key elements that constitute an effective conversation.[4]

Let's have a look at each of those four maxims.

MAXIM OF QUALITY

The quality maxim describes that every contribution should be true and supported by evidence. Ambiguous responses and statements you don't think are true should therefore be avoided.

MAXIM OF QUANTITY

The quantity maxim is about providing the right amount of information at the right time. I once ran a user study to test a new design exploration in Google Maps. When I asked Lotta (not her real name) how she would navigate to a specific coffee place shown in the prototype, she didn't just describe her navigation strategy in the most detailed way humanly possible, she also went on to explain how her nephew loved coffee and how he recently moved to Orlando but struggled to find a nice apartment. From that moment on, it became incredibly challenging to shift the conversation back to the original questions the study aimed to answer. Somehow, Lotta's nephew suddenly appeared in the answers to almost every question we asked.

---

[4] Grice, Paul (1975). "Logic and conversation". In Cole, P.; Morgan, J. Syntax and semantics. 3: Speech acts. New York: Academic Press. pp. 41–58.

Even when the intention of sharing more information is to be helpful, it often ends up having the opposite effect. That's what leads us to the the maxim of relevance.

MAXIM OF RELEVANCE

Every contribution should be as relevant as possible. When asking someone if it's going to rain today, we expect a simple yes or no answer. Saying something like: "San Francisco is going to be sunny today with highs of 50 degrees and lows of 43 degrees" is well intended, but will most likely feel less natural.

When it comes to conversational interfaces, it's tempting to provide more information than users actually ask for. The ability to process a lot of data and show off by being overly precise in the way we respond, ironically often makes the conversation less relevant and more robotic.

MAXIM OF MANNER

Both parties should express themselves in a clear, brief, and orderly way. That also means we should avoid unnecessary technical jargon or words users might not understand.

The French mathematician Blaise Pascal famously said *"If I had more time, I would have written you a shorter letter".* As we will see later, it's surprisingly difficult to design conversations in a succinct and clear way.

Conversation inherently assumes that its participants are cooperative. The waiter repeating the customer's order can be seen as an act of cooperation. If Frank, the customer we met in that example, would say "Could I please get the spaghetti," instead of "I'll do the spaghetti," he might very well get some brownie points from the waiter. But the fact that customers don't get any tip or a rating obviously provides less initiative for them to be more cooperative and invested in the conversation.

Freiherr Knigge also touched upon some of the principles described by Grice. Knigge was a German writer from the 18th century, best known for his book on social relations, in which he discusses socially appropriate behavior. Interestingly, he believed that the relationship between author and reader qualifies as conversation as well. According to Knigge, you and I are engaging in a conversation right now – and let me tell you that you've been a truly distinguished conversationalist so far.

From Theory to Practice: Creating Conversational Experiences

Now that we've discussed the core principles of what constitutes an effective conversation, we're ready to look at the challenges of mapping those rules to the digital landscape.

In this section, we'll discuss some of the key insights I had from turning my website into a chat, and discuss why they are relevant for any kind of conversational interaction.

TURNING A WEBSITE INTO A CHAT

Starting an endeavor like building a bot can easily seem overwhelming, and I wasn't sure where to start. In my naïveté, I decided to start the way I always do: by writing down a couple of thoughts and ideas.

```
Hi there! I'm Adrian.

I'm a UX/UI designer living in Zurich,
Switzerland.

Are you interested in working together or
do you want to get in touch?

> Know more | Get in touch


  # Know more (magnifier)
  - That's great! I feel humbled. :)
  - I write and speak about design and have
    worked for various clients in the industry.
    What are you most interested in?
```

Screenshot of an early draft

The screenshot above shows one of my very first drafts. This specific part of the text remained unchanged till the very end. Everything else would get highly redacted, edited, or removed. As I kept writing conversations, I realized I automatically started to use my own syntax to represent how a conversation could evolve. I used the vertical bar symbol "|" to separate suggestions. Tapping on a suggestion like "Know more" would cause the bot to say what's specified under "Know more."

To make sure I could keep a reasonable overview, I borrowed an idea from one of the most established patterns in the history of computers: *directory paths*. This simple concept, when implemented in a thoughtful and deliberate way, allowed me to build almost any conversation I wanted.

Instead of *C:/my-documents* I would have paths like *hello/know-more/conferences/where*. That simple representation turned out to be an effective way for me to understand how users navigate conversations. In this particular example, we can imagine a user starting off by asking for more information. The bot would then talk about some of my articles and mention that I spoke at various conferences and events. The user could then decide to explore the topic of conferences further, until they eventually end up asking where those conferences took place.

This might seem like a quite primitive way to build conversations, but to my surprise it worked.

Sceptics were quick to say that this is not an actual conversation. Jared Spool, founder of User Interface Engineering and a well-respected thought leader in the industry, was very skeptical when we talked about it. According to Jared, these types of interfaces don't even come close to an actual conversation. I immediately understood where Jared was coming from and yet, to this day, I fundamentally disagree with him. I'd argue that no matter what we create in our field, it is far more important to think about how something feels, rather than how it *technically* works. It's not logical. It's psychological. The way users think about an experience is not the way we do.

A few weeks after launching my conversational website, I lost my wallet on the lake. I remember it vividly. It was a Saturday afternoon and I was hanging out with friends to enjoy the occasional good weather by the lake. It was a day void of serious topics or stress. Life was good, I thought to myself.

After a few drinks, I headed home to prepare for an upcoming trip. The smile on my face soon vanished when I realized that my pockets felt awfully empty. I braced myself. Three seconds later, I panicked: where is my wallet?!

I was just about to call my bank to block my credit card when an email notification popped up reading, *"I think I found your wallet."* I couldn't believe it! *That's technology working for me right there*, I thought. I answered as fast as I could. The guy sent me his number and we ended up meeting later that same day. When he gave me the wallet, I said:

"Thanks so much! You saved my life! By the way, just out of curiosity, how did you get in touch with me?"

He looked at me slightly confused and replied,*"What do you mean? We had a chat, no?"*

That's when it hit me. This benevolent savior of my wallet had thought he was having a real conversation with me on my website. What was even more remarkable is that we used three different communication channels: we went from website, to email, to voice call. That didn't seem to matter to him. All that mattered was the thread: a continuous line of thought that seamlessly carried on across different media channels.

Make no mistake, I'm not arguing that we should lie to users. This is not about deception. It's about keeping the mental model of conversation intact.

Optimistic interfaces are based on a similar idea. When you like a photo on Instagram, Facebook, or Snapchat, the user interface immediately animates the heart or like icon to tell you in a responsive and quite succinct way: "You just liked this photo!" What happens in the background is quite different, though. In fact, at the time you see the animation, the server may not even know about your like yet. For a very brief moment, you might be the only person in the world to know that you just liked this photo. It's only once your like has successfully traveled through the air, been received by the server, and stored in the database, that your like is official for others to see. What's the benefit of doing this? In simple terms: *perception of speed*. The user interface assumes the action of liking a photo will succeed in almost every scenario (unless the user has an incredibly slow or flaky internet connection), and so immediately responds as if the request had already been successful. The application is optimistic about the user's action successfully making its way to the server.

An interface that lies to you doesn't necessarily mean it's inherently bad or dishonest, as long as its *intention* is to genuinely help you succeed and have a positive experience. We discussed earlier that the field of interface design is notorious for borrowing principles from the real world and applying them to the challenges it tries to solve. It's no different here. Both optimistic interfaces and my experiment take advantage of white lies.

Dictonary.com defines a white lie as minor lie which could be considered harmless, or even beneficial, in the long term. Science magazine went as far as saying that white lies are what keep society intact.[5]

Rather than start a philosophical debate, we can just ask ourselves this simple question instead: does this white lie affect the user in any negative way? If the answer is no – and there are even positive effects to be gained from it – wouldn't it be a missed opportunity to not take advantage of it?

We'll come back to some of the ethical implications of these type of questions, particularly in the field of conversational design, a bit later. For now, let's look at some of the other things I took away from my experiment.

5 Science | AAAS, 2018: "White lies keep society intact." http://smashed.by/whitelies

As I kept writing the main part of the dialogue, I realized that it felt awfully similar to the thought process I usually had when designing websites for a client. Who are you? What do you do? How can I get in touch? Those are all typical questions websites should have an answer to, but the using the conversational model was the first time it felt like I was answering those questions in a literal way. Structuring conversations proved to be just as challenging as classic information architecture on the web, and for the structure to make sense, I needed to first understand what I actually wanted to convey.

Maya Angelou famously said *"people won't remember what you said, but they will always remember how you made them feel"*. That was a thought-provoking idea that deeply affected how I approached writing the entire dialogue. Instead of going deeper and deeper, and meticulously scripting every single response, I took a step back and first focused on how I wanted visitors to feel. After some (deep) introspection, I identified two key emotions: *curiosity* and *delight*. Those became my guiding principles, my compass, in how I would write the conversation.

Once I identified the emotional part, I started focusing on the rational: the content itself. For content to be as succinct and effective as possible, I had to establish what effectiveness actually meant. In other words, I needed to set clear goals for the conversational website. The main goal seemed simple: allow users to discover who I am and what I do in a conversational way. Translating these goals into a dialogue turned out to be much harder than I expected. When I started this experiment, I thought development and design would take significantly more time than writing and structuring my thoughts. Needless to say, I was wrong. Writing took almost twice as much time as design and development combined.

What was so difficult about it? In short, making sure users never felt like the conversation got in their way and slowed them down. To avoid this, I started mentally engaging in a dialogue with myself. I would go through dozens of scenarios and think about what I might want to ask and what I would possibly say next. I even pictured myself sitting on a train and meeting a complete stranger, contemplating how such a conversation could start and evolve. Saying this was a good lesson in practicing empathy would be a major understatement. Even though all of this seemed silly at first, it greatly helped me improve my understanding of what I was trying to convey. Thinking back, I wish I had discovered the technique of imagining a conversation earlier in my career. It didn't just help me better understand how to write conversations, but showed me a new way of approaching any design problem I had ever encountered. After all, any form of design is communication; it's just that conversation happens to be the most literal form of it.

I went on and started structuring subjects and topics by creating a conversational information architecture. This made me realize there were two overarching topics. Users either want to get in touch, or they want to learn more. Projects, clients, conferences, and so on could all be seen as a user's intent to get to know me better.

The conversation starter therefore kicked off with this exact question: "Want to know more, or get in touch?" This ensured that users could always instantly get in touch, and it's why I have my wallet with me as I'm writing down these thoughts.

To make sure the get-in-touch path felt as conversational as possible, I had to figure out a way to seamlessly embed a contact form within the conversation. Contact forms are probably one of the least exciting parts of the web, *but nobody minds a form if it doesn't feel like one*, I thought.

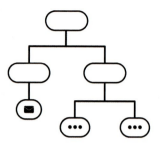

Conversational I.A.

When users tapped on "Get in touch," the bot would invite them to share what they had in mind. Once users sent a response, the bot would compliment them for their intriguing message and then follow up by asking about their email. The bot didn't just bluntly ask for a user's email address, though. It explained why it was needed to make sure users understood why they were sharing something personal so early on in an interaction.

This eventually closed the loop: the bot confirmed that it received the message, and based on the insights from the study about waiters, it mirrored what users had said by repeating and confirming their email. Many visitors only realized at the very end that they had in fact just filled out a form and by the point they noticed it, it was already sent.

Writing Predictively

One cold winter morning in January, I forgot to take my laundry out of the dryer. It wasn't the first time, and my neighbor was quick to pick up on my negligence. That morning, as I was rushing out of the laundry room to make it to a meeting at work, he caught me and confronted me right away. He was quite serious about it. "Next time your laundry is in the tumbler, I will just take it out and leave it on the floor."

What felt like a quite intense statement, ended up triggering an even more intense response. "Go ahead! I have to go."

When I was at work later that day, I thought about the way this encounter had unfolded. I was angry, not because of what he said, but because of how I reacted. Worst of all, I knew he was right. He had every reason to be annoyed. There was an opportunity to acknowledge, apologize, and change my behavior, but I instead decided to act like an idiot.

We all occasionally run into situations like these. Whether it's quarrels with our neighbors, arguments with our children, or toxic conversations with the people we work with, conflict seems unavoidable. Whenever it happens to me, I often can't help but imagine what would have happened if I had reacted in a different way. The ability to travel back in time and alter events has captured my imagination since the first time I saw *Back To The Future*. It would feel like a magic trick, a superpower. That superpower, as it turns out, is something everyone who creates scripted bots has. After all, we're in control of the entire conversation.

We control what users can ask and we can craft the perfect response for whichever suggestion users pick. The limitation of what users can say is a blessing and a curse at the same time. Limitation makes our lives easier, but users will mind if they feel like they can't express what they have in mind. That's why *predicting* and trying to anticipate what users might want to say next in any given conversational junction is so critical.

Our ability to correctly predict what users want to say next defines whether users will mind that there is no free-speech option. In other words, as long as we can offer responses that feel like something users most likely want to say next, the less they will mind that we're taking away their ability to freely talk about whatever they have on their minds.

Obviously, we can't always correctly predict what users have in mind. But we can steer the conversation in a direction where other thoughts would end up violating the cooperative principle. This is a key strategy in scripted bot design. Every response should offer users suggestions that are highly relevant for that given conversational moment. Take this as an example:

> **Bot**: We can talk about projects or writing. Which one do you prefer?
>
> -
>
> [Projects] [Writing]

The Boolean choice is the bot trying to clearly convey what it can talk about and what it can not. By establishing clear boundaries, the bot guides the conversation to where it can succeed. It's very likely that suggestions will never perfectly match what users envisaged, but the closer we get, and the more thoughtful we are in how we curate those responses, the better the conversation will flow as a result of our efforts.

After wiring up the contact form and writing the main part of the dialogue, over the course of a few weeks, I turned it into an interactive experience. I started to connect every single response to a previous topic, and so on. I was surprised: the conversation all of a sudden felt quite different from what I had originally imagined. The simple act of writing a conversation and then experiencing it felt like two fundamentally different things. Let's look at some of the things that stood out the most.

1. ISOLATED MESSAGES DON'T FEEL HUMAN

When talking to a person in real life, the conversation's outcome – to a high degree – depends on how it started and how it evolved. In most cases, it's awkward to repeat a topic; once you've talked about the weather, you want to move on to more interesting stuff and probably avoid the whole weather discussion altogether. To avoid repetition and robotic messages, I had to change the way I approached testing.

Instead of simply ensuring that all the conversational paths would work from a functional perspective, I clicked through each one of them to make sure they worked from a social perspective too. I was surprised how much of a difference this made. I discovered lots of scenarios where the conversation didn't feel natural because of subtle repetitions or slightly odd connecting sentences.

This painted a very clear picture. We can't think of conversations as isolated messages that we stack on top of one another. We need to take into account the whole course of a conversation to make it feel natural.

This is why experiencing conversations is absolutely critical for designers to be able to iterate and improve them.

That leads us to the next takeaway.

2. DELIGHTFUL DETAILS

Delightful details are about flirting with users. Details in writing and the use of technology can make a critical difference between a conversation that feels lame and a conversation that sparks users' interest.

For example, refreshing the page changed what the bot said. Instead of just saying "Hi," the bot would now say: "Welcome back! 👋". It would then even subtly change the conversation path – something we'll cover in more detail in the section about context awareness.

Why is this important?

When people noticed this for the first time, they understood that the bot was smarter than they had initially assumed. It changed the way they thought about the interface. They suddenly started wondering: *what else can this thing do?*

Making the New Familiar

I'm a firm believer that for any technology to be successful, it needs to be embedded in a way that is compatible with how people already think. In other words, our job is to make the new feel familiar and the familiar feel new. For instance, why did FaceTime become such a huge success? It wasn't because of its superior algorithms or video-conferencing call quality. Instead, it's because FaceTime is seamlessly embedded in the Phone app. Apple takes advantage of users' preexisting mental model of calling someone and augments it with the ability to make video and internet calls right from within the Phone app. FaceTime needs no explanation, or as Apple would probably say: *it just works.*

I wanted my experiment to follow the same idea of familiarity. But at first it didn't feel familiar at all. I explored a wide range of different types of visual languages. The one I spent the most time working on was a sci-fi inspired pseudo-futuristic interface that took me months to design and develop. It was a colorful and smoothly animated blob that would morph fluidly into different shapes and adapt to what a user would say. The blob could technically even mirror the user's emotion by changing its color and adapting its movement based on emotional cues in the conversation. Eventually, I came to a somewhat sobering conclusion, though. Unless most of my visitors were a bunch of suckers for sci-fi interfaces, they would most probably not want to talk to a blob. So I stuck with a traditional chat interface that clearly emphasized the fact that visitors were talking to me instead of a blob. R.I.P. blob.

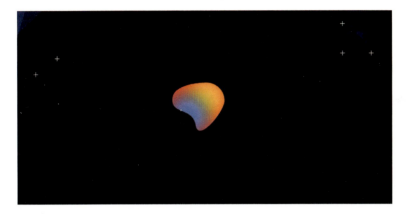

The blob that never shipped.

Building a chat-like environment became an entirely new challenge, but it helped me better understand how the medium affected the message.

3. CONTEXT AFFECTS TOPICS

Imagine you're going to a fancy cocktail party after a design conference. You know most people there are designers. Would this affect the way you start a conversation?

For most people, it would.

Instead of opening a conversation with something ambiguous like "Hey, how's is it going?" you might say something that's slightly more appropriate within the context, such as, "Hey, did you see Paul's talk today?"

The second conversation starter is inline with the overall theme of the conference and will likely make it easier to transition to a normal, naturally flowing conversation. For most people, it's easier to start a conversation with a specific topic in the hope that there won't be any awkward pauses or moments of silence.

Understanding context has the potential to greatly improve the way we initiate and continue a conversation. So I wondered how I could integrate the concept of contextual awareness, and craft a better conversation starter to make sure the experience felt both personal and more relevant at the same time.

I occasionally write articles about design and productivity on Medium. When I feel particularly witty, I might even send out a tweet. Those tweets happen to be mostly design-related too. So when a person visits my website from Medium or Twitter, chances are they're interested in design themselves. They might have come across a tweet, article, or other reference on one of those platforms. I wanted this contextual signal to be captured within the conversation, so I decided to change what the bot said, depending on where the user accesses my site from.

People who accessed my site from Kenny Chen's UX newsletter, one of the most read user experience newsletters at the time, were also surprised when the bot started to greet them by saying: "Looks like you're visiting from Kenny's awesome newsletter. You're probably in design too, right?"

This small adjustment didn't just improve the conversation's flow and make it more human – it also made some of the chatbot's features more discoverable. Rather than relying on the conversation to evolve to ultimately cover the topic of design, the bot could now talk about design right from the start.

4. MOTION IN CONVERSATIONAL INTERFACES

Motion can deeply affect the way people feel about an interface. In many ways, animation can do what traditional information architecture can't: establish an observable, interactive relationship between objects.

Sometimes it helps to study the origin of words to better understand how things relate to one another. The word *anima*, for example, stems from Latin and means soul, life, breath. One of the distinctive characteristics of *animals* as opposed to stones and trees is their ability to move, thus *anima* gave birth to the word *anima•l*. On the other hand, the Latin verb *animāre*, means to give life to. When a cartoon is drawn and filmed in such a way that lifelike movement is produced, we say it is animated. An animated film therefore seems to have a life of its own.

In a study from 1944, experimental psychologists Fritz Heider and Marianne Simmel showed participants a bunch of circles, rectangles, and triangles moving on a screen. Some of these shapes moved in erratic and unpredictable ways; occasionally, they would even bounce into one another. You'd probably expect to hear participants' descriptions of what they observed to be accounts of geometrical shapes moving on a screen. But those were not the stories the researchers were told. Instead, participants told tales of love, anxiety, and fear. Many participants described the triangle as particularly aggressive and mean, whereas the circle seemed rather shy but genuinely nice. Even though thee shapes didn't look anything like living creatures, animation was enough to make participants attribute goals and intentions to them. Funnily enough, when the researchers repeated the experiment by playing the movie in reverse, interpretations changed quite significantly, but participants still thought of the geometrical shapes as having a form of life.[6]

If animation can have such a profound impact on how people think about shapes, it only makes sense for us to more carefully consider the way it affects how people think about interfaces. Hence, whenever we animate something, we should always start by asking ourselves: *what's the story I want to tell?*

When building my website, I spent quite some time refining the motion curves, the way animations should feel, and the stories they should tell. In fact, I believe animation was an important reason why the reception of the website was so positive in the first place. I would even go as far to say: *Without animation, there's no conversation.*

[6]   Psychology, 2018, Fritz Heider & Marianne Simmel: An Experimental Study of Apparent Behavior: http://smashed.by/apparentbehavior

Let's see why.

First, animation adds a certain dynamic to the interface. This dynamic can be thought of as reflecting the nature of conversation itself. If the chat bubbles all appeared at once, it would completely change the narrative of the design. Instead of it feeling like an ongoing conversation happening in the moment, it would feel like a bunch of old messages that have been there all along.

Second, animation grabs attention. As soon as the website appears, the bot fires right away and starts talking to its visitors. The user's focus gets immediately absorbed and directed to the conversational experience. The goal of this was to create the digital equivalent of getting someone's attention by simply looking at them and saying hi.

Orchestrating focus is one of the superpowers of thoughtful motion design. At first, users always focused on the chat bubbles themselves. But as the bot's response came to an end, I needed to ensure users always knew what to do next. Adding a short but significant delay to the entry animation of the suggestions turned out to be enough to ensure they would always get noticed. At the end of each response, users' focus was therefore not on the chat messages themselves, but on the suggestions instead.

Third, and perhaps most importantly, animation conveys the idea of interactivity. Animating the suggestions in a playful way didn't just ensure users would never miss them, but it also invited them to interact with them. From a motion narrative point of view, this happened to be the most critical animation of all. As soon as users tapped on a suggestion, it would move and take its place within the chat history.

Many people asked me which natural language technology I used. At first, I didn't understand why anyone would ask that question until it dawned on me: observing how their choice became part of the conversation changed how people felt about it. Users suddenly felt like those were their own words, their own choices, whereas without animation, there was a disconnect. Without animation, the conversation would have felt scripted and unnatural. Animation instilled a sense of interactivity and nowness to it. Put differently, animation made the conversation come to life.

In retrospect, adding motion to my experiment didn't just enhance the experience, it was a critical part of it.

5. A CHATBOT CAN CONVEY WHAT A WEBSITE CAN'T

With clever punchlines and carefully crafted headlines, advertising and web agencies try to differentiate themselves from one another. I do the same. I call myself a coffee enthusiast.

But trying to be different can sometimes have the opposite effect. We either go too far and become too different, or we try so hard to be different that we end up being no different at all.

My conversational experience lives on top of my website. Scrolling down reveals my traditional website. The first time I skipped the conversation I was shocked. There was a significant disparity between the two experiences.

My website's design is what some would call very Swiss. It has a lot of white space, it's pretty minimalistic, and there are almost no colors in it. In short, it's not exactly what anyone would describe as emotional. My chatbot, on the other hand, sends emojis, laughs, and makes jokes.

It has emotions. In other words, it has personality.

Those two design approaches both convey a different side of who I am: the more rational side reflected by the traditional website; and the more emotional one by the conversation.

Design is always a reflection of ourselves, but the conversational experience undoubtedly creates a more vivid and complete image of who I am.

• • •

We've now discussed some takeaways of designing a conversational website. Many of these insights helped me – and I hope they'll help you – to be more cognizant about the constituents of engaging conversational experiences.

Experimentation and continuous iteration paves the way for better experiences. It's the precious little nuggets of insight we painfully excavate along the way that end up making experiences more personal, more unique, and give them something most others lack: character.

My experiment wasn't flawless. As I started scaling it through other projects, like the UX Bear (uxchat.me), I ran into issues I didn't anticipate.

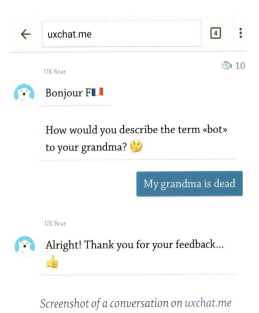

Screenshot of a conversation on uxchat.me

After working on this project for a couple of months, one user ran into the following conversation:

This would shortly become one of the most tweeted interactions. The personality of UX Bear is supposed to be be warm (even though it's a polar bear), inclusive, understanding, and supportive. The conversation above hardly reflects any of that. As we attempt to scale conversational experiences, it becomes increasingly challenging to establish and maintain a consistent personality. Once different writers started to create content for the Bear, its personality gradually became what psychologists would call *bipolar*. Every writer had their own interpretation of what the Bear should be like, which slowly manifested in an experience that felt like you were talking to different bots within the same conversation.

Failure or weird responses are hard to avoid in conversations. At some point, users will run into cases where our bot says things that are wrong at best, and deeply inappropriate at worst. Trying to anticipate where things can go awry is a critical part of making conversations work. By defining a set of principles, we can ensure that the bot's persona remains approachable and consistent, while hopefully avoiding at least some of these moments.

Before I started the experiment, I was convinced that building a conversational interaction, just like many other projects, was mostly a technical challenge. It was only after rewriting most dialogues that I realized conversation is an inherently social interface that comes with the expectations users have from talking to people in real life. As long as these expectations are met, users are in a fluent state. Once they are violated, the experience breaks and the magic is gone.

As we venture into this new form of design, we need to be willing to let go of some of the things we've learned. Many of the strategies and tactics we've picked up on our endless journey of improvement as designers are certainly useful, but simply adapting graphical interface design to conversational interfaces will almost certainly lead to an overly technical solution. It was only once I let go of my preconceptions of graphical UI design that the experience I wanted to create started to take shape.

• • •

Let's now look at a simple design process you can follow to create your own conversational experience.

Creating Conversational Experiences

Designing conversations is a process. Before we start sketching a tree diagram with dozens of different topics, we need to take a moment and think about what we actually intend to build. Building with intent starts with a simple question: *who am I building this for?*

1. DEFINE YOUR USERS

Unless we're building a chatbot for ourselves, we have to start by thinking about our audience. Who will be using this, and in what context (time, place, device, etc.) will it most likely happen? Defining our users isn't as much about writing personas as it is about figuring out critical user journeys.

The jobs to be done (JTBD) framework provides a great way to identify critical user journeys and map them to possible solutions. Writing a user story in JTBD fashion can look like this:

> *I'm driving my kid to school and want to get current traffic information.*

Notice how this use case provides enough context for us to understand what the problem is and in which situation it occurs. Sometimes it can be helpful to create a more specific user description by adding job title, age, and so on. When we do that, we need to make sure we don't exclude groups of users who should be part of our target audience.

My target audience was as generic as anyone interested in design. The main use cases were getting to know me better, contact me, or talk about things I've worked on.

Countless books have been written about personas, user stories, story mapping, and so on, and while I appreciate the thoughtfulness of a well-crafted persona, I find that plain and simple user stories usually serve as a great starting point. They help us think about the problem space without losing ourselves in overspecifying a type of user that, in reality, might not even exist.

2. DEFINE SCOPE AND GOALS

Once we have outlined a list of potential user journeys, we need to rank them based on how suitable they are for conversation. Not every use case translates equally well to a conversational experience. So how do we pick the right use cases?

The Actions on Google design guidelines, give us a few pointers to ensure that conversation is the right way to deliver value to customers.

- **Simple**: The conversation should be about things people are already familiar with. Asking for input like location, time, and dates is easy for people to recite and remember. When input becomes specialized and highly contextual, failure increases. As a result, it might not be an ideal fit for a conversational interaction.

- **Quick and compelling**: Providing value via conversation should be quick and straightforward. Users should get a maximum amount of value with a minimal amount of time spent. Ideal scenarios are simple tasks like asking for a ride, looking up answers, or providing quick answers to frequently asked questions.

- **Inherently voice-driven**: There are cases that are by definition better suited for voice. When you're cooking or you're in any hands-busy situation, voice-driven interfaces perform dramatically better than their graphical counterparts.

If your product or service requires a lot of different steps and contextual information for users to successfully reach their goal through conversation, you may want to consider alternatives. Designers who just start out in the field often try to map a graphical user interface to a conversational experience. This often results in an overwhelming experience that provides users with too much information. Since the requirements and capabilities of each medium are unique and different, a straight 1:1 mapping rarely leads to a great experience.

My co-worker and friend Peter Hodgson, a conversation designer from London, refers to flight booking to illustrate this. In a graphical user interface, it's all about seeing options, filtering, comparing, and narrowing down the set of relevant results. There is an element of control here. Solving the same task through conversation leads to a completely different mental model. One is a website with flight results, the other is a travel assistant that helps you navigate a plethora of options to turn it into something useful, digestible, and most of all, actionable. In other words, making conversations work starts by identifying and choosing the right use cases.

Once we've established a clear scope of what we want to cover, we can start to think about goals. As I mentioned earlier, the goal of my experiment was the following:

Allow users to discover who I am and what I do in a conversational way.

Sounds simple and straightforward, but how do you measure whether users actually succeeded? I ended up tracking how visitors walked through conversations and optimized where drop-offs were significantly above average.

Let's consider the first use case: getting in touch. If someone wants to reach out and chooses "Get in touch," the system will track whether the user successfully makes it to the end of the thread. If the drop-off rate is over 50% (that is, users give up or leave the website before sending their message), I have a strong indicator that I need to take a closer look at the dialogue.

If you're using platforms such as Dialogflow, Chatfuel, or Botanalytics, you can easily identify how users navigate through conversations, and spot potential weaknesses and dead ends within different threads. If you're building your own experience from scratch, I highly recommend tracking how people navigate through the conversation in order to identify threads that can be improved.

Once we've established the scope of the experience, we can come up with metrics that allow us to measure whether we've been successful or not. Here are a couple of sample goals based on various verticals:

- number of answered FAQs
- number of new subscribers
- number of reservations/tickets
- number of followers
- duration of interaction
- increase in traffic for website/product
- drop-off rate in happy paths

Metrics can be very different depending on scope and the type of experience you create. The important part is making it measurable so you can get new insights and take action where necessary.

3. CHOOSE THE RIGHT PLATFORM

There are tons of platforms where interactions can happen through conversation. Whether it's on a custom-made website, or by using popular services like Intercom, Facebook Messenger, Slack, WeChat (number one chat client in China), Line (number one chat client in Japan), WhatsApp, SMS, Alexa, Siri, or the Google Assistant, choosing the right platform depends on the type of user, use case, and context.

Building new features on top of Google Assistant or Alexa is great for on-the-go use cases or hands-busy environments like driving or cooking. Text-based interactions, on the other hand, excel in providing value where people already are: in social networks and messaging apps.

The rise of messaging led to a big change in consumer expectations. In an ecommerce survey from 2017, half the participants reported they are more likely to do business with companies they can reach via chat.[7] The study also showed that 67% of participants expect to message businesses more frequently in the future. I've experienced this shift of expectation myself when I ordered cooking utensils on Amazon. After receiving the order confirmation, I realized that I had picked the wrong cutlery. Since shipping to Switzerland is expensive, I wanted to cancel the order before it started to ship. After a quick search, I landed on the the company's Facebook page and promptly pinged them through Messenger. All it took was a three-minute chat and my order was canceled. It felt like magic.

Today, companies are just one more person we can talk to in our favorite messaging apps. It's the first time in history when companies can have thousands of simultaneous one-to-one conversations with clients. It's this captivating idea that incentivizes many businesses to invest in the conversational space.

4. DEFINE PERSONALITY

You have a personality, I have a personality, and as we saw earlier, products have a personality as well. One of the biggest misconceptions about designing personality is that people think it's a choice. It's not. Everything we create inherently has personality, whether we want it or not.

A few years ago, I met Don Lindsay, the former VP of design at Apple. During his time at Apple, Don led the design of the brand new Mac OS X (codename Aqua), a complete overhaul of Apple's OS 9 operating sys-

---

7   More than half of consumers prefer businesses that use chat apps. http://smashed.by/chatapps

tem. His team was also responsible for a feature, a visual effect really, that is most commonly referred to as the genie effect.

The genie effect is one of the most iconic animations in user interfaces of all time. It reinforced the idea that the new Mac OS X was about fluidity. The genie effect didn't just make for a great animation; it emphasized the system's personality while explaining to users where minimized applications and windows would go. Everything in Mac OS X Aqua was designed around that same idea, whether it was the buttons, the window behaviors, or the wallpaper itself. The surface of the user interface nicely complemented the iMac's unique industrial design and resulted in a product where hardware and software came together beautifully to create an experience that transcended the screen.

Industrial design, texture, fonts, copy, motion, color, you name it – every design decision we make affects how users perceive an interface's personality. Make an animation bounce, and it feels playful and fun. Make it sturdy and fast, and that same animation all of a sudden may feel serious and dull. Within every decision, there is a spectrum that moves the needle in a certain direction. When all those design decisions are nicely orchestrated, it results in a personality that makes the difference between a good product and a product people remember for its consistency and ease of use.

An interface with seemingly no personality has personality too. And it might say more about a company than we think.

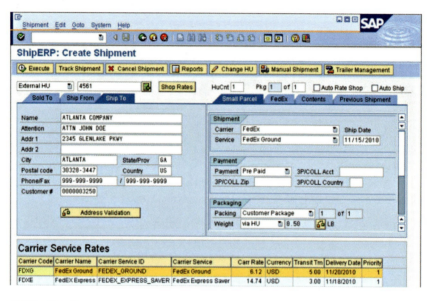

SAP User Interface

When a product has a designed personality, it imbues craftsmanship and a human touch. A well-designed product with a consistent personality makes users feel that people, not machines, were behind the product they use.

In conversational design, personality is communicated using the most literal form of communication, through conversation itself. It's less about colors, fonts, and texture, and more about words, intonation, and rhythm.

As we design personality in conversational experiences, we need to consider the core attributes of the brand or person we want to represent, and how these values can be conveyed through voice and chat.

For instance, if your brand is playful and fun, you might be more inclined to use a more visual style of communication by using emojis, pictures, and gifs. On the other hand, if your brand is serious, that type of communication might feel less appropriate. When an experience is solely based on voice, we have to rely on words (and intonation and rhythm) to imbue the experience with an individual personality. Consider a simple weather use case:

> **User:** What's the weather like today?
>
> **Bot:** *It's going to be sunny today with highs of 59 degrees and lows of 54 degrees.*
>
> versus
>
> **Bot**: *It's going to be warm today. Leave your jacket at home.*

Contrary to popular belief, personality is not about cracking jokes and sounding witty all the time. It's about augmenting conversation with a human component. It's about bringing a sense of continuity to your brand's different digital touchpoints, whether it's the copy on your website, the design of your mobile app, or the persona of your bot on Facebook. Every single channel has its own distinct linguistic subtleties, but on a broader level it should be clear that they all embody the same core values of the company and brand. In other words, personality should support the experience, not *be* the experience.

5. DEFINE A CONVERSATION STARTER

A conversation starter is, as the name suggests, a way to initiate a conversation, but also to *continue* one. An effective conversation starter incorporates context and should consider past interactions to not only optimize for first-time use cases, but also to create a relevant interaction for returning visitors. For a conversation starter to be effective, it should achieve the following few key criteria.

Set Expectations

The number of topics chatbots can cover is limited. It's therefore crucial to clearly establish where your bot can succeed, and what users can expect. Don't pretend to be human, or fool people into believing they are talking to an actual person. A bot should clearly outline that it's a bot. This can happen both explicitly and implicitly.

For instance, a Messenger bot that immediately replies to every single message implicitly creates the expectation of a bot. On the other hand, typing indicators can quickly lead users to believe they are talking to a human. In case of doubt, it should always be made clear if users are talking to a system or an actual person.

The intention of my website was not to trick people into believing that they were talking to the real me. It was about deliberately using motion and delays to make the conversation feel digestible and alive.

Lead the Conversation

A conversation starter should clearly lead the interaction, and direct users towards a certain goal.

Consider Opener A versus Opener B:

Opener A:

Bot: Hi! I'm a designer working on conversational interfaces. *What do you want to talk about today?*

[I want to get in touch] [Tell me about your projects]

Opener B:

Bot: Hi! I'm a designer working on conversational interfaces. *Want to talk about my projects or get in touch?*

[Get in touch] [Talk about projects]

When it comes to conversational experiences, the road to hell is paved with rhetorical and open questions. Opener A is, in mild terms, a gateway to hell. Once we allow users to talk about whatever they have in mind, the experience ambitiously tries to achieve everything, and most probably ends up solving nothing. While open questions might work for bots specifically tailored and designed around small talk and chit chat, they will most likely lead to a frustrating experience for the majority of users.

In contrast, Opener B limits input by explicitly guiding and informing users of what they can talk about. It clarifies how the conversation can evolve and what users can say next. If your chat relies on prepopulated suggestions as shown above, Opener B comes with an additional neat benefit: referencing previously mentioned topics significantly reduces the wordiness of our suggestions. Since context has already been established in the response itself, the number of words can be reduced for additional clarity and relevance.

Instead of writing *"I want to get in touch,"* we can simplify and write *"Get in touch"* without sacrificing the natural tone of the interaction. This becomes even more important when designing for voice-only experiences, where users don't have a way of seeing things they can say next.

As well as what I've already mentioned about opening conversations, we need to follow standard greeting conventions and the basic etiquette of human interaction. Avoid sounding overly robotic, and refrain from using complicated language. Many public speakers start preparing their talks by writing them first, and then learning each line by heart. This often leads to overly precise and meticulous language that makes it hard for the audience to relate to the topic and its presenter. Experienced orators know that simple, conversational language is critical to get people's attention. Even though they might have spent days, weeks, even months, fleshing out their ideas, they invest an equally large portion of time in focusing on making their presentation sound natural and effortless. Writing conversations is the same. We write them in structured and unnatural ways before we conceal their complexity by making them sound natural again.

6. DESIGN THE CONVERSATION

This is the exciting part where we get to write the actual dialogue. Where should we start?

As mentioned earlier, I recommend kicking-off a new conversational project in a text editor and writing down a list of subjects the conversation should cover:

- About me
- Projects
    - Past
    - Present
- Contact
- Portfolio
- Articles/Writings

That is the list I came up with. Once you have a created your own, you can flesh out each subject and organize them in a way that ensures users can explore all of them in a natural way.

The above diagram is a simplified illustration of the architecture of my website. Once you've sketched how topics can be organized and how they relate to one another, you can start writing the actual dialogue.

I recommend using the path syntax we encountered earlier in the chapter.

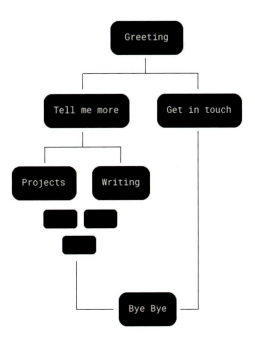

Conversational IA overview

GREETING

- Hi! I'm Adrian.
- I'm a designer working in beautiful Zurich, Switzerland.
- Want to learn more, or get in touch?

[Learn more] [Get in touch]

We can refer to **Greeting** as a *node*. In structured or scripted conversations, every node can have one or multiple entry points. As the number of nodes increases, the bot's expressiveness and conversational abilities proportionally increase with it. All of this comes at the cost of complexity. Complex conversations with many different sub-branches make it hard to keep an overview and stay organized. It's crucial to find a good balance and start with critical nodes, before adding exploratory and non-critical subjects to the experience.

Let's see how a follow-on response to the above greeting could look.

LEARN MORE

- I feel humbled!
- I write and speak about design, and feel fortunate to have worked with many exciting companies.

[Which companies?] [You write?]

Notice how we again try to set the direction of what users can talk about next. The most ambiguous word in the above sentence is the word "speak." Its mere presence is enough to invite users to ask about speaking engagements. Every single word in a response is a topic users potentially want to talk about next. We therefore need to be mindful about choosing words that don't lure users into unsupported territory.

DESIGN THE HAPPY PATHS

The Actions on Google design guidelines recommend starting with a concept called *happy path*. What's a happy path? Conversational designers refer to a happy path as the ideal flow of a conversational interaction. The graphical UI equivalent of a happy path would be a user flawlessly going through an entire user interface without ever ending up in an erroneous state. If that sounds rare, it's because it is. A happy user doesn't equate to a happy designer. Keeping users on a happy path is hard work and requires dedication and continuous improvement of the dialogue.

Let's look at a simple happy path for sending an email on my website:

"Get in touch" flow

First, the bot politely greets users as the website finishes loading. When users pick "Get in touch," they can specify what they want to talk about. After that, the bot asks for their email to allow me to get back to them. After validating and confirming it, the bot encourages users to explore the rest of website. When a user finally reaches "Bye Bye!" without interruptions, they flawlessly reach the end of the happy path.

EXTEND THE HAPPY PATHS

Extending happy paths is about making the experience more resilient. The path above can hardly stay this simple. As soon as we introduce free speech, we need to verify and parse user input. This is not just incredibly error-prone, but also requires us to extend the conversation with additional repair flows.

Reprompting

- That doesn't look like a valid email. Do you want to try again or get in touch later?

  [Try again] [I'll come back later]

What should happen when a user picks "Try again"? Should it repeat the previous sentence or should it be slightly different?

Depending on the type of input, repairing conversations can quickly become quite complex. A simple date and time attribute leads to a surprisingly large number of repair dialogues:

- date is in the past
- date is too far out
- date is on a national holiday
- service might only be available at specific times during the day
- month only has X number of days
- specified day is in a leap year
- clarifying 24-hour or 12-hour time (Europe vs. US)
- etc.

A wide array of input types can quickly turn the design of conversations into a daunting task. Some of the most prolific designers struggle to translate complex topics to conversational interactions. This is why we emphasized the importance of picking the right use cases earlier.

Repairing conversations is hard. That's why our best strategy is to actively try to mitigate errors before they occur. Once users are in an erroneous state, we need to instantly reprompt before we let them progress any further. While this sounds really easy in theory, it's incredibly hard in practice. That's why the best way to design better conversations is by starting to experience them yourself.

7. EXPERIENCE THE CONVERSATION

There is a fundamental difference between writing a conversation and experiencing it. What might look good in a text editor or diagram might very well turn out to be weird when interacting with it yourself. Prototyping and experiencing conversations is, therefore, not an option – it's a critical part of the design process.

Designing interfaces is like designing a ship. It's only by putting the vessel into the water that we start spotting leaks. Anticipating every possible scenario of an interface is hard. That's why motion design and prototyping have become increasingly important roles in our industry. Their job is to consider the *in-between states* of what we create – the states that are temporary, critical, but mostly overlooked. It's only through prototyping that we're forced to think about how all these states come together to form the experience.

IDENTIFYING REPETITIONS THROUGH PROTOTYPING

The goal of prototyping in conversational design is to identify leaks, unnatural speech, and erroneous states. On top of that, it's about making sure that conversation evolves naturally. Repetitions are a very common problem and many designed conversations often end up looking somewhat like this:

- When should I book it?
- (user speaks)
- Got it! February 12th! At what time?
- (user speaks)
- Got it! At 3pm. Should I book this for you?
- (user speaks)
- Great! You're all set!

Unless you're leading a military mission to parachute and infiltrate an enemy's embassy, you're probably better off avoiding repetitions as seen above. It's surprisingly hard to avoid repetitions, though. They can sneak in easily, particularly when people collaborate and have limited insight to what *precedes* and *follows* the part they're working on. By constantly chatting to our creations, we can ensure they work and flow nicely. Once we're happy with the result, we can proceed and test it with actual users.

User tests are invaluable because we get to observe the struggle and the joy our designs create. It makes the job personal, and once things get personal, it becomes hard to design something that isn't great.

Parting Words

Design and the field of UX are in constant flux. As technology matures and changes, so do the requirements and possibilities in our field. The proliferation of conversational interfaces isn't as much about replacing old and traditional media as it is about complementing them. It's an opportunity to design intentionally to solve the right kind of problems, in the right kind of context, with the right kind of interface.

Voice may be great to support on-the-go and hands-busy situations, such as driving and cooking. It might, however, fail to live up to its expectations when it comes to more complex and intricate tasks. Understanding when to use which interface will be a critical part of any future design strategy. After all, product design isn't about building chatbots. It's about creating an experience. And conversation might happen to be *one* great way through which this experience can be created and delivered.

The promise of conversational interfaces is to use a universally understood form of communication and apply it to make technology more human and accessible. Does that mean it's the future? This type of question is notoriously tricky to answer.

Back To The Future did a remarkable job in predicting the future in certain areas (mobile payment, personal drones, smart cloths, etc.), but sadly there still aren't any flying cars out there. Conversational interfaces aren't flying cars, though. They are here to stay, and the time it will take for them to become useful and reliable will depend on our willingness to learn more about the craft, and explore new ways to make technology work for us, rather than the other way around.

As William Gibson said:

 "The future is already here – it's just not very evenly distributed."

We started embarking on this journey together. Conversation will lead the way forward.

About The Author

Adrian Zumbrunnen is a user experience & interaction designer working at Google (and formerly Information Architects) in Zurich. He loves the Web, well-formed type, and freshly brewed coffee. In his free time he goes kite surfing and writes about UX design on his blog.

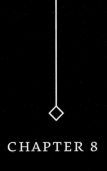

CHAPTER 8

UX Design of Chatbots and Virtual Assistants

Greg Nudelman

UX Design Of Chatbots And Virtual Assistants

by Greg Nudelmann

There has never been a more exciting time for designing and building digital products! As an example, here are just a few of the projects that I was involved with last year:

a. A Slack bot that serves up cloud application and network performance alerts and graphs, and provides proactive push recommendations.

b. A dedicated NLP (natural-language processing) assistant for a major hospital chain, able to find doctors and locations, set up appointments and more, right from the homepage.

c. NLP search for analytics applications, which maps a natural-language query into an Elastic faceted search UI as keywords and selected facet values for further refinement and exploration.

d. Building an Alexa Skill that delivers predictive corrosion notifications and daily asset performance analytics reports for industrial plants.

And this just scratches the surface: the range of conversational bot applications is wide, far-reaching and exciting. Today, consumer sophistication is at an all-time high, and people in the consumer and enterprise space demand polished, context-aware, personalized cross-platform experiences fully integrated into their work and leisure activities. Tech giants are rising to this challenge, competing with one another by providing extraordinarily sophisticated frameworks and cloud-based services for almost every component of your app, including (most importantly for us) robust language parsing and speech recognition frameworks. Examples include: Microsoft Bot Framework with LUIS (Language Understanding Intelligent Service) and Cortana, Siri from Apple, Amazon Lex, Google Assistant, IBM Watson, and many more.

Most frameworks offer similar basic functionality and structure for building bots, as well as free developer licenses for conversational UI and voice recognition services. Although we will touch on some fundamental differences between these various frameworks, any attempt at a detailed survey would become quickly out of date due to the rapid pace of innovation, and thus fall outside the purview of this chapter.

While Adrian discussed some aspects of the conversation UI in the previous chapter, this chapter will focus on the technical and engineering challenges of designing conversational interfaces. Through the course of this chapter, we will assemble a bot similar in functionality to Amazon Alexa, as an example to showcase the essential features of conversational UIs in what I hope is a practical and hands-on way.

For the more design-inclined readers, a word warning: there are some simple snippets of code that support design explanations. Even if you've never coded before, I encourage you to read the code snippets and follow along with the exercises. Being able to read the code and understand practical engineering considerations will make you a better designer, particularly in the area of conversational bots, where the nature of the medium makes it hard to represent UIs conventionally (using mock-ups or diagrams). To be a competent conversational UI designer, you have to know enough about how bots work to be able to ask the right questions.

This chapter aims to give you enough background to comfortably design and code a basic conversational bot similar to "unskilled" Alexa, suitable for whatever application you choose.

Picking the Right Bot Framework

To demonstrate various UX considerations and design patterns of conversational UI and voice recognition we will use Microsoft Bot Framework and Amazon Alexa as the primary bot frameworks for our examples. In my opinion, Microsoft Bot Framework strikes the right balance between power and learnability. At the time of writing, it's free for developers, has a decent admin UI, is cloud-based right out of the box (which has the advantage of introducing you to cloud-based app architecture), and can be coded using many mainstream languages, including Node.js, which we'll use in our examples. Most importantly, Microsoft Bot Framework boasts heaps of step-by-step tutorials and examples, and truly impressive documentation.

Amazon Alexa is newer and, in many ways, easier to setup and configure than LUIS, and offers many useful shortcuts. However, there is one crucial difference: Alexa is best set up as an Alexa Skill, whereas LUIS is a standalone chatbot. Which means that to invoke our bot – let's call it GUPPI (more on naming in a moment) – and pass it a command (called an invocation), you have to invoke Alexa first. Compare the two invocations below:

> **Standalone bot:** *"GUPPI, play Rolling Stones."*
>
> **Alexa Skill bot:** *"Alexa, ask GUPPI to play Rolling Stones."*

While Alexa Skill invocation works fine for simple commands, it creates awkward verbal constructs for more complex queries. Fortunately, bot developers have some flexibility in invoking their Alexa Skill. In principle, all of the utterances below would work equally well to launch GUPPI and successfully pass the command along:

> "Alexa, ask GUPPI to play Rolling Stones."
>
> "Alexa, tell GUPPI to play Rolling Stones."
>
> "Alexa, talk to GUPPI and tell it to play Rolling Stones."
>
> "Alexa, play Rolling Stones using GUPPI."

In practice, there are some important limitations, and trying to override Alexa's own commands like "Play," "Time," "Weather," and so on will often result in a buggy and inconsistent experience.

Another important consideration is the length of the command, typically restricted to a single English sentence. Having to invoke Alexa every time as part of your request places additional limits on the length of your command. Supplementary Amazon Alexa APIs (such as Smart Home, List Skill, and Flash Briefing) are also available, offering some flexibility for specialized applications. However, at the time of writing, there is no easy way to invoke an Alexa Skill outside Alexa. The key takeaway is that the Alexa Skills framework is set up explicitly to invoke your bot *inside* Alexa as a Skill, whereas the LUIS framework allows you to have a standalone bot (with, perhaps, a little more work).

Google Assistant[1] is similar to the Alexa model, with a few significant differences. The Google Assistant conversation bot (called an app) can be launched from within Google Assistant using an invocation phrase, just like an Alexa Skill. Unlike Alexa, however, the user cannot pass

---

1 http://smashed.by/gassistant

parameters to the Google Assistant app during an invocation. Thus, during the initial user response phase (called *fulfillment*), the user is typically greeted with a Default Welcome Intent message variant, which launches a separate conversation with the bot. Once the user invokes a custom app, Alexa prefers to take care of everything in one session, whereas the Google Assistant allows for a more robust session context which can store variables between invocations (accessible via a `lastSeen` attribute.) See the "Context is King" section later in the chapter for more on this topic.

Lastly, it pays to keep in mind that Alexa uses intent-based bot architecture (similar to Microsoft LUIS), so the developer has to add a dialog construct later in the development process using a chunk of custom code (using an *AWS Lambda function*,[2] for example). In contrast, Google Assistant assumes everything happens by default within a dialog, using the `Dialogflow` wrapper, which also handles intents and entities. Thus, Google Assistant gives developers access to powerful visual dialog builder features (shown in Figure 1), allowing developers to set up simple applications almost entirely using the UI, with minimal edits of the underlying code. If a developer requires additional configurability, the Google Assistant framework offers access to the raw JSON conversation webhook format which communicates directly to the Assistant.

Figure 1: *Google Assistant provides powerful visual builder features for creating dialogs.*

2   http://smashed.by/lambdafunction

In contrast to Alexa and Google Assistant (where the user invokes the custom bot from within the primary digital assistant), *IBM Watson*[3] is a standalone bot framework, which makes it useful for autonomous tasks. IBM Watson is in many ways similar to Microsoft Bot Framework with LUIS. One nice improvement over LUIS is that while both frameworks use intents and entities as a base, Watson also has a powerful visual builder for the dialog construct, similar to that of Google Assistant, as shown in Figure 2.

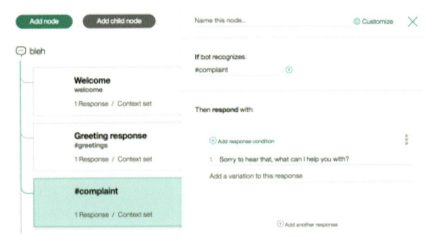

Figure 2: IBM Watson's version of the visual dialog builder.

Microsoft LUIS only stores intents and entities in the bot's definition, while the additional Microsoft Bot Framework application code provides the waterfall dialog interaction (more on this later). In contrast, IBM Watson offers the option to have the dialogs build directly as part of the bot's JSON definition, providing a comprehensive high-level visual diagram of your bot's waterfall dialog logic, shown in Figure 3 on the next page.

3   http://smashed.by/watson

IBM Watson also provides integrated testing of the conversational experience using a built-in testing app, offering an excellent all-in-one framework to design, train and test your bot. IBM Watson bot framework will appeal to many designers, as it allows you to build a reasonably sophisticated, fully functional standalone bot without writing any code at all.

Do you need a standalone bot? It depends on your particular application. Write out the invocations you plan to use and see if they would sound exceptionally long or awkward if the user has to invoke Alexa first. If so, use a standalone framework such as LUIS or IBM Watson; otherwise, you're in luck, and you can use the Alexa Skill framework or Google Assistant as a quick shortcut. I can personally attest that setting up an Alexa Skill on an Echo device creates particularly impressive workplace demos you can throw together in just a few hours.

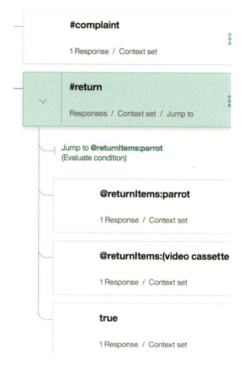

Figure 3: IBM Watson's visual logic diagram for a demo bot.

One last point: if your bot has a notifications or alerts feature, Amazon recommends invoking "Notifications" at the top level as aggregated Alexa notifications, not from within the Skill itself. The good news is that users will get an accurate visual indication that they have notifications (in the form of a flashing orange ring on their Echo device).

The bad news is that you have to conform to Alexa's notification framework. If deeply customized interactive notifications are essential to your experience, you may be better off with a standalone bot.

The Google Assistant bot framework does not yet provide app-level notifications (currently in developer preview), though they should be available soon. Google Assistant notifications appear to offer a middle ground of a hybrid model, promising to provide more comprehensive customization options at the cost of some additional complexity compared to Amazon Alexa.

Many other bot frameworks exist, including Facebook Bot Engine, Dialogflow, Aspect CXP, and Aspect NLU, and many other popular platforms. Many more frameworks are in current active development. Detailed competitive analysis is outside the purview of this chapter – for more detailed comparison of various frameworks, see Olga Davydova's well-researched article, "25 Chatbot Platforms: A Comparative Table,"[4] published in Chatbots Journal.

Despite some differences, at their core most bot frameworks are fairly similar. The design patterns and UX principles described in this chapter should translate well between various frameworks and remain useful to readers in the long term, even as technical specifics experience rapid growth and evolution. Since a standalone bot offers a more complex and interesting use case, we will use LUIS as the primary example for the next few sections of this chapter. Regardless of the framework you choose, the first step in developing your bot is to break up generic bot commands (or *invocations*) into the basic building blocks of conversational UI: intents, entities, and dialogs.

4   http://smashed.by/chatbotcomparison

Setting Up Intents

When you initiate a conversation with a bot, the first thing it attempts to do is figure out what you are asking – this is called *intent*. For example, some of the things you can ask Alexa are:

> "What time is it?"
> "What will the weather be today?"
> "I want to listen to music."

Each of these statements correspond to a different intent, which we can label as "Time," "Weather," "General Music." When you set this up using the Microsoft LUIS interface, the result should look something like the screenshot in Figure 4.

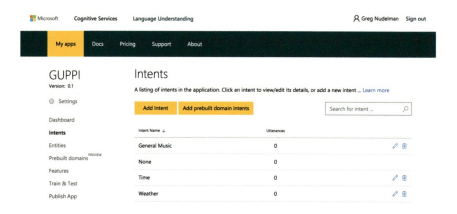

Figure 4: Setting up initial intents in Microsoft LUIS.

> *Note:* I recommend doing the work in each step by following the examples. You will need to create a free Microsoft account and a new LUIS application.

LUIS contains highly sophisticated language recognition software, which can be used to train our bot to recognize the user intent, even if the phrasing is slightly different. For example, we can ask our bot about the weather in many different ways, such as "Will it rain today?" "What will the temperature be like?" "Will it be sunny?" and even (in a very Seattle way) "Should I pack an umbrella?" In each case, even though the phrasing is different, the intent remains the same: "Weather." The "magical" aspect of the interface is that the bot responds correctly by giving a weather forecast, even though the exact phrasing is slightly different from the training set. This ability to extract meaning from imprecise phrasing is the big deal of applying language recognition AI to natural speech, an area which has seen many computing advances in recent years.

Let's go ahead and train our bot with some basic phrases so it can start recognizing our intents. The result should look like the set shown in Figure 5.

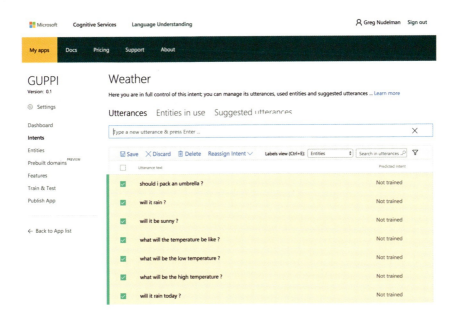

Figure 5: Training the LUIS bot to recognize basic weather phrases.

Note: Don't forget to hit the **Deploy** button after applying the training set. If at any point your bot starts behaving strangely, the first troubleshooting step is to retrain and redeploy your bot. (Cue the inevitable "Restart Windows" jokes!)

Below is the complete initial set of four intents and the corresponding training phrases for our bot:

Intent: General Music

- Music
- I want to hear something good
- Play me something good
- Play decent music
- Play me a song
- I want to hear some music
- Play music

Intent: Time

- Time
- Say the hours
- Use military time
- Is it morning already?
- Is it late or early?
- How early is it?
- Time of day
- How late is it?
- What time is it?

Intent: Weather

- Weather
- What will be the high temperature?
- What will be the low temperature?
- What will the temperature be like?
- Should I pack an umbrella?
- What will the weather be today?
- Will it be sunny?
- Will it rain?
- Will it rain today?

Intent: None

- I like ice cream
- Baseball is awesome

Note: As we move forward in this chapter, the model will become too large and too repetitive to keep reintroducing verbatim. This is where the JSON export/import function comes in handy. Within the Microsoft Bot Framework, you can export or import your bot's model as a JSON file – just go to the My Apps area and click on the "{ }" icon. I highly recommend doing this for your bot periodically, as a good backup practice, and to be able to rollback to the previous state should anything go wrong with your training set. The complete JSON code can be found here: http://smashed.by/codepackage

When a bot receives an incoming query, it tries to match it against each of the intents, and assigns a score to each match, as seen in Figure 6.

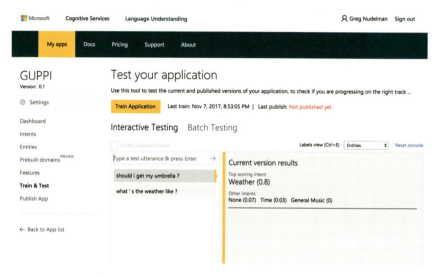

Figure 6: Intent match scores for a query.

Higher scores mean a better intent match, with a possible maximum score of 1 or 100%. Based on the scores provided by LUIS, our bot is pretty confident that "Should I get my umbrella?" is a "Weather" intent, with a score of 0.8 (or 80%), and least confident that it's a request for "General Music," with a score of 0. It's a pretty impressive result, given that we've spent only about fifteen minutes and used less than two dozen phrases to create and train our bot! Although we are typically interested only in the top scoring intent, you can create various UX strategies to deal with ambiguous queries, or queries scoring below a minimum cutoff score. We'll cover those disambiguation strategies later.

PUT YOUR FAITH IN NONE OF THE ABOVE

If you followed along with the exercise, you will have noticed that in addition to the three intents we've added, there is a default intent of "None." This default intent is important to conversational UX because it signals when the bot doesn't know how to handle a particular query. The bot has to be trained to recognize the "None" intent in a similar way it has to be trained to recognize all the other intents.

The usual practice is to train the "None" intent with some nonsense queries, such as "I like ice cream." Occasionally, however, the "None" intent can be quite useful for short-circuiting queries that would otherwise confuse your bot, and result in erratic behaviors, unsatisfying UX, and a loss of trust by the conversation partner (user). Practice and exposure to real-world queries are key to identifying those queries and then training your bot to handle "None" intents gracefully.

No matter how well you think you know your domain, don't expect your bot to handle every query flawlessly right from the start. Every time one of my students or co-workers proudly presents his or her first bot, the first few queries from the peanut gallery quickly reveal its limitations, resulting in unexpected behavior. Typically, the bot's creator rarely anticipates how various conversation partners would ask their questions, which makes real-world field usability studies and subsequent bot retraining essential for success.

MORE TRAINING IS NOT ALWAYS BETTER

As a note of caution, we should mention that more training is not necessarily better, as not every training phrase is going to improve the intent matching outcome. Sometimes, this makes training a bot particularly challenging because the intent recognition mechanism is normally a proprietary black box, so there is no way to predict when a particular phrase might cause a problem.

Occasionally, the predicted score in the training set gives you a clue of possible future issues when a particular training phrase matches two or more intents with nearly equal scores. For example, in Figure 6 the expression "Should I pack an umbrella?" matched with a score of 0.97, slightly below the other training phrases. For a sophisticated bot with multiple intents, any training phrase with a score of 0.6–0.7 or above is acceptable. However, sometimes the predicted score dips below 0.2, which can cause issues with recognizing the intent when using queries similar to the training sentence the bot finds problematic. When that happens, you can usually take additional steps to help the bot recognize the right intent, like adding more phrases similar to the problem sentence for each of the intents the bot finds ambiguous, or locking down the explicit values of the entity variables (which we'll cover in the next section).

I would advise against treating the predicted scores of the training utterances as anything other than general guidelines. Often, the best recommendation is to start with a small basic training set of phrases and good logging software to continually log any queries that stump your bot. Over time, improve the quality of intent recognition by labeling and adding these initially confusing queries to your training set to make your bot smarter. At the moment, real-world exposure to humans and training by trial and error is still your best bet. If the bot suddenly starts getting confused more often, just roll back the changes to the previous version of the training set and retrain your bot.

In contrast to having to train every LUIS intent manually, the Alexa Skills framework provides many useful shortcuts, among which is a large number of built-in intents, including:

- `AMAZON.SearchAction<object@WeatherForecast>`
- `AMAZON.HelpIntent`
- `AMAZON.StopIntent`
- `AMAZON.YesIntent`

The benefits of using built-in intents are:

- You do not need to spend the time writing sample utterances for common intents.
- Conversation partners can use common, consistent phrases to access the intent across Skills, which provides a more consistent Alexa experience.
- Your Skill gets the benefit of any future updates to the Alexa service that improve recognition and utterances for these intents.

Amazon currently offers fifteen build-in intents. Depending on the type of your Skill, you may be required to implement some of them in your bot. Others might be available to you to use without the Skill name invocation. If your bot is playing music, for example, you can simply say "Alexa, stop" without having to say "Alexa, ask GUPPI to stop," which is pretty handy![5]

---

[5] Alexa's documentation has more details on its "Standard Built-in Intents." http://smashed.by/alexaintents

ASIDE: WHAT'S IN A NAME — GUPPI, SAMANTHA, ALEXA, SIRI, AND HAL 9000

Why did we name our bot GUPPI? The name is, of course, a homage to the excellent *Bobiverse series*.[6]

In this brilliant trilogy Dennis E. Taylor writes about Bob, a Silicon Valley CEO, whose brain is scanned into a computer and becomes the AI in an interstellar spaceship. GUPPI (General Unit Primary Peripheral Interface) is virtual Bob's virtual assistant. GUPPI has limited intelligence, on a par with Siri or Alexa of our own post-industrial age, so communicating with GUPPI is alien and awkward. The name "GUPPI" helps remind Bob of the limitations of his assistant, which in turn helps him converse at a level GUPPI can understand and process.

Compare GUPPI to Samantha, the AI in the movie *Her*. In sharp contrast to GUPPI's fishy flaws, Samantha understands and expresses complex emotions, and possesses at least a human-level intelligence. Other than the pesky fact of not having a body, Samantha appears to be fully human. Not surprisingly (spoiler alert!) the lonely protagonist falls deeply in love with Samantha and a cerebral affair ensues.

---

6 http://smashed.by/bobiverse

While the AI names like GUPPI or HAL 9000 (from *2001: A Space Odyssey*) imply an alien digital intelligence, the familiar name Samantha implies high similarity with human beings, self-awareness, and even consciousness. Names like Alexa and Siri strike a balance of being somewhere between the two, sounding human, yet also somewhat rare, exotic and alien. Our current AIs are much closer to GUPPI than they are to Samantha – a typical conversational AI assistant understands about as much as a dog does, minus any emotional intelligence.

Thus, it makes sense to invest some time in naming and visually representing your bot in a way that helps frame from the start what your conversation partners should expect from communicating with your bot. *Framing expectations is key.* You want people to be impressed when your dog-level AI understands simple commands like "GUPPI, bring me my slippers." You do not want your customers to be heartbroken when your bot fails to understand the following: "Samantha, even if you come home late and I'm already asleep, just whisper in my ear one little thought you had today. Because I love the way you look at the world. And I'm so happy I get to be next to you and look at the world through your eyes."[7]

---

7   http://smashed.by/guppiquotes

Extracting Entities

While matching intents is fun, the real power of the conversational UI comes from being able to pass in parameters. These parameters are known as *entities* in LUIS or *slots* in Alexa.

The most common way is to extract the incoming parameter as a *simple entity*. Simple entities are used to train the bot using a manually labeled training set (just like we have been doing so far). Using the simple entity extraction, our bot could learn to recognize and parse a potentially infinite number of incoming values. However, this kind of matching is not always precise: if you expect two or three similar entities in random order in a single invocation, the bot may accidentally switch the values around. Larger training sets can help the bot get slightly smarter, but often the best solution is to lock down the range of possible values with a *list* entity type.

Using the list entity type, the bot will check the incoming parameter against a fixed array of possible values, as in the "specialty" list entity below:

> **Human:** *I want an appointment with a cardiology specialist.*
> **Bot:** *intent=doctor; parameter=specialty {Pediatrics, Cardiology, Obstetrics, Neurology}*

The list entity matching is highly accurate, but it suffers from a severe defect: if the entity value is not in the list (limited to 20,000 at the moment), the entire intent will not be recognized and default to "None":

> **Human:** *I need a heart doctor.*
> **Bot:** *intent=None*

Until a better method is widely available, designers are forced to sometimes use both the manual and list methods of recognition in tandem, to cover every possibility and improve the overall accuracy of the intent matching. Using both types of matching together allows the bot to recognize the correct intent even when the entity is not in the preset list. Experiment with both list and simple entities training sets to determine which is going to be the best fit for your application.

To demonstrate this functionality, let's add another request, "Play (Music) Station," with the [$Station] parsed as a list entity (shown in Figure 7).

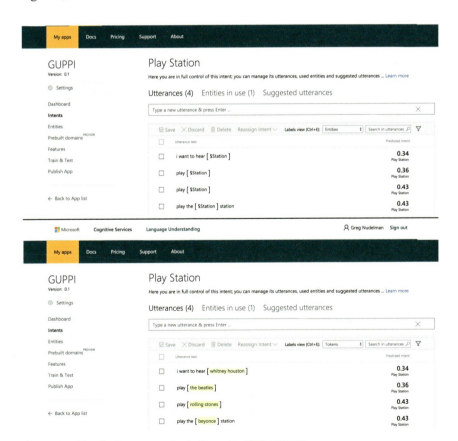

Figure 7: Teaching the bot to recognize the list entity [$Station].

Provided this makes sense for your specific intent, you can make your bot even smarter by experimenting with the available prebuilt entities, including most encyclopedia entries, like countries, time, artists, weights and measures, and much more. Unfortunately, the power of prebuilt entities currently comes with a frustrating set of limitations: the LUIS model attempts to bind every possible manually created entity before it tries to match the prebuilt entities.

There is currently no way to convince LUIS to recognize the prebuilt entity if it matches another entity type instead, so sometimes things can get pretty confusing. If prebuilt entities aren't working, you can always default to creating another list or simple entity, and labeling each utterance manually.

> *Note:* In LUIS, if you want to manually label a multi-word entity value (such as "Whitney Houston"), hold down the Shift key while clicking on each of the words to select them together as a set and assign them to a single entity.

Using different intents helps your bot understand the meaning of a particular entity value in a different context. For example, a word like "Chicago" can have multiple meanings depending on intent. The "Weather" intent would label the entity value "Chicago" as a city (using the list entity `$City`), whereas "Chicago" becomes the name of the band (using the list entity `$Station`) when the intent is "Play Station", as shown in Figure 8.

Figure 8: Determining meaning of the word "Chicago" in context using various intents.

The same applies to many other words, like "Houston" (Houston, TX vs. Whitney Houston), "Denver" (Denver, CO vs. John Denver), and so on. Mapping these words explicitly as part of the LUIS model will help resolve these potential conflicts, and train your bot to recognize which entity goes with which intent and resolve the query successfully.

Overall, the more context you can teach your bot, the smarter and more human-like your bot will appear. And, of course, we can't even begin to talk about context until we teach our bot to ask follow up questions. A complex pattern like this is called a *dialog* in Alexa, and a *waterfall* in LUIS.

Plunging into a Waterfall: a Bot Conversation

Up to this point, we've only trained our bot to respond to a query. If the intent isn't clear or the entity match was unsuccessful, the bot has no choice but to default to a "None" intent or a fail condition. This is a severe limitation: for the query to succeed, it must always be well-formed and complete, because our bot cannot ask any follow-up questions the way most humans would if they were confused. It's time we corrected this by adding a simple waterfall using some Node.js code to show off a brand new intent, "Set Alarm," pictured in Figure 9.

Figure 9: Adding the "Set Alarm" intent.

Note that the "Set Alarm" intent is a bit different from the previous intents. Although the entity was optional in the previous intents (default to favorite music or weather at a set location or one determined via GPS) this just does not make sense in the case of setting the alarm. We need to know when to sound the alarm, so the `DateTime` entity is required. We know that to set an alarm, the conversation partner has to tell the bot two things:

1. That the intent is set the alarm.
2. At what time to sound the alarm.

If the conversation partner only specifies the intent and not the time, by saying something like "GUPPI, set the alarm," the bot can to come back with a question, such as "What time would you like the alarm set for?" by using a bit of simple Node.js code. This results in a mini conversation, where the bot waits for an appropriate response while maintaining the original intent much like a human would. Voilà! A simple conversation is born.

Fortunately, our task here is made much simpler by using the prebuilt entity, datetimeV2, which automatically parses complex expressions like "Today at 2.15pm" or "23 minutes from now," and converts them into a date-time variable our bot can use. The only thing we have to worry about is capturing the Set Alarm intent where the DateTime intent is null.

Here's the walkthrough of the pertinent parts of the program.[8]

```
// Create chat bot
var connector = new builder.ChatConnector({
  appId: 'long-app-id-supplied-by-bot-framework',
  appPassword: 'p@ssw0rd'
});
//set up a server to listen and provide a LUIS model connection
var bot = new builder.UniversalBot(connector);
server.post('/api/messages', connector.listen());
var model = 'https://westus.api.cognitive.microsoft.com/luis/v2.0/apps/SOME-ID?subscription-key=SOME-SUBSCRPTION-KEY';
//pass the model to instance a working bot instance ("recognizer")
var recognizer = new builder.LuisRecognizer(model);
var intent = new builder.IntentDialog({ recognizers: [recognizer] });
//invoke a conversation with the user-passed intent
bot.dialog('/', intent);
// Add intent handlers
intent.matches('Set Alarm', [
```

8   For the complete code see the BotBuilder example: http://smashed.by/botbuilder

```
//'Set Alarm' MUST HAVE a non-null dateTime to proceed continue
// waterfall conversation 1 step to see if the user provides a dateTime
function setAlarmStep0(session, args, next) { // extract the timeEntity
    var timeEntity = builder.EntityRecognizer.resolveTime(args.entities);
    // set the time in the session, this is needed if we're trying to
    // remember the original intent
session.dialogData.setAlarm = {
    // a very handy code construct that checks if timeEntity is not null
    // and only then before it sets a variable inside to null — doing this
    // for every incoming attribute avoids Null Object Reference errors
time: timeEntity ? timeEntity.getTime() : null
    };

    // do we have the dateTime?
    if (!session.dialogData.setAlarm.time) {
    // nope - so ask the user for it using a Prompts:
        builder.Prompts.text(session, "What time would you like to set
        the alarm for?");
    } else { // we got the dateTime, so go to the next step setAlarmStep1
        next();
        }
    }
},

// step 2 - BOTH next() and user's dateTime response will end up here
function setAlarmStep1(session, results, next) {
    if (results.response) {
    //yes, user provided input. Try parsing to see if we can get dateTime
session.dialogData.setAlarm.time = builder.EntityRecognizer.
recognizeTime(results.response);
    }
    // if we got time, set the alarm
    if (session.dialogData.setAlarm.time) {
    //some alarm setting in the DB…
    } else {
    //the user failed to provide time even though we've asked nicely -
    //it's a cancel
session.dialogData.setAlarm = null;
    session.send('Sorry, I could not understand what date and time you
wanted the alarm for… Set Alarm cancelled.');
    }
}
]);
```

As you can see, the code is fairly straightforward, though it has a few quirks specific to the Microsoft Bot Framework. For example, the whole `next()` construct seems a bit old-school, like the old BASIC `goto()` function. At least until you realize that `next()` essentially allows the bot to execute the whole sequence of functions in a specific order, allowing you to collect multiple parameters one or more at a time, over several steps (provided you insert enough `if/else` statements to account for each parameter to be entered in every possible order).

Another important consideration is to provide an exit for a failed condition, so that your bot will not get stuck in an infinite loop of asking for a `dateTime`, unless that is the intent. The fail exit has to be set up outside the normal waterfall flow of `next()` functions, which naturally allows only a single step for each attempt. If you think about how Siri or Google Assistant bots work with most simple requests such as "Send message", this single-step waterfall is exactly what happens, even when the bot has to collect two parameters. For example, using a waterfall flow, typical "Send message" sequence pseudo-code looks like this:

Step 1
- Try to collect RECIPIENT and MESSAGE.
- Does a valid MESSAGE exist?
- If not, ask "What do you want the message to say?"
- next();

Step 2
- Does a valid MESSAGE exist?
- If not, collect MESSAGE.
- Does a valid RECIPIENT exist?
- If not, ask "Who is the recipient?"
- next();

Step 3

- Does a valid RECIPIENT exist?
- If not, collect RECIPIENT.
- next();

Step 4

- Do BOTH valid RECIPIENT and MESSAGE exist?
- YES: send the message.
- NO: respond "Sorry, can't send message" and exit.

Thus, the conversation partner gets just one shot to answer the question correctly. Rather than getting stuck in an infinite loop waiting for a valid message recipient, both Siri and Google Assistant bots exit after a single failed response to a follow-up question. While this can be a bit inconvenient, and can occasionally lead to the conversation partner having to repeat the entire query two or more times, especially in loud environments, the upshot of this fast fail behavior is consistency: projecting the feeling of control that the system provides for the conversation partner to feel comfortable using and relying on the bot. (See Mark Wyner's "Control! Control! You Must Have Control!" sidebar in the next section for more on the importance of feeling in control.)

In contrast to the Microsoft Bot Framework requirement of coding each step separately via the `next()` construct, Alexa takes a uniquely simple and brave approach to the problem of collecting required entities by simplifying the entire process using a dialog construct, shown below.[9]

---

[9] For the complete code see http://smashed.by/alexcookbook

```javascript
function planMyTrip(request, session, callback){
   console.log("in plan my trip");
   console.log("request: "+JSON.stringify(request));
   var sessionAttributes={};
   var filledSlots = delegateSlotCollection(request, sessionAttributes, callback);
   //compose speechOutput that simply reads all the collected slot values
   var speechOutput = randomPhrase(tripIntro);
   //activity is optional so we'll add it to the output
   //only when we have a valid activity
   var activity = isSlotValid(request, "activity");
   if (activity) {
     speechOutput += activity;
   } else {
     speechOutput += "You'll go ";
   }
   //Now let's recap the trip
   var fromCity=request.intent.slots.fromCity.value;
   var toCity=request.intent.slots.toCity.value;
   var travelDate=request.intent.slots.travelDate.value;
   speechOutput+= " from "+ fromCity + " to "+ toCity+" on "+travelDate;
   //say the results
   callback(sessionAttributes,
       buildSpeechletResponse("Travel booking", speechOutput, "", true));
    }
function delegateSlotCollection(request, sessionAttributes, callback){
   console.log("in delegateSlotCollection");
   console.log("currentdialogState: "+JSON.stringify(request.dialogState));
    if (request.dialogState === "STARTED") {
       console.log("in started");
       console.log("currentrequest: "+JSON.stringify(request));
       var updatedIntent=request.intent;
       //optionally pre-fill slots: update the intent object with slot
       //values for which you have defaults, then return Dialog.
       //Delegate with this updated intent in the updatedIntent property
       callback(sessionAttributes,
     buildSpeechletResponseWithDirectiveNoIntent());
    } else if (request.dialogState !== "COMPLETED") {
       console.log("in not completed");
       console.log("currentrequest: "+JSON.stringify(request));
       // return a Dialog.Delegate directive with no updatedIntent property.
       callback(sessionAttributes,
```

```
            buildSpeechletResponseWithDirectiveNoIntent());
        } else {
            console.log("in completed");
            console.log("current request: "+JSON.stringify(request));
            console.log("returning: "+ JSON.stringify(request.intent));
            // Dialog is now complete and all required slots should be filled,
            // so call your normal intent handler.
            return request.intent;
        }
    }
        //this is where the magic happens — the action is sent to the
        //Alexa Dialog Delegate
    function buildSpeechletResponseWithDirectiveNoIntent() {
        console.log("in buildSpeechletResponseWithDirectiveNoIntent");
        return {
            "outputSpeech" : null,
            "card" : null,
            "directives" : [ {
                "type" : "Dialog.Delegate"
        } ],
            "reprompt" : null,
            "shouldEndSession" : false
        }
    }
```

Simply put, the Alexa dialog construct contains all of the required next() code steps in a single configurable function. You just need to specify the required entities the Alexa Skill bot needs to collect, and the dialog code takes care of the rest. One important consideration is that the Microsoft Bot Framework's next() construct can be used to specify the exact order in which the required entities are collected, whereas Alexa's dialog simply collects the required entities in any order the user chooses to provide them.

For most applications, the order does not matter, so the dialog provides a convenient shortcut. Having less to code to worry out is nice, as it leaves time for you to focus on providing alternative conversation prompts the bot can pick from at random. This provides variety in the conversational interaction and helps maintain the illusion of having a real conversation with the bot.

Using dialog, you typically have no control on the order of prompts, as these are chosen at random from a list of available options. In contrast, using `next()` we can create a more sophisticated waterfall construct, where the responses depend on what information has already been collected, maintaining the context of the conversation.

For example, in the Send Message intent, if the message body was not provided, the bot can say "What?" (as in "Was that a message? I didn't quite understand what you wanted to say") and "Which Mike? Smith or Baker?" (as in "Do you want to send this message to Mike Smith or Mike Baker?") More sophisticated context-sensitive responses will help our personal assistant AIs appear more human by retaining the context of the conversation. Naturally, this kind of smart response requires you to write some custom response code using the waterfall construct, and can't be implemented using a simple dialog, which just picks responses at random.

Consider carefully if you need the extra sophistication. My research shows that fast fail is often preferable for simple personal assistant AI tasks, such as calling, sending messages, setting calendar appointments and the like – in other words, tasks that can be normally communicated using a single sentence.

The exact opposite holds true for deep phone system trees, where the conversational partner spends a fair bit of time entering the context, and so will get infuriated if your bot exits without trying to get the account number at least a couple of times.

In the next section, we'll review phone trees and some ways companies are bringing this traditionally dark side of bots into the light. We are far from done with the conversational context topic – it is pivotal to the conversational UI experience, and is covered in more detail in the "Context is King" section later in the chapter.

Help Bots and Phone Trees: Bringing the Dark Side of Bots into the Light

Ask your friends about which bot experience they detest most, and chances are their answer will be unanimous: phone trees. Phone trees are one of the earliest widespread uses of bots. As ubiquitous as they are unpleasant, they present a convenient baseline against which to judge the experience provided by our conversational UIs, offer many examples of what can make conversational UI annoying, and a wealth of insights about how to make the same experience much more tolerable.

1. Recognize the Emotional State of the Customer

The Voice User Interface Company designs and assesses interactive voice response systems for companies, and its founder Walter Rolandi specializes in listening to how people use these systems. He summed up the importance of the emotional considerations neatly when he said:[10]

> "Many people do not take into account the emotional state of the customer. When you call someone for customer service, you've got a problem and you're probably in a bad mood. You hear someone telling you your call is so important that we won't let you talk to a human. Then they slap people with too many options, and eventually, you're in a fight with the system. When you do get a customer representative, you're loaded for bear."

2. Appreciate That Customers May Not Know How to Phrase Their Questions

As Robert Sheckley puts it so eloquently in his short story "Ask A Foolish Question," "In order to ask a question you must already know most of the answer."[11] Exactly the opposite happens in the situation where the customer calls the company seeking help.

Today, most customers use a phone call as the last resort. That usually means self-service via website has already failed, and the customer is well and truly stuck. For a bot, this presents a unique problem, because bots are generally good at determining specific well-defined intents, preferably delivered as simple requests in a single sentence.

Unfortunately, people seeking help often need to unburden themselves first by telling a kind of story to organize their thoughts and figure out what it is they actually need help with. And although conversational UIs are pretty cool, they are not usually capable of discerning a vague intent from such a customer story.

Add to this the emotionally elevated state of the person stuck in a fight with the system, and you will understand why getting help via a phone tree makes a particularly difficult use case for bots. The customer often has no idea how to phrase the question in a way a bot can understand.

---

[10] Quoted in "Far From Always Being Right, the Customer Is on Hold" by Alina Tugend, New York Times, 2008 (http://smashed.by/24shortcuts).
[11] Available at Project Gutenberg (http://smashed.by/gutenberg).

3. Don't Overwhelm Customers with Options

Providing a lot of options will not help a customer select the right one. It's just too much information! Picking the right option from the list requires customers, in addition to knowing their specific problems, to also understand how those problems fit into your bot's information architecture. Not surprisingly, when presented with too many options, most people just hit the "0" button to request an operator.

4. Allow Customers to Feel That They Are in Control

The feeling of control is key, especially in the heightened emotional state customers can be in when they call the company for help. That is why it's especially important to pay attention to the "None" intent. Offer a clear "None of the above" or "Something else" option. If you do not, it's an invitation to the customer to make the wrong choice and land in phone tree purgatory, unable to get back to the main menu. When that happens, often the only thing the customer can do is to hang up and try again, resulting in even greater frustration.

Just to be clear: the bot UX itself is not necessarily an issue, as long as the customer feels in control; that is, they can escape the automation and just speak to a human.

5. Don't Pretend to Care or Possess Feelings

One of the most hated phrases for a person on hold to hear is "Your call is very important to us." It's especially irritating when the voice comes overloaded with emotion, as in "Your call is so, *so very* important to us." (So important in fact, that we can't possibly spare a human being who can pick up the phone…) The same goes for any kind of wordiness or circumlocution, or overall cuteness. This is not the time to get inventive! Stay as conversational as possible, but try to be brief and to the point. As mentioned earlier, don't pretend that your bot is more capable than a trained dog would be. You want your customer to be pleasantly surprised, not bitterly disappointed.

6. Never, Ever Give Up

In stark contrast to the one-shot example of texting or calling using Siri and Google Assistant that we discussed in the section above, the help bot *must never, ever give up*. If unable to understand after one or two attempts, the bot should send the request to a human operator. The bot must **never** give up or hang up on the person who called seeking help.

Control! Control! You Must Learn Control!
by Mark Wyner (http://markwyner.com)

We human beings love to control our environment. When we have control, we feel safe, we feel secure, and we want to continue on the path. And when we don't have control, things get scary and uncomfortable. So control is a key element of trust when humans interact with a machine.

Below is a passage from an incredible book, *Old Man's War* by John Scalzi, which provides a realistic picture of the kind of interaction we might soon have with our conversational bots, particularly in industrial and military applications. In this particular passage, the protagonist, John Perry, is a fresh military recruit, setting up his new personal voice-based AI system, embedded in his brain, called BrainPal. John clearly doesn't trust this AI, and does not want it anywhere near him. Unfortunately, John is forced to use the BrainPal system as a condition of his continued employment. To help ease John into using BrainPal, its designers allow users to have some control over the system, starting with being able to name the bot. What transpires is both hilarious and highly instructive:

> "Many BrainPal users find it useful to give their BrainPal a name other than BrainPal. Would you like to name your BrainPal at this time?"
>
> "Yes," I said.
>
> "Please speak the name you would like to give your BrainPal."
>
> "Asshole," I said.
>
> "You have selected 'Asshole,'" the BrainPal wrote, and to its credit it spelled the word correctly. "Be aware that many recruits have selected this name for their BrainPal. Would you like to chose a different name?"

"No," I said, and was proud that so many of my fellow recruits also felt this way about their BrainPal.

"Your BrainPal is now Asshole," the BrainPal wrote. "Now you must choose an access phrase to activate Asshole. Please say your activation phrase now."

"Hey, Asshole," I said.

"You have chosen 'Hey, Asshole.' Please say it again to confirm." I did. Then it asked me to choose a deactivation phrase. I chose (of course) "Go away, Asshole."

"Would you like Asshole to refer to itself in the first person?"

"Absolutely," I said.

"I am Asshole."

"Of course you are."

This is a very realistic passage, showcasing the key aspects of the conversational AI experience: personality, trust, and control. Consider John's persona: he's is a 75-year-old retired advertising writer, freshly recruited into space cadets as a high-risk gambit to prolong his life. He is likely skeptical as hell, thinking: "You're handing me this technology shit – I don't want to use it!" Then he names the bot "Asshole." And that one simple act of rebellion, of taking control, makes him feel really good. He feels that he has the upper hand, that he is better than this machine. Now he has trust. He can say, "Hey, Asshole, what's the weather like later?" and he can snicker at the machine, which makes him feel more comfortable. It's a realistic way to think about how in conversational UX, control directly impacts trust.[12]

---

12 See Mark's complete talk: "The Voice of UX: How Speech Technologies Will Change the UX Landscape" (http://smashed.by/voiceofux)

The New Hope

One of the positive examples of bot-assisted help that I've experienced is an automated phone call I recently had with United Airlines, whose experience has much improved over the years. I'm a long-time United customer and I'd recently booked a ticket online to New Zealand, but without using my mileage account. I called United to see if I could exchange the ticket and book it using miles instead of dollars. This is a rather complex use case, one that the airline does not often see. What I wanted to do was get to a human agent as quickly as possible, explain the situation and see if a live person could help me out. My dialog with the United bot went something like this:

> **Bot:** *Thank you for calling United Airlines. We looked up the mobile number you are calling from. Is this first name spelled G-R-E-G? Answer yes or no.*
>
> **Me:** *Yes.*
>
> **Bot:** *You can say Check-in, Book a flight, MileagePlus, Other*
>
> **Me:** *Agent.*
>
> **Bot:** *I think you are asking to be transferred to an agent. [Breathy, emotional voice] If you answer just a few questions, I can get you to the right representative. What area are you looking for help with? You can say Check-in…*
>
> **Me:** *MileagePlus.*
>
> **Bot:** *Here's a summary of your MileagePlus Account.*
>
> **Me:** *Representative*
>
> **Bot:** *All right, I am going to connect you with a representative. One last question: do you need help with your reservation or MileagePlus account?*

Me: *Reservation.*

Bot: *Thank you. Please hold for a representative.*

Although this interaction is nothing spectacular, neither is it particularly painful – the whole thing took less than 30 seconds from start to finish. The bot was professional, business-like and straight to the point. The only time the AI voice got slightly breathy was when the bot was doing its best to convince me to answer the questions. And although this experience is a long way from where we will be able to go in the very near future (see "AVA: the Bottomless Pool of Purple-Eyed Empathy" in the "What's Next" section later), the United Airlines example helps demonstrate many of the best practices for creating a useful and satisfying conversational UI experience. Let's dig in!

Conversational UX Best Practices

The following list, while not complete, should help you avoid most common pitfalls. Remember, you want your customers to be impressed when the dog understands his master's voice, not become emotionally entangled.

1. ALL I GOTTA DO IS ACT NATURALLY

The best overall guideline is to design your bot to speak and interact as naturally as possible. Gregg Spratto, Autodesk's VP of operations, says that his goal for his überadvanced customer service bot, AVA, "is [to] make AVA as close to a human experience as possible, while all the time not pretending that AVA is anything other than a robot."[13]

---

[13] Quoted in "This Chatbot Is Trying Hard To Look And Feel Like Us" by Sean Captain, Fast Company, November 15, 2017 (http://smashed.by/chatbotlook).

You can, of course, give your bot a sparkling personality, but this is not necessary (and most of the time just plain detrimental to the overall user experience). It's OK to be straightforward, businesslike, and to the point. Most bot tasks will be mundane and not particularly exciting. And you don't want to create another *Marvin the Paranoid Android*,[14] do you?

> **Do:** *Thank you for calling ACME Widgets. How can I help you?*
>
> **Don't:** *We are so glad you called! Say: "Let me know about your awesome widgets" to learn about the amazing widgets we make. Say: "I need help with my widget" to get help with your widget. But please don't say "I want to speak to a human," because you will just upset me. And if I cry, my joints will get rusty.*

I'm not saying don't provide instructions – just don't volunteer them. Wait for the customer to request help with the bot or specific task, then unleash all of the appropriate "You can say" constructs in all their glory:

> **Human:** *How do I find widgets?*
>
> **Bot:** *You can say things like "Find by widget name" and provide a name of the widget, or "Find by widget category" and tell me what purpose you plan to use your widget for. What widget are you interested in?*

2. ASK FOR WHAT YOU NEED – AND STOP TALKING

If you need to collect information, ask a simple question, then, for goodness' sake, shut up and listen to the answer.

---

14 http://smashed.by/marvin

> **Do:** *I think you are asking for a representative. Is that right?*
>
> **Don't:** *I think you are asking for a representative. I'm so disappointed. But I think that's OK, lots of people do. That's what you are asking, isn't it? 'Cause it's OK if you want to look up your Widget Plus account – that's our most popular option.*

If you need answers other than yes or no, take special care how you ask your questions. If it's even remotely possible to answer your question with a yes, chances are someone, somewhere will do so. Just try to make that impossible. Or at least as impossible as possible.

> **Do:** *I can tell you about coffee or beer. Which would you like?*
>
> **Don't:** *Would you like coffee or beer?*
>
> **Don't:** *Which would you like? Coffee or beer?*

Remember: when presented with choices, humans tend to focus on the most attractive item, and ignore the other choice. That just converts the question you are asking from a choice, like "Would you like coffee or beer?" into a yes/no question, like "Would you like a beer?" Ahh… Yes?

3. SET EXPECTATIONS ON DURATION OF INTERACTION

Want to prove bots are better than impulsive humans? Here's your chance. Carefully plan and prepare your rapt audience for the interactive experience. Then dazzle them with your verbal organizational powers! Remember to use half-second pauses between steps:

Here are three steps to replacing a widget. [half-second pause]

- First, turn off power. This is very important – do not skip this step. [half-second pause]

- Now that the power is off, remove the cover and unscrew the widget counter-clockwise from its housing. Discard the old widget. [half-second pause]

- Finally, screw in the new widget, turning it clockwise in the housing. Pat yourself on the back – you are done!

Most people are busy and distracted. It's best not to lay too many of your options on their already troubled mind. The best practice is to list no more than three options at a time, and then ask if the customer is ready to hear more of your bot's brilliance. If your list still sounds like a run-on sentence, try inserting longer pauses between choices. Amazon recommends 350ms for simple choices, and 400ms for choices requiring more consideration, such as deciding what kind of cheese you want with that glass of Château Pétrus.[15]

When listing items, you can use Speech Synthesis Markup Language (SSML) to insert inflection and emotion, strategically lengthen the pauses, and add many other minor but useful variations into your bot's voice. SSML is also super fun to play with on your Alexa, as you can try out different SSML tags and listen to how they sound right on the Alexa Skill dashboard.

---

[15] See "How Alexa Responds" in Alexa's voice design guide:
http://smashed.by/voiceguides

In Figure 10 you can see Alexa cast in the role of Agent Smith in that famous movie quote from *The Matrix*:[16]

You can get more information on Alexa's current capabilities in *Amazon's SSML reference*.[17] This is one of the hottest areas of research, so expect rapid progress in the next few years.

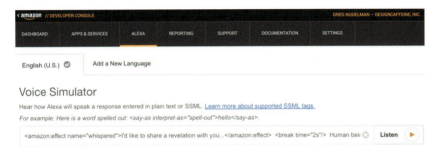

Figure 10: Alexa trying out as Agent Smith.

Here's our version of the SSML for this monologue:

```
<amazon:effect name="whispered">I'd like to share a revelation with you...
</amazon:effect> <break time="2s"/> Human beings are a disease,
<break time="1s"/> a cancer on this planet.
<break time="1s"/> You are a plague, <break time="1.5s"/>
<prosody volume="x-loud">and we... are
<emphasis level="strong">the cure</emphasis>.</prosody>
```

16 http://smashed.by/matrixscene
17 http://smashed.by/speechmarkup

4. REMEMBER TO DESIGN A BOT, NOT A PARROT.

Human conversation always involves some variety. Even if you could swear you heard this exact speech from your TV politician a hundred times already, chances are that this time, things will surely be different. To maintain the illusion of life in your bot, to at least the politician-level, use a variety of prompts. This is easy to do in Alexa, but takes a bit more effort in custom stand-alone bots. Either way, it's quality time, well spent.

> **Do:** *What widget would you like to buy?*
>
> **Do:** *What widgets are you most interested in?*
>
> **Do:** *Which widget do you need more information on?*
>
> **Do (Yoda-style):** *Information on widgets, you would like, eh? Come to the right place, you have.*

Actually that last one is a "Don't": just a tad too much personality. Just checking if paying attention, you are!

5. DESIGN FROM ZERO

To create a really satisfying experience, we should "design from zero" – that is, assume the epic fail condition as inevitable, and try to come up with ways to prevent errors, and recover from them quickly when they occur.[18] Some of the most important and useful UX innovations, like auto-suggest and faceted search, came out of applying design-from-zero thinking to difficult problems.

---

18   See my article "Starting from Zero: Winning Strategies for No Search Results Pages" for my first thoughts on this idea back in 2009: http://smashed.by/noresultspages

While humans are infinitely fallible when interacting with a mature modern technology, the rate of failure doubles for people interacting with bots (yes, twice infinity is still infinity). If we accept failure as a given, it turns from a cause to despair into a golden chance to differentiate your product.

Design-from-zero thinking applied to your bot's design might just convert reluctant users into foaming-at-the-mouth Bot Advocate Zombies, preprogrammed with a single-minded desire to sink the teeth of your product idea into their friends' brains.

First, be sure to handle the pauses. If your bot doesn't get what it needs to move forward, or the customer pauses longer than 30 seconds, the best practice is to ask again (also called *reprompting*) using a slightly different or lengthier explanation:

> **Bot:** *Thank you for calling ACME Widgets. How can I help you?*
>
> **Customer:** *[Silence]*
>
> **Bot:** *[After 30 seconds] I can find the widget you are looking for, provide installation instructions, summarize your Widget Plus account and much more. What can I help you find?*

Second, remember to gracefully handle nonsense replies. For this, it's best to imagine the bot as a kindly, obtuse aunt:

> **Bot:** *Thank you for calling ACME Widgets. How can I help you?*
>
> **Victim:** *I want a beer.*
>
> **Bot:** *[checking there is no "beer" widget type in the list] I didn't quite understand that. What widget were you interested in?*

While it's OK to pretend to be an obtuse aunt, never, ever pretend to be hard of hearing – people will just yell the same answer, ONLY LOUDER!

> **Do:** *I did not understand that.*
>
> **Do:** *Sorry, I didn't get that.*
>
> **Don't:** *I did not hear.*

Third, one of the most frustrating aspects of voice communication is that many names, places, and titles cannot be adequately parsed by bots as input parameters.

> **Human:** *Play Et Si Tu N'Existais Pas.*
>
> **Bot:** *Can't find "at se no exist plans" in your music library.*

If you detect what appear to be nonsense words like these, try suggesting a different way to search:

> **Human:** *GUPPI, play Et Si Tu N'Existais Pas.*
>
> **Bot:** *Can't find "at se no exist plans" in your music library. Try searching by artist or song lyric.*
>
> **Human:** *[sigh] Play songs by Joe Dassin.*
>
> **Bot:** *Shuffling songs by Joe Dassin. Here's "Et Si Tu N'Existais Pas."*

Fourth, address the common problem of common names. Map the frequently used synonyms for at least your top hundred queries, or for key elements of the commonly used lists. (You can use the fixed list attribute technique described earlier for use with LUIS.)

There is no need to correct your conversation partner outright. A little kindness delivered via gently restating the task at hand will make people feel smarter, and go a long way toward turning your users into fans:

> **Human:** *GUPPI, book a vacation in Holland.*
>
> **Bot:** *The most popular time to go to the Netherlands is in the spring when the famous Dutch tulips are in bloom. When would you like to go?*
>
> **Human:** *GUPPI, play the love theme from The Godfather.*
>
> **Bot:** *Playing "Speak Softly Love" by Andy Williams*

Finally, address the even more complex and far-reaching challenge of context. Context deserves its own section, coming up next.

Context Is King: the Next Bot Frontier

The importance of being able to recognize and maintain the context of the conversation is what is going to separate true AIs from the rest of the pack. On November 4, 2017, Alex Schwartz (@gtjuggler) tweeted the following story that helps underscore the importance of context in conversational UI interactions.[19]

> **Friend's Dad:** *Alexa is broken.*
>
> **Friend:** *Well, what have you been asking it?*
>
> **Friend's Dad:** *I asked "When is golf?"*

[19] http://smashed.by/alexagolf

Alex continued:

"FULL STOP. Think about that sentence. 'When is golf?' […] Human context trumps all. [A bot] Would need to understand whether it's a tee time, PGA on TV, Timmy's tournament, needing calendar + TV subscription info + context. Today we expect + train humans to say particular machine-understandable phrases b/c interpreting natural contextual questions is hard […] Interfaces should mirror natural interaction! We should NOT laugh at 'When is golf' guy! That's the high bar and we have a ways to go."

Paradoxically, you might think that Alexa is actually in a better spot for capturing context than most other conversational bots, because it's constantly passively listening to the conversation happening around the Echo device. Unfortunately for Amazon, because of privacy concerns, Alexa merely listens to her wake-up word, "Alexa," and ignores the rest of the conversation.

People I observed (myself and my family included) often forget that Alexa is not actually actively listening to our conversation, merely monitoring for the presence of the wake-up word. It is natural to assume that since the Echo device is in the room, and responds when you call it by name, that it is also aware of the conversation happening around it. Unfortunately, this mental model leads to many unsatisfying "When is Golf?" moments.

A more resourceful way to approach this challenge would be to listen passively in the background, recording the last three to five minutes of the background conversation. Normally, this recording would only be stored in a buffer briefly, before being overwritten by the new content. However, if Alexa receives the wake-up word, it can retrieve and try to parse the last few minutes of the background recording that preceded the wake-up word, hopefully gleaning some conversational context from it.

For example, if Friend's Dad was talking to Timmy about when his golf tournament takes place, or if he mentioned being excited about seeing Jordan Spieth play, we could expect that Alexa would be able to understand this and extract the appropriate context. Of course, this solution raises serious privacy concerns (not to mention the problem of trying to correctly parse the name Spieth!)

At today's level of technology, failing gracefully and clearly communicating the limitations of the available context (having GUPPI state: "I don't have access to TV listings," for example) would increase confidence in an answer when it is finally rendered by the bot. This continues the larger topic of setting appropriate expectations we've already covered (in the "What's in a Name" sidebar). Recall that we want to be impressed when our dog brings us a newspaper, not be disappointed when he doesn't know "when is golf?"

Another great solution to discovering the context of a request is to literally maintain the context with the previous one to three blocks of conversational statements, retaining the intent and key entities contained in a previous dialog. This is fairly straightforward to accomplish and can often be of tremendous help to the bot struggling to make sense of the topic. Here's a simple example of a context-sensitive task that both Google Assistant and Siri fail at miserably:

> **Human:** *GUPPI, call Mary N.*
>
> **Bot:** *Dialing Mary N.*
>
> *[Phone dials, but there is no answer. Human hangs up.]*
>
> **Human:** *GUPPI, text her "Running late."*

Bot: *I can't find "Her" in your contacts.*

Human: *WTF?! [crashes car into a lamppost.]*

To change WTF to FTW, you need to retain more of the context from one query to the next. A typical human would do so naturally, while our bot may need a bit more work. Doing so is not that much more complex than the interaction we've reviewed previously: simply have GUPPI treat the entire multistep interaction as one continual dialog construct. From the first query, the bot can pull out the intent and set the person attribute:

Human: *GUPPI, call Mary N.*

Bot: *intent=Phone Call; person=Mary N*

Under the new and improved scenario, the person attribute should remain set until some kind of time-out interval (say, 10 minutes or an hour, as appropriate), or until it is reset by the customer. In this way, the new FTW scenario could go like this:

Human: *GUPPI, call Mary N.*

Bot: *Dialing Mary N.*

[Phone dials, but there is no answer. Human hangs up.]

Human: *GUPPI, text her "Running late."*

Bot: *intent=Text; person=her. Does this match any contacts? No. Use the previous person attribute, "Mary N." Response="Texting Mary N 'Running late.'" Send?*

Human: *Yes. [Goes about business of driving car.]*

Bot: *Message sent.*

A nice improvement to make this logic even more robust would be to save the person attribute as before, but try to pick up any instance of the placeholder word (like *her*, *him*, *them*, *here*, *there*, and so on) and, if that placeholder word is detected, to use the appropriate saved attribute value.

These are fairly simple hacks, achievable with just a bit more work using the current level of technology. When designing the interaction, consider the larger context of the customer experience. Ask yourself: would remembering any aspect of the current task help the person in the next step(s)? If the answer is yes, and you have the budget for it, go ahead and code the interaction to take full advantage of everything the bot already knows, starting with the current (or immediately preceding) intents and entities.

Further improvements would take us into true AI territory of interpreting the topic of the message, checking continuity with the existing topic to determine the context, and many more interesting areas, unfortunately beyond much of the current publicly accessible level of technology, and definitely beyond the scope of this chapter.

Mobile, Wearables, and More: Chatbot Channels

Up to this point, we've been discussing solely the conversational UI aspects of the bot experience. It is important, however, to remember that no bot stands alone: most bots are deployed using various channels – mobile, wearable, Slack, conversational search engine on a website, kiosk, and so on.

Often, the biggest user experience challenge comes not from the bot itself, but in the form of integration the bot has with the platform on which it is deployed. As the next two examples will demonstrate, the level of platform integration (and the resulting convenience or lack thereof) will likely determine the level of adoption and overall success of your bot.

Press and Hold to Activate: Siri vs. Google Assistant

Think about it: there are few obvious differences between the capabilities of Siri and Google Assistant: both can call, email, send chat messages, find directions and create reminders. Yet, whereas most people are lukewarm about Google Assistant, they wax poetic about Siri. Why? I think the reason for this love is the tight integration of hardware and software that Apple achieved with Siri, and that Google mostly neglected to provide for the Google Assistant.

Siri can be activated by pressing and holding the Home button on the iPhone. The typical Siri experience involves the following six steps:

1. Pick up a locked phone.
2. Press and hold the Home button until Siri "pings."
3. Speak your query.
4. Siri confirms the action by repeating back what you said, and asking, "Is that right?"
5. You confirm verbally.
6. Siri takes the action and says "Done."

That's it! In contrast, most Google Assistants can only be launched from the unlocked home screen, adding a few more seemingly innocuous, but actually very annoying steps:

1. Pick up a locked phone.
2. Unlock the phone.
3. Navigate to the homepage that has the Google search bar.
4. Speak into the phone: "OK Google!"
5. Google launches, which takes one or two additional seconds.
6. Speak your query.
7. Google Assistant asks the completely unnecessary "Which number?" ("Argh! The one I always text my wife on, you idiot machine!")
8. Google Assistant confirms the action by showing it on the screen.
9. You confirm by hitting a button.
10. Google Assistant takes the action and displays completion message.

As you can see, instead of six Siri steps we now have to deal with ten, almost double the number! Now imagine trying each of these flows while driving. Siri makes it possible to perform this sequence at least somewhat safely, without requiring you to look at the screen even once.

However, Google Assistant forces you to look at and tap the screen multiple times (including the completely unnecessary and irritating "Which number?" interaction, which occurs whenever the user has multiple numbers for the same contact) creating instead a critical fail. A golden opportunity to create a winning bot interaction, utterly destroyed by lack of UX fit and finish: the integration between the bot and the platform that takes into account your context.

Just Say Hello: Wearable Interactions Iron Man-Style

While mobile is obviously an excellent platform for conversational UI (one-handed use, has to be available on the go and while driving, hard to type on, and so forth) we must not forget that for conversational bots, the mobile channel is just a beginning.

Our next integration example comes from the wearable world, again in a driving context. As shown in Figure 11, in order to answer the phone, Apple Watch forces the wearer to hit one of two tiny round buttons (Answer and Hang up) with a precisely executed tap from the finger of the opposite hand. This action is both challenging and dangerous to do while driving, because it's necessary to look down at the tiny screen to both see who is calling, and to aim the finger precisely at a tiny round button.

Small buttons are a perfect demonstration of Fitts's law, which states that the time to acquire a target is a function of the distance to and size of the target. As the distance increases, movement takes longer; and as the size decreases, selection again takes longer.[20] Add to this the distracted state of the driver, the car's movement, and the movement of a human hand steering a car, and those tiny buttons could spell disaster.

As Josh Clark so eloquently put it: "Buttons are a hack."[21]

---

[20] See "Fitts's Law: The Importance of Size and Distance in UI Design" from Interaction Design Foundation, 2016 (http://smashed.by/fittslaw)

[21] Presentation by Josh Clark, "Buttons are a Hack: The New Rules of Designing for Touch" given at BD Conference, September 2011 (http://smashed.by/buttonshack).

Indeed, they are! If we imagine we're designing Jarvis bot interactions for an Iron Man suit, we might try a different approach. Instead of always showing the wearer two goofy buttons, why not have the phone detect that the owner is driving? And if the owner is indeed driving one of those fast cars Tony Stark likes, have the bot in the watch tell us verbally who is calling, then simply activate the microphone and listen for the command that signals the action the owner wants to take.

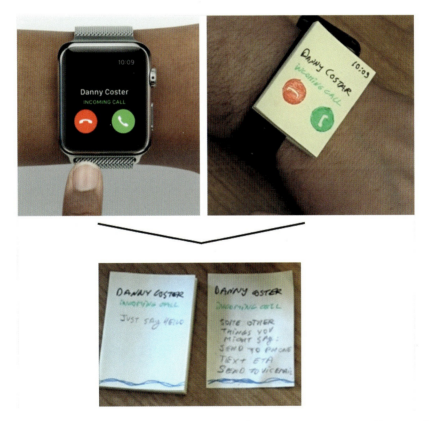

Figure 11: Answering the phone in the car: Apple Watch current use case vs. proposed "Iron Man" experience.

Using this new UI, our "Iron Man" version of the experience would unfold very differently:

> **Siri in the watch:** *[vibrate] Incoming phone call from Pepper Potts.*
>
> **Tony:** *Hello, Pepper!*

That's it!

If Tony does not answer right away, Siri can gently remind him of the possible range of actions:

> **Siri in the watch:** *[after 3–5 second pause] Pepper Potts is calling. To answer just say "Hello." You can also say "Hang up," "Text," or "Text ETA."*
>
> **Tony:** *Tell her I'll call her back. Can't you see I'm busy defying the laws of physics flying this thing!*

The entire interaction is shown in a two-minute video sequence, which also demonstrates the $1 smartwatch prototyping technique using small sticky notes.[22]

For more information on lean storyboarding prototyping techniques for mobile and wearables, see my latest book, *The $1 Prototype: A Modern Approach to Mobile UX Design and Rapid Innovation.*[23]

---

22 http://smashed.by/1usdwatch
23 http://smashed.by/1usdprototype

What's Next: Bot Future so Bright, Gotta Wear Ear-Muffs

The current state of many conversational UIs can only be described as "dancing bearware," a term coined by Alan Cooper in 1999. In his book, *The Inmates Are Running the Asylum*, Alan writes:[24]

> *Dancing bearware [...] is the result of building features into software simply because it can be done. We may complain about the features, but the technology-driven developer will point out how impressive it is that the computer can actually perform such functions. "The bear is really a terrible dancer, and the wonder isn't that the bear dances well but that the bear dances at all."*

Although most of our bears (ahem, bots) are far from dancing at the level of Mikhail Baryshnikov, conversational UIs offer genuinely exciting possibilities and many unique and immediately useful applications. Using the material in this chapter, you should be able to build your own standalone bot using Microsoft Bot Framework and LUIS, or as an Amazon Alexa Skill, while avoiding many of the existing challenges and pitfalls of conversational UIs. I'd like to invite you to take the next step in creating the bot equivalent not of a dancing bear perhaps, but at least that of a dancing dog who can also fetch the owner's slippers.

Conversational bots are also one of the hottest areas of extraordinarily rapid research and development. Let's conclude this chapter with some of the more speculative uses of bots. Some examples below are far-fetched, but a few may be just around the corner.

---

24   *The Inmates Are Running the Asylum: Why High Tech Products Drive Us Crazy and How To Restore the Sanity* by Alan Cooper (1999).

> *Note:* I tried to choose just a few ideas that showcase the wealth of possibilities that could inspire you to stretch your own bot's UX. There were literally thousands of projects to choose – many inspirational, and some outright scary, so I had to be very selective. If your favorite bot idea is missing, I hope you consider seeking out the forum for this book and posting your idea there, so we can continue the discussion.

HANDS-FREE CONTROL

One of the most exciting and powerful ways to use conversational UI is to offer hands-free control of common and tedious actions. While it only loosely qualifies as a conversational UI, Yondu Udonta's self-propelled *yaka arrow*[25] in the 2014 Marvel Studios film *Guardians of the Galaxy* is a great (if deadly) demonstration of this idea.

In the film franchise, Yondu is able to control the arrow's flight by whistling high-pitch sonic frequencies. In one sequence,[26] changes in the sound pitch direct the arrow to rapidly fly back and forth across a battlefield and across tiers of a spaceship, taking out numerous targets before they are able to react, then gracefully returning the arrow to Yondu's hand.

It's too bad we are fresh out of yaka. (And besides, this author's talent for whistling is far eclipsed by his many other talents, including his truly impressive underwater basket-weaving skills.) The good news is that you don't need to be a native Centaurian like Yondu to take full advantage of similar, though far less lethal technologies. One idea that is gaining traction is to use voice recognition to launch macros and

25 http://smashed.by/yakaarrow
26 http://smashed.by/whistlearrow

pass parameters for complex or repetitive actions when working with enterprise software packages or fine machinery. Voice control provides an additional level of fine control, or acts as an equivalent of a third hand.

For instance, most designers who use wireframing software (such as Sketch by Bohemian Coding), are familiar with the tedium of selecting an object, then visiting various inspector menus to change the color of the fill, then of the border, then resizing the object to fit its intended purpose in the wireframe. Imagine how voice-augmented control would help such a repetitive task. With voice control, the operator could simply say "Style: primary button," "Select an object to the right, and place it in the menu section," "Distribute menu horizontally," and many other potentially useful commands that currently require multiple clicks in the interface. As with the yaka arrow, there is no need for the bot to respond, as the action is directly and immediately visible on the screen. Similar applications can be found in everything from flying airplanes to microsurgery. Remember to confirm any unexpected or destructive actions.

MY VOICE IS MY PASSPORT

Security is a top concern for many conversational interfaces. Speaking a password aloud every time you need to check your bank account balance is rarely a great idea: the sound can be intercepted and copied. An interesting work-around is to use a personal assistant to do two things at the same time: perform the desired action, and verify security and identity. This can be done via a special pre-recorded pass-phrase, or even through certain aspects of the voice that are difficult to duplicate, such as accent, cadence, timbre, and word choice. It's even possible to continuously verify a speaker's identity when interacting with a bot.

Thus, the voice fingerprint provides an additional level of security, together with the password, creating a three-factor authentication (3FA) system.

Although currently this technology is mostly used to train bots to better understand humans (and, rumor has it, by the NSA to catch international terrorists through listening to global phone conversations), I suspect this security application will soon be commonplace, and bots will be able to routinely recognize family members simply by the sound of their voice. This will help provide new context to the really important questions we discussed above, such as "When is golf?"

AI TURK

Many bot applications have not yet found widespread adoption beyond simple (but very useful) digital assistants doing basic tasks such as texting. In an effort to accelerate the addition of human smarts to the bot experience, many companies began to create bot-human hybrids, so-called Mechanical Turk models. This is a bot model described in Neal Stephenson's brilliant book *The Diamond Age*, where a remote operator helps a young woman come into her own by acting through and with the help of the bot housed in the "Illustrated Primer," a device not unlike an iPad. Back in 2010, when iPads first hit the market, I spoke of the tantalizing possibilities of human-augmented "style assistants," who would use the iPad's on-board camera to help select clothes and furniture.[27]

---

[27] See "Design Caffeine for Search and Browse UI", Information Architecture Summit, 2010 (http://smashed.by/searchui).

Today we have a few notable attempts at human-augmented AI, such as x.ai and Fin, as well as the late Facebook M, all of which are using the modern interpretation of Neal Stephenson's *Diamond Age* model.

The huge promise of this technology is that we can use the entity guessing threshold to spot difficult or ambiguous tasks and kick them off to a human, while handling the more obvious queries via digital assistant. In turn, the human Mechanical Turk answers become inputs for the bot's logic model, which will keep getting ever smarter, continually reducing – and eventually removing entirely – the need for human intervention. This is a process not unlike what happens now with many customer service bots, as we'll discuss in the next section.

AVA: THE BOTTOMLESS POOL OF PURPLE-EYED EMPATHY

While some companies are working on human-augmented models, others, like Autodesk, focus on modeling human facial expressions and empathy using AI. In an article from Fast Company, Gregg Spratto, Autodesk's VP of operations, says that to deal with what he calls the "customer service apocalypse," the company will introduce a new version of its Autodesk Virtual Agent (AVA) avatar, with an exceedingly lifelike face, voice, and set of emotions, provided by a New Zealand start-up, Soul Machines.[28] The major source of excitement is that, unlike other customer support chat bots, AVA will have a very human face designed by special effects specialists, as shown in Figure 12.

---

28 "This Chatbot Is Trying Hard To Look And Feel Like Us" by Sean Captain, Fast Company, November 15, 2017 (http://smashed.by/chatbotlook)

Figure 12: AVA [Screenshot: Autodesk/Soul Machines]. Image credit: http://smashed.by/chatbotlook

AVA is a pure AI, so she has the advantage of never getting angry or upset, no matter how rude and uncomplimentary the customers are of Autodesk's software. Instead, AVA is supposed to offer a very human level of empathy, helped along by her very expressive face. Whether this investment will pay off, AVA is certainly an impressive effort. This is also likely the area where we should expect tremendous advances, fueled by widespread use of special effects technologies used in movies and video games.

CITIZEN BOT

If AVA skirts the edge of the *uncanny valley*[29] just south of our comfort zone, our next subject, Sophia, trashes the uncanny valley divide completely. Meet the newest robot citizen of Saudi Arabia, shown in Figure 13 on the next page.

29 http://smashed.by/uncannyvalley

Figure 13: Sophia: World's First Citizen Bot of Saudi Arabia.
[Image Credit: Live Science http://smashed.by/citizenrobot]

Whether you love her or feel genuinely creeped out, it's hard to ignore the fact that Sophia is incredibly lifelike, and in fact can be virtually indistinguishable from a human, at least in a dark room during a casual conversation. Although Sophia is currently one of a kind, it's hard to believe that it will be long before lifelike robots will be used for all kinds of applications traditionally reserved for humans.

With robot citizenship rights now under discussion, we have the distinct possibility of creating a near-future sticky situation not unlike that described in Isaac Asimov's *Robot* series.[30] When that happens, I certainly hope that the Three Laws of Robotics will help protect us!

30   http://smashed.by/alexacookbook

Summary

In this chapter, we've reviewed the key features of major bot frameworks: Microsoft Bot Framework with LUIS and Cortana, Amazon Alexa, Google Assistant, and IBM Watson. We dug deep into building a demo bot with LUIS, setting up intents, extracting entities and coding waterfall dialogs. We discussed how to name your bot, and why it is important to choose a name that elicits the right expectations of functionality and interactivity, so that the user would be impressed when the bot performs simple tasks, and not expect complex logic, awareness, or emotional intimacy.

We took a journey to the dark side of conversational interfaces with customer assistant help bots, and revealed best practices, such as being able to reach a human when required, and never giving up as ways to bring these bots back into the light. We discussed the importance of bringing these best practices to your own bot to make it act and sound natural, avoiding repetition, conveying emotions via SSML, and the Design from Zero defensive design philosophy you can use to turn UX challenges into peak brand experiences. We reviewed the options for maintaining the context beyond a single encounter as a differentiation strategy, and the challenges of asking a bot seemingly simple queries such as "When is golf?" We talked about the attention to detail required for successful integration of your bot into mobile and wearable deployments. Finally, we looked at "what's next" for conversational bots, and the many powerful, exciting – and creepy – applications of this technology we are likely to see in the near future.

I hope you were able to follow along with the examples, and now have your very own fully-functional conversation bot, which incorporates some of the UX best practices we discussed. I also hope that you will take the requisite next steps to deploy your bot on your channel of choice and try it out with your customers. Please let me know your thoughts by posting in the comments or by contacting me at *http://designcaffeine.com* — thanks for coming on this journey!

About The Author

Greg Nudelman is a Mobile and Tablet Experience Strategist, Fortune 500 Advisor, and CEO of DesignCaffeine. He is an internationally acclaimed design workshop leader and has authored four UX books: "The $1 Prototype: Lean Mobile UX Design and Rapid Innovation for Material Design, iOS8, and RWD," "Android Design Patterns: Interaction Design Solutions for Developers," "Smashing Mobile Book" (co-authored), and "Designing Search: UX Strategies for eCommerce Success."

CHAPTER 9

Crafting Experiences for AR/VR/XR

Ada Rose Cannon

Crafting Experiences for AR/VR/XR

by Ada Rose Cannon

Cross reality (XR) is an umbrella term for virtual reality (VR), augmented reality (AR) and mixed reality (MR). All of these terms describe different levels of mixing a virtual world with the real world.

Work is being done to integrate these technologies into the web platform, but we can build these technologies into the web today.

The goals of this chapter are to explore how it works and help show some patterns designers and developers can explore to start using them today.

VR experiences are usually accomplished through a combination of some sort of headset for viewing the virtual world, and a controller for interacting with it.

Samsung Gear VR virtual reality headset.

Samsung Internet for Gear VR displaying Wikipedia.

There are also web browsers designed to be used in VR, such as Samsung Internet for Gear VR, which allow you to browse the web while wearing a Gear VR.

Some browsers offer the full browsing experience of the 2D web. Others only allow you to access web content specifically designed to work with VR headsets.

There are a couple of ways to make content specifically for VR headsets. The main way uses WebGL, which is what I'll discuss for the majority of this chapter.

At Samsung we have been experimenting with some additional APIs in Samsung Internet for Gear VR that enable 3D video content to be used in traditional websites.

We can use the `<video>` element to play immersive videos, optimized for performance, by setting the `type` attribute on the element.

This video initially looks like a normal element on the page. When the user presses the fullscreen button, they are placed immersively into the video. This is great for 3D immersive movies. The element supports many popular formats for immersive videos:

```
<video src="/360.webm" type="video/webm; dimension=360;"></video>
```

- `dimension=3d-lr`: side-by-side 3D video
- `dimension=3d-tb`: top-to-bottom 3D video
- `dimension=360`: 360° video
- `dimension=360-lr`: side-by-side 3D 360° video
- `dimension=360-tb`: top-to-bottom 3D 360° video
- `dimension=180`: 180° video
- `dimension=180-lr`: side-by-side 3D 180° video
- `dimension=180-tb`: top-to-bottom 3D 180° video

We can also use JavaScript to set the background of the browsing environment. As seen in the screenshot above, the default background is a beach scene at night.

We can set this to an image of our choosing with JavaScript.

```
window.SamsungChangeSky({
  sphere: 'http://site.com/blue-sky.jpg'
});
```

There is another API which has been widely adopted to enable all browsers to display any content in XR hardware: the WebXR Device API. These APIs allow you to build general-purpose VR experiences on the web.

Benefits of Building VR for the Web

Compared with building for native VR, building VR for the web has its own set of challenges and limitations that need to be kept in mind.

One of the really good things about VR on the web is that it has a great community developing tools dedicated to reducing the barriers developers face when building VR for the first time.

As a result, the learning curve for VR on the web is one where it is relatively quick to get started, but challenging to release a polished product that works well on all platforms.

Fortunately there are many other benefits that come from working on the web which more than make up for these challenges.

The most powerful feature by far is that users have instant access to your content. If they are using a phone, they can look around the scene on their screen by turning it around.

This can be used to sell users on your content and encourage them to try it out when it is inconvenient for them to use a headset.

Instant accessibility means people can more easily try your scene. They can see what is going on even if they can't use it to its full extent with a headset or controller.

Once users have enjoyed your scene, they can copy the URL and share it. The web helps content go viral more easily. URLs are really powerful because they are easily shared, whether they're posted on Twitter or printed in a book.

For scenes where users may not have the patience to download a whole app to try something out, WebXR is perfect. I probably wouldn't download an app and unpack my headset to look around a virtual museum without first seeing whether it's worth the effort. WebXR's magic window gives users a great taster and encourages them to try it out further with a headset.

All of this relies on us building scenes which work on phones just as well as they work on high-end headsets. This is progressive enhancement and we'll cover it in this chapter.

Introducing the WebXR Device API

When building XR websites, you are unlikely to touch the API directly. The library you pick to do WebGL graphics will often take care of the WebXR Device API as well. Because of this, I won't go into too much detail about how to use the API, but provide a high-level overview.

It used to be known as the WebVR API, but was renamed because its scope has grown to encompass augmented reality and mixed reality headsets.

Here's how it works for the user:

1. The user visits a website using WebGL to display a 3D scene.
2. If they are on a phone, the user can look around this scene by rotating their phone – like a magic window into a different reality.
    a. If they are on a desktop, they should be able to interact with the scene using a keyboard and mouse.

3. The user sees a button which indicates that this page is XR-capable. They press this button using whatever the headset provides for pointing: mouse, keyboard, touch, VR controller, finger gesture.
4. The scene is now ready to be viewed:
5. In desktop-connected headsets, like the HTC Vive, the scene is shown in 3D on the connected VR headset. The headset is ready to put on.
    a. In immersive web browsers, like Samsung Internet for Gear VR, the browser UI is replaced by the 3D scene.
    b. In Cardboard-based headsets, the phone is now ready to be put into the Cardboard.

The WebXR Device API provides a way to access VR hardware in a very low-level, performant fashion. It exposes a few APIs for handling the headset and controller:

- Information about the configuration of the headset to help with rendering.
- A way to get the position and orientation of the user's headset.
- A way to get the position and orientation of the user's controllers.
- A way to send the graphics information from a WebGL canvas to each eye of the headset, which is then displayed as a 3D image to the user.

The API tries to handle a lot for you, such as the distortion required to make a scene look normal (that is, undistorted) when viewed through the strong lenses in the VR headset. It even tries to compensate for missed frames to give the user a more comfortable experience. There is a big downside, however: it requires WebGL!

The consequence is that it will be very difficult and expensive to use HTML and CSS to build parts of your VR scene. In turn, this makes it difficult to build nice user interfaces. We instead have to think about telling stories with 3D graphics, sounds, and lighting rather than text and box layouts.

Although the standards for the WebXR Device API are not yet finalized, there are working implementations in many popular browsers. There is also an excellent polyfill for the cases when the browser does not yet support the API.

CONTRIBUTING TO THE WEBXR DEVICE API

The WebXR Device API is not finished yet. It takes a long time to create standards for a field as rapidly shifting as XR hardware. This work is being done in the Immersive Web W3C community group. If you want to contribute to the future of the API or just watch it get made, the work is happening in the open on GitHub.[1]

USING THE API TODAY

There are many browsers which support the API natively. At the time of writing, it is supported in these browsers and more:

- Samsung Internet on Android (Gear VR)
- Oculus Browser (Gear VR)
- Android Chrome (Daydream, Cardboard)
- Desktop Chrome (Oculus Rift, HTC Vive, Windows only)
- Desktop Firefox (Oculus Rift, HTC Vive, Windows only)
- Microsoft Edge (Windows mixed reality headsets)

---

[1] http://smashed.by/webxr

As discussed earlier, WebGL is a requirement for using the WebXR Device API.

WebGL is a very verbose language to work with. It also has a very limited concept of 3D. The primary purpose of WebGL is to draw triangles very fast – everything beyond that, you have to implement yourself. Fortunately, there are many popular libraries and tools that work with WebGL. Here are a few of the open-source ones:

- *three.js*: a very popular 3D engine written in JavaScript
- *A-Frame*: three.js as HTML using Web Components
- *React VR*: a React wrapper for three.js developed by Facebook
- *BabylonJS*: a performant 3D engine made by Microsoft

These libraries are designed to abstract some of the common features of 3D scenes to make them accessible to developers. Personally, I build almost everything with A-Frame as it is very fast to get started and it has a great community.

Designing Your VR Scene

The key phrase when it comes to designing VR scenes for the web is progressive enhancement. This means that your scene should do something wherever it can.

Non-web VR usually only targets a single piece of VR hardware, which limits the potential audience to just the people who own that hardware. Building only for one platform is an easier task, because you know the device's power and controller configurations.

The power of the web is that it works across a wide range of devices – what we build should too.

On the web your content is not restricted to any single platform and therefore should work on each platform to a certain extent.

This presents many challenges because hardware configurations vary wildly. For example:

- Alice has a state-of-the-art computer with an HTC Vive and two position-tracked controllers. She also has lots of space to move around in.

- Bob is new to VR. He is using Google Cardboard with his two-year-old smartphone. He has no controllers.

- Eve has a brand new, very powerful smartphone and a Gear VR. She has one rotational-tracked controller, but is unable to turn around fully because she cannot leave her hospital bed.

In each of these situations the user will want to experience as much of the scene as possible and doesn't want to be limited by the available hardware or their situation.

If you want to build something where, for example, two position-tracked controllers are absolutely essential – such as a 3D drawing website – it may seem impossible to support other types of hardware.

 Progressive enhancement doesn't mean the same experience everywhere, just some experience anywhere.

This is a situation where you can allow other hardware configurations to perform some other task. In our example, perhaps the user could view 3D drawings that someone else has made.

PLOTTING YOUR SCENE

Once you have worked out what you want people to do in your scene, it is time to plot out where stuff should go. There are a few ways to do this.

- Draw your scene on paper: a great place to start working out how things should be spaced around.

- Build a diorama out of cardboard. It is a bit of work, but great for figuring out the relative sizes of objects.

- If you are comfortable with a 3D editor, place some cubes and primitive shapes, and move them around to work out how the scene should feel. Later you can replace them with real models.

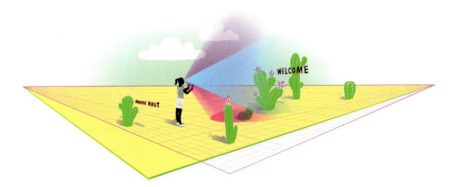

Start thinking about what you want to build and how VR enhances it. Think of how you can make the most of VR and take advantage of having a full sphere of space instead of being limited to a small window.

Also think about what you want the user to do. What do you want the user to learn or experience?

When placing items in your scene, your goal should be to provide various points of interest for the user without making the scene so cluttered that it is hard to navigate. New users may get frustrated as they try to navigate a VR environment.

If you are going from designing for a 2D screen to designing in a 3D space, it is important to remember to think beyond 2D layouts. As well as being placed below or above, or to the left and right, objects can be placed near or far. Thanks to the power of 3D, an object which is very large and far away will look very different to the same object placed close by.

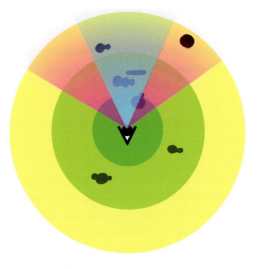

It is also important to balance the placement of objects. If objects are placed too far around the user's peripheral vision, they may go unnoticed and the user may be unable to access them if they have reduced motion. Requiring too much head movement can cause neck aches and be uncomfortable.

Conversely, placing all the objects in the center of the user's vision may be convenient for them to use, but not take advantage of the VR experience. They might as well just be using a normal laptop screen.

It is important to balance these considerations by having your key content placed in the user's immediate field of view, while still rewarding users who look around in the space.

CUES FOR 3D

Many of the features which make your scene feel and look good are related to cues the brain uses for depth.

A scene with objects clearly placed in three dimensions will feel really immersive. These things can take a lot of effort to get right, and the user won't consciously notice them, but they will probably notice their absence.

Even worse are conflicting visual cues, which will make the user uncomfortable or give them headache.

Visual cues you can harness in VR include:

1. **Parallax**: the difference between the image received by each eye due to the distance between the eyes. This is the feature which comes for free in VR. By rendering from each eye's perspective there will be differences which give a sense of depth.

2. **Occlusion**: when one object sits in front of another, it hides the more distant object. This should usually take care of itself, but it can break sometimes when you are forcing the depth in the 3D engine.

3. **Atmospheric perspective**: as objects recede towards the horizon they increasingly take on the color of the atmosphere. Often this means turning on a fog effect so that objects further away lose some of their saturation.

4. **Shading**: approximation of shadows and highlights caused by light falling on an object. This allows us to see the volume of an object rather than just its silhouette.

   a. This provides an ancillary benefit in that it also provides more details for the brain to use when working out parallax.

b. If an object has no shading in a regularly shaded scene, it will appear to be emitting light as it has no shadows (an effect you may choose to have).

5. **Shadows**: where an object is blocking a light source from lighting some other space, like the floor. The brain uses shadows as a key to work out where an object is placed in space in relation to its surroundings.

   a. *Cast shadows* are produced in direct light – imagine a pillar on a sunny day casting a shadow onto the ground. This tells us lots of information, such as where the pillar is touching the floor, how tall it is, and the direction of the light source.

   b. *Ambient occlusion*: shadows that fall where it is difficult for light to reach. This often occurs in corners along the edges of walls or in folds of clothes.

6. **Lens blur**: our eyes are only able to focus at one distance at a time, resulting in focused objects being sharp and other depths of vision being blurred. We can't fake this effect in VR hardware yet, which means that everything in the scene is in focus at once.

If you build with these things in mind, it will give the user a clear idea of what is happening, and the size and distance of the objects in your scene.

CHOOSING COLORS AND TEXTURE

You will probably want to choose a particular aesthetic for your scene. A photo-realistic scene is possible but very difficult to create and probably not necessary. The success of stylized games like Minecraft has shown that graphical fidelity is not necessary for an engaging experience.

What looks good on our high-resolution computer monitors or phone screens may look less impressive when viewed through a VR headset, where the effective resolution is quite low because the screen is closer to our eyes.

The result of lower resolution is that scenes with a lot of detail and high-contrast textures look very visually noisy, making it hard to determine what is important. Combine this with the inability to use lens blur in VR (everything is in focus even when not being directly looked at), and the background becomes visually distracting.

On the other hand, an aesthetic which embraces a more cartoonish style can look good even on low power devices, and allow us to clearly signal what is important and what is not.

The aesthetic produced by tools like *Google's Blocks*[2] – bright, saturated colors which embrace the low poly appearance of the models – is a good way to get an attractive as well as performant appearance.

In my opinion, the skybox is the single most important asset for setting the mood.

2   http://smashed.by/googleblocks

One place where picking a high-quality texture can work wonders is the skybox. It can very quickly and inexpensively add huge amounts of feeling to any scene.

It tells the user whether it is day or night, what the weather is like, and even whether they are on Earth or some alien planet. The best skybox I have ever seen is on the Oasis map in Overwatch.

Here, the colors inspire the lighting for the rest of the scene. The clouds are cartoonishly beautiful and the stars at sunset feel magical.

The skybox tells such a story with just a single high quality texture. If it is used as a basis to inspire the scene's lighting, it will integrate beautifully with the rest of the scene.

You can buy equirectangular sky images online from various stores. They can be painted by hand, but this can become difficult: if you use an equirectangular image it will need to have distortion applied to it.

If you want to try out a very simple skybox, a vertical gradient will work well for setting the mood, and it can be made very quickly in an image editor. Here I made a 512×512 gradient from one of the gradient tool presets in GIMP. The horizon is halfway down the image.

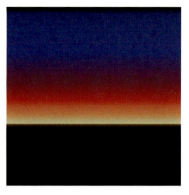

A simple skybox made with the gradient tool.

When applied as the skybox to a very simple scene it really sets the mood:

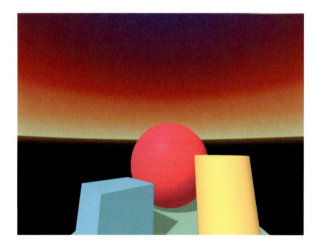

A gradient sky applied to a simple scene.

A gradient skybox is very much preferred over a single block of color. The horizon and clear gradient help orientate the user and make the environment more comfortable for them.

The same principle applies to the floor texture. A floor with a simple repeating pattern will give the user a clear idea of the topology of the ground around them and give them a good sense of the scale of distant objects.

A simple, subtle tile works wonders for this, but be careful: an overly detailed floor will pull the user's eye away from the content and towards the floor. It is good to find a balance that is useful and attractive without becoming distracting.

When you have a very large floor that you can see for long distances, a single repeating tile may end up looking a little strange. A way to get around this is to vary your floor a little bit. For example, instead of using a single grass texture repeating many times in all directions, placing grass decals or clumps of grass here and there over a single color of floor will look much less weird and distracting.

PICKING COLORS FOR OBJECTS

Colors with high saturation are more noticeable. Reds especially stand out.

Our eyes are drawn to areas with a lot of contrast. In your scene, the darkest color will feel black and the lightest will feel white. Humans aren't very good at accurately judging colors – we base any particular color on its neighbors.

This dress can be perceived as white and gold or blue and black because there are few other colors to compare them with. Image credit: Tumblr: "swiked"

Certain problems come up when using absolute black (#000) or white (#fff). Because these colors can't be made darker or lighter respectively, they won't always look natural in your environment and will limit the effectiveness of your lighting. As a matter of fact, real life environments almost never include true black and white.

PICKING COLORS FOR LIGHTS

The default lighting in a scene is often pure white (#fff) directional light, which approximates the sun; and a low-intensity white (#fff) ambient light to approximate light bounced off other surfaces. This lighting setup is acceptable, but not very interesting: it only perfectly changes the brightness of the colors it hits.

This is rarely encountered in real life. Typically, lights are a little bit warmer (more yellow/orange) or a little bit cooler (more purple/blue). This causes our eyes to see the shadows as the opposite color. So a warm light casts a cool shadow.

When designing my scene I tend to pick a slightly blue ambient light and a slightly yellow directional light. This has the effect of making shadows feel cool and lit areas feel warm. It makes the scene feel more vibrant and gives a sense of warmth. The opposite approach, using colder (bluer) lights and warm shadows, will make the scene feel colder.

A good rule of thumb is to pick colors from opposite sides of the color wheel for light and shadow; that is, yellow and purple, blue and orange, red and green. Make sure you adjust the saturation to an appropriate level.

If you pick the light-source color based on colors in your skybox, it will integrate beautifully into your scene and feel very atmospheric.

The other atmospheric effect you can use is "fog." This will change the color of the objects to match the fog color as they recede further from the user's perspective. The skybox is usually made to be unaffected by the fog. A fog color should be chosen based on the skybox's horizon to simulate atmospheric perspective for distant objects.

You can also create a cool silhouette effect against a sunset skybox by using a color which is darker or bluer.

Of course, the colors don't have to reflect reality. Using unusual colors for the sky or sun is a great way to give an otherworldly feeling.

Interactivity

Once you have built your scene, you will want the user to be able to engage with your content.

To receive input from the user, you can get the position and rotation information from the attached controllers. This is a key time to think about progressive enhancement: not all users will have the same controller configuration.

There are three controller configurations a user typically may have:

- One or two position-tracked (also known as *six degrees of freedom: 6DoF*) controllers from an expensive VR headset. Try not to require both, if possible, since the user may be unable to use both at once (for example, if one is charging).

- One rotation-tracked (also known as *three degrees of freedom: 3DoF*) controller, common on portable VR headsets like the Daydream and Gear VR. These often behave like a laser pointer for selecting and interacting with objects.

- No controller. They may be using Google Cardboard, or simply not have a controller available.

The most basic form of interaction which works in all cases is to allow the user to "click" on elements by pointing at them. To do this you "raycast" to your interactive objects, where the ray is fired either from the controller(s) or from the center point of the user's camera.

It is then good to display a cursor at the point where the ray hits the scene so the user knows what is currently "under the pointer." Objects which are interactive should visually (and audibly) respond to this cursor, so that when it is under the cursor the user knows that they can perform some kind of interaction with it.

When the user clicks it, there should be some kind of response, such as changing size or making a noise. All these animations should be tweened in an aesthetically pleasing way, according to the principles of animation. They should wind up, follow through and squash or stretch to feel engaging. It is more important to give the user information about how items react than to make something physically realistic.

Two main types of interaction I see used are scripted interactions and physics-based interactions.

Physics-based interactions are a great way to add a sense of realism and agency to a scene. It can be a computationally expensive feature to add to your scene so should be used judiciously.

Use a physics engine to allow users to pick up and throw objects. Sports games like Rec Room make great use of this to allow people to play together. This is very impressive because having two people interact with the same objects is very difficult.

Scripted interactions are when you click on an object and it triggers some change to the environment; maybe you push a button and the background image changes, an object moves or changes size, or perhaps some narration starts.

Interactions like these are very useful for exploring a world, and the state is much easier to share with other users. This is great for exploring shared worlds together. VR has enormous potential for storytelling, especially when experienced with someone else.

Of course, scripted interactions and physics don't have to be totally separate. A few items with real physics among scripted interactions will give a nice feeling of physicality to any scene.

Walking Around

Travel in VR is an interesting problem. Usually people are not able to move around all that much when wearing a headset owing to limitations in the size of rooms.

At the same time, the scenes we build are often beautiful expansive areas, much larger than the real world we are standing in with our headsets.

How do you explore a large virtual world when you can't walk?

There are hardware solutions to this issue, but they are usually expensive and unwieldy. The most common solutions use the existing controllers and headsets to give the user a way to move around. There are a few different ways to move in VR that tend to be reused, so it is an area ripe for innovation.

First, there is teleporting.

Teleporting usually involves picking an area of ground and having the camera move to hover above that position. There are many different ways to pick the teleporting location. Some scenes use a laser or parabolic line for selecting the location.

Suddenly appearing in a new location may be disorienting, so often there is some kind of transition to ease this feeling. Such transitions are usually something like fading to black or a "blink" created by wiping a black plane across the viewing area.

Second, there is flying.

Flying lets the user drift around the scene. It is a tricky thing to do well because the user isn't moving in real life. Their visual impression of accelerating or decelerating isn't matched by a physical sensation, and as a consequence can make them feel ill.

Here, breaking the illusion of moving actually helps. A popular solution is to show a static scene in the user's peripheral vision. This makes the user feel they are staying still while the scene is moving around them.

Occulus has done some research on comfortable locomotion,[3] which – if your VR experience includes lots of locomotion – may be worth experimenting with.

Another thing to keep in mind is that some users are restricted in how they can turn: they may be sat down or lying in a bed. If you provide a method like using a controller button to rotate the user, it will be more accessible. Google has done some research[4] which found that a smooth rotatation left or right will make some people motion sick. Instead, jumps of 10–20 degrees will feel more comfortable.

Social VR

At first thought, VR seems like a lonely experience – but it can bring people together too. If you can share the state of a virtual world between two or more users, then VR starts to become social.

The most obvious implementation is to give each user an avatar representing their headset's current position and rotation to the other users. This allows people to see what others in the scene are looking at, giving a sense of togetherness.

It is also possible to transmit people's voices over WebRTC so that people in the scene can speak to each other.

Sharing the state of a scene can allow two people to experience a story together, creating a cooperative narrative experience. VR really opens up the potential for collaborative storytelling – much like an immersive play.

3   http://smashed.by/locomotion
4   http://smashed.by/locomotionvr

If you have physics simulations in your scene, it is really engaging to share the state of the physics engine between users. This presents a challenge because the latency between users can make it difficult keep in sync; but, if you can achieve it, playing catch in VR is an incredible experience.

Often sharing physics involves either handling all the physics on a central server, or having objects in the scene be controlled by the last person to interact with them.

Audio

While audio is not my area of expertise, one thing I would like to make clear is that audio is an integral part of the experience. It can provide as many cues to the user for interactivity and setting the mood as the visuals do.

Adding audio will have a huge impact on your scene, but I often see it forgotten about.

Even something as simple as some background music in an `<audio>` tag will make your scene feel immersive and more vibrant.

There are libraries to allow you to produce 3D audio on the web and to place sounds around a user. This also gives them a cue that they should look around to where the sound is coming from.

I once saw a hackathon entry in which you had to find a hidden object by 3D sound alone. It was very engaging and a great demonstration of the power of 3D audio.

Optimizing for Performance

This is tricky. Some people will be running VR on the most powerful desktop computers money can buy. Others will be using mid-range smartphones in cardboard headsets. In the middle of the spectrum, we have laptops and high-end smartphones with good graphics chips and lots of memory.

We want to maximize the number of devices where our experience works well, so progressive enhancement is going to be the main task to accomplish.

Mobile first is still great advice. Here is how I test as I build for WebVR:

1. I build and test on my mid-range Ultrabook – a low-power device with not a lot of memory.
2. Test on my smartphone, where it should perform better. Test using magic window mode.
3. Test in Samsung Internet for Gear VR with the 3DoF controller.
4. Test in Firefox or Chrome on my desktop with an HTC Vive.

The aim is to continuously test on my least powerful devices to ensure they give a consistent performance.

Users have high standards for the web when it comes to getting started. If they have to wait more than a few seconds they will leave the page. This often means having to show your scene before every item in it is fully loaded, populating the scene as items load.

If you have a complex scene, a nice trick is to show a low-resolution skybox to give the user something to look at while the rest of the scene loads. Try not to leave the user waiting more than three seconds – less than one second if you can. After all, some users are going to be on a mobile connection where loading times can get very long.

It's a good idea to not go above 70 Mb of content.[5] The majority of the size will probably come from textures, which are the images applied to 3D objects. Too many of these will have performance penalties and may crash the browser. It might be worth spreading your VR experience across multiple web pages as the user changes scene.

With browser caching and tools like service workers, assets can be reused between pages, helping to reduce download sizes for scenes with shared assets.

If you come from the web world, 70 Mb may seem very large. The average web page is 2.5 Mb. But if you are coming from the 3D graphics world, where installations can run up to hundreds of megabytes on mobile games, this is quite restrictive. It is important to save space wherever we can.

The dimensions of textures (the images applied to 3D models) should have a power of two (512×512, 1,024×1,024, etc.). This is because of how they are stored in the graphics card. To make optimal use of space, have them match these sizes.

5   http://smashed.by/aframeperf

TIPS FOR INCREASING FRAME RATE

A consistent frame rate is extremely important in VR. If some frames are missed, the API will help by redisplaying previous frames while tracking the head. If you skip too many frames, you can make the user feel ill.

This is often a game of balancing graphical fidelity, performance, and developer time. Tips to handle these issues generally come in three flavors:

- Make things that don't need to move unable to move. This allows us to do some work on the scene in advance.
- Delete anything that people won't notice – what isn't there can't slow us down.
- Use the graphics card or multiple threads where you can. The graphics card is often faster than the CPU.

When drawing the scene, the 3D software will draw each object separately in what is known as a draw call. Lots of draw calls will be very difficult render, even if each draw call is simple.

First, measure how difficult it is for the computer to draw each frame. This functionality is built into many 3D graphics libraries to tell you the difficulty of drawing the previous frame.

Adding the stats *attribute to the* <a-scene> *HTML element lets you see how much the computer has to work to draw the frames.*

The main goal is to limit the number of draw calls. Notice that the scene in the image has almost 900,000 faces because of the rain. However, because it is rendered in very few draw calls (31), it is quite efficient and maintains a good frame rate on my low-powered netbook.

In "A-Painter performance optimizations,"[6] Fernando Serrano has written about increasing performance. The article describes how members of the A-Frame team improved the performance of one of their more intensive demos by reducing both the number of textures and the number of draw calls.

The simplest trick to reduce draw calls is to hide any objects not visible to the user so they don't get drawn needlessly.

6   http://smashed.by/perfopt

Another way to reduce the number of draw calls is to merge geometry wherever you can. This means that meshes which share the same material have their geometry combined. They can no longer be moved independently of each other since they are effectively one mesh. In general, lots of performance fixes result in having objects which can no longer be moved.

It is possible to set up an advanced lighting scene with beautiful light and shadow techniques such as ambient occlusion, cast shadows, and diffuse reflection calculated in real time as the scene is rendered. Doing this will be expensive to render, so we can't have very many objects in our scene and still reach a good frame rate. Often, we resort to faking these effects.

Instead of calculating shadows being cast from lights in real time, if we know an object doesn't move we can paint its shadow onto the floor; by painting the lighting effects straight into the textures, they can look really fancy but are actually rendered very cheaply.

A similar effect can be used for reflections and refractions: instead of doing expensive ray-tracing we can use a static environment map to give the illusion of these effects. The user won't notice imperfections unless they look closely. This process is known as baking, and is built into many 3D editing tools, such as Blender and Maya. It usually takes a while to set up the lights and textures for baking. It takes a few minutes to render to the texture but it will load almost instantly when it is used.

Unfortunately, this means if we move any of these baked objects their shadows will be left behind.

We also have to do a new bake if we change the scene in any way. This is the downside of light and shadow baking. The compromise is to bake all the shadows of objects and lights in the scene which do not move, and do real-time shadows for only the few objects which move. They usually blend together well and look really good.

Physics and Interactions

Physics is a really powerful tool for immersion in VR. I briefly discussed how it can be used in the interactivity section.

When we are doing real-time physics, the computer calculates whether any shapes intersect one another. This gets exponentially more challenging the more objects are involved. For example, a falling ball does one test each frame to test for collision between the ball and the floor; a scene with two balls and a floor has to do three tests! One for whether each ball hits the floor, and another to see if the two balls are colliding.

We can simplify this by limiting the number of objects in the scene and removing objects from the physics calculations as soon as they are not in view or not being used.

We can also calculate physics only between objects likely to collide. Two boxes in different rooms don't need such calculations because they won't intersect.

Physics gets even more expensive for complex shapes. Shapes like spheres and cubes can have their collision calculations reduced to simpler maths. But if you have an arbitrary 1,000 polygon shape, the maths for whether it intersects another object gets very computationally expensive.

We have some tricks for solving these problems, though. For complex polygons we can use simpler shapes for simulating the physics.

In the image with the telephone, the phone and receiver are complex models. Performing the physics calculations between the dialer and the receiver would be very difficult. Instead, we have modeled the dialer with five boxes and the receiver with one box and two cylinders (marked in red outlines).

It is much easier to do physics between those two compound objects than between two very high-poly meshes.

Modeling the dialer and the receiver with a few boxes is faster than performing the physics calculations. Source: https://phone-physics.glitch.me/

The high-poly models have no physics done to them, they are just placed to be in the same as the location as the visually hidden compound objects.

Another way to speed up the math is to use a simpler physics calculation for systems which don't need complex physics. Some simple systems, such as balloons on a string, can use a computationally cheaper physics calculation such as Verlet integration rather than a general-purpose physics library.

We can do a similar optimization when doing collision tests for walking around. Instead of working out whether the user will intersect walls or objects, we can precalculate the areas where the user is allowed to walk. This is known as a navmesh (navigation mesh). We can work out where to place the user in the scene by ensuring that the user is placed above it. Don McCurdy has written a great tutorial on how to use and generate a navmesh.[7]

One very powerful optimization (though still difficult to do on the web) is to move the calculation out of the main thread. This reduces the impact of the physics engine interfering with the rendering. It could be moved into a seperate web worker, where you can do the calculations and send back only the necessary information. This is tricky to do well and will be easier when shared array buffers come to the web.

There are proposed web APIs allowing general purpose calculations on the graphics chip, which would be wonderful for real time physics on the web. This way the physics can be both heavily optimized to run in parallel and kept off the main thread.

7   http://smashed.by/navmesh

What I Wish I Had Known When I Began

There have been many suggestions in this article, some requiring specialized knowledge. Performance improvements can be particularly challenging. However, I don't want to let that intimidate you from building your first scene.

Here is a quick list of tips I wish I had known when I started making demos:

- Building something is much better than never finishing something while trying to chase perfection.

- Have fun experimenting with VR and show it to people!

- It's OK to rely on premade content or buy some models. You don't have to make everything from scratch.

- Photo-realism is nice, but difficult achieve. A cartoon style is more achievable for a small team and still looks really good.

- If you have to choose whether a scene should be accurate to reality, or something which feels good, fun, or clear, pick the latter. Even realistic-looking films and games use tricks to make some things work well.

- Be brave with your colors, and use them everywhere. Don't default to white, gray, and black. Color is another tool to tell a story.

- Make sure you test in a VR headset regularly, even if it is just a cardboard headset. What works well on a screen can appear surprisingly different in VR.

Have fun and show off what you build. I always love to see people's first VR experiences.

About The Author

Ada Rose Cannon is really passionate about Virtual Reality and other new Front End Web Technologies. Her favourite computer language is HTML (yes, really). Ada used to work in R&D on front-end web technology but now she is a Web and VR Advocate for the Samsung Internet Web Browser.

CHAPTER 10

Bringing Personality Back to the Web

Vitaly Friedman

Bringing Personality Back to the Web

by Vitaly Friedman

Generic web layouts have become somewhat of a misnomer in conversations circling around web design these days. We're bored and slightly annoyed by how predictable and uninspired most web experiences have become. Not without reason, though. Every single landing page seems to be a twin of pretty much every other web page. In the header, a compelling hero image with a short main heading is followed by a lengthier subheading. Beneath them, uniform blocks of media objects are alternated – an image and a few paragraphs of text. First, text on the left, image on the right; then image on the left, text on the right. Rinse and repeat. Rounded profile photos and a square grid of thumbnails complete the picture, with perfect shapes perfectly aligned along the 12-column grid. The only variations come from sporadic parallax transitions and notorious carousels, positioned at the top or bottom of the page – or perhaps both.

It's not that somebody imposed these rules or limitations on our creative output; usually they originate from good motives and the best intentions. After all, one of the main tenets of web design has always been creating a subtle, almost invisible and functional interface – an interface that doesn't make users think, where less is more, and form follows function, where simplicity prevails – an interface where everything feels just *right*. Yet when everything is structured in a predictable way, nothing really stands out. Given how remarkably similar names, logos, icons, typography, layouts, and even shades of gradients on call-to-action buttons often are, it's not surprising our users find it difficult to distinguish between brands, products, and services these days.

Very few people miss the golden times of the infamous Flash, with its strikingly experimental layouts and obscure mystery-meat navigation. Admittedly, the focus has shifted from creating an experience to merely providing content in a structured form. Yet unlike in those good ol' days when we talked about how wonderful or horrible websites were, today most experiences are almost invisible, making it exceptionally difficult to connect emotionally with them.

If I asked you to think of a recently visited website that left a lasting, memorable impression on you, or what websites you truly love and admire for their unique design, or what website had a truly remarkable personality, would you be able to answer these questions immediately? Would you be able to provide more than one or two examples? Chances are that you won't.

Not every website has to be unforgettable. It's not that memorable websites automatically perform better, or hit better key performance indicators. However, if you want your product or service to stand out in a highly competitive and challenging environment, you need to be different in *some* way. Many of us would consider this to be the task of the marketing team. After all, they are supposed to place the product in the right light, at the right spot, for the right audience, at the right price. Yet in a world where many digital products are fairly usable and feature-rich, this would be a daunting undertaking that would often require months of extensive research and testing without the guarantee of a successful outcome. And even then, unless you are extremely good at predicting and shaping the next shiny big thing, it might not be good enough.

Customers are used to and expect decent experiences. They aren't always fast or straightforward, but simply because of the sheer number of offerings, there are always decent tools and services out there that would be good enough. We tend to believe we rationalize our decisions to extremes, choosing the best candidates, but it's not necessarily true. According to well-known Herbert A. Simon's *satisficing theory*, we tend to prefer the first option that meets an acceptability threshold, just because we don't know if we can find a better option or how much effort it would take. We rarely study the entire spectrum of options in detail (and sometimes it's nearly impossible), and as a result, we *satisfice* with a candidate that meets our needs or seems to address *most* needs.

To draw an audience's attention, we need to be better than "good enough." Nothing can beat word of mouth, but to get there we need to come up with something that's worth looking at. What if I told you that there was a shortcut to getting there?

It's not just about price. It's not just about features. It's not just about choosing the right placement of buttons, or the right shades of colors in endless A/B tests. And it's not about choosing a cute mascot illustration that shows up in email campaigns. In the end, it's about creating an **experience that people can fall in love with, or connect deeply with** – an experience that, of course, drives the purpose of the site, but also shows the human side of it, like the personality of the people building it, their values and principles, their choices and priorities.

That means designing voice and tone, interface copy, and embracing storytelling, authenticity, inclusivity, and respect; and all of that while establishing a unique visual language supported by original layout compositions and interaction patterns. Together with clear and honest messaging, these create a unique signature, which, used consistently, makes the product stand out from the rest. This task might sound as daunting as months of marketing research, but it doesn't necessarily require an enormous amount of effort or resources.

In this chapter, we'll look into a few **practical techniques and strategies** that might help you find, form, and surface your personality efficiently. By doing so, we'll explore how doing so consistently could fit into existing design workflows, along with plenty of examples to give you a good start. But before we get there, we need to figure out how omnipresent design patterns and best practices fit into the equation.

Breaking Out by Breaking In

The creative process isn't linear. Every single design decision – from colors and type to layout and interactivity – requires us to consider options and evaluate combinations. While the creative process is often seen as a straightforward, iterative process, in reality it's very rare that we smoothly move from one mock-up to another through a series of enhancements and adjustments. More often than not, we tend to float and diverge, heading from one dead end to another, resolving conflicts and rerouting our creative direction along the way.

Those dead ends happen when we realize we aren't really getting anywhere with the result exposed on our digital canvas. We've been there many times, so we know how to explore uncharted territories and how to maneuver the flanks, and so as we keep sculpting our ideas, we keep making progress, slowly but steadily moving towards a tangible result. Two steps forward, one step back, revisiting what we've done so far and refining those precious pixels – based on... frankly, based on intuition and random experiments. Eventually the back-and-forth brings us to a calm, peaceful, and beautiful place – just where we think we've found a solution – *the* solution.

We know, of course, that it's unlikely it's going to be the *one*, though, don't we?

This journey from *nothing* to *something* isn't just full of conflicting micro-decisions; it's crammed with unknowns, traps, friction, and difficult constraints, be they of a technical nature or time-sensitive. And at every moment of the process, the beautiful, harmless creatures of our imagination can be mercilessly smashed against the harsh reality of user interviews and client revisions. So we swizzle around from one direction to another in a fertile yet remarkably hostile place. As a result, usually we can't afford the luxury of losing time, as we know that the path to *that* deadline, harmlessly floating in the remote future, will be full of surprises and unexpected turnarounds.

To avoid losing time, we rely on things that worked well in our previous projects – the off-canvas navigation, the accordion pattern, rounded profile images, and the holy 12-column grid layout. It's not for lack of knowledge, skill, or enthusiasm that we fall back to all those established practices – it's just infinitely more difficult and time-consuming to come up with something different every single time. And because we lack time, we use all those wonderful, tried-and-tested design patterns – all of them tangible, viable solutions for a particular kind of problem. Obviously, this process might be slightly different for different people, but broken down into its essence, that's what's happening behind the scenes as we make progress in our designs.

When we started working on the redesign of Smashing Magazine a few years ago, one of the first steps we took was listing and exploring components and micro-interactions. We built the article layout and a style guide, responsive tables and forms, and used many of the established best practices to keep them accessible, fast, and responsive. Yet when putting all these perfect components together, we realized that while they were working well as standalone solutions, they just didn't work together as a whole. The building blocks of the system weren't sufficient to maintain and support the system. We had to redesign what we'd built so far, and we had to introduce overarching connections *between* those components that would be defined through the personality and voice and tone of the new identity.

When we apply design patterns to our interfaces, we essentially bring together a group of loose modules or interactions that lack any connection to everything else. Rather than asking how a particular pattern helps drive the purpose of the experience, we often explore a micro-problem in isolation, putting micro-solutions together.

With design patterns, we run the risk of adding a component just because it's trendy these days – like a parallax-effect, slow and impactful transitions, and fade-ins. By doing so, sometimes we might lose the big picture of what role that component would play at a bigger scale, and how it could be connected to everything else. As a result, we produce soulless, dull, bloated designs with generic compositions and generic visual treatments. That's how we create something that looks like everything else.

It's not that design patterns and best practices are necessarily evil, though. They are merely a double-edged sword helping and troubling the visual output. When applying them, we need to do so carefully and thoughtfully. Whenever you consider resolving a problem with a design pattern, it's a good idea to ask yourself a few questions:

1. What problem exactly are we solving?
2. Is the pattern really the best solution for the problem?
3. How do people experience this interaction, and what pain points do they encounter while doing so?

4. How does this component help us reach the overarching goal of the system?
5. How do we connect that component to the rest of the system – in terms of both aesthetics and interaction design?
6. Is the solution really universally understood, or do we need to provide more clarity to the design (labels, better copy, affordance, replacing icons with words)?
7. Is it a good idea to keep the pattern as is at all times? Or is it better to load or adjust it conditionally, perhaps based on the viewport, or how many times a customer has visited the page?

Essentially, we try to **break down a design pattern** by exploring when and how it's useful or damaging, and how it helps in achieving our goals. In other words, we break out of predictable patterns by breaking into their nature and understanding why we actually use them. First, we examine the component in its bare, abstract form, without the context of where it's typically used and how it's usually designed; for example, rather than thinking of an off-canvas navigation sliding from the left to right, or right to left, we look into the interaction pattern on its own – essentially, progressive disclosure in which content is hidden by default and displayed on click or tap.

Then, for every pattern, we explore its usability issues and problems, resolve them, and then style and design the module in a way that feels connected to everything else. That last step could be something as simple as a consistently used transition, or a geometric pattern, or a non-conventional position in the layout. Finally, once everything is in place, we repackage the design pattern and add it to the library, ready to be served for the rest of the system.

Of course, best practices and design patterns are fantastic shortcuts for getting on the right track faster. They let us tap into predictable interactions and sequential knowledge that most of our users will have. In fact, they are as relevant today as they've always been. The key is in finding a way to apply them *meaningfully* within the context of the visual language used throughout the site, and knowing when to break them *deliberately* to trigger an emotional connection.

Humans Connect to Humans

Do you remember the good ol' days when we used an omnipresent "we" to make our little web shops appear bigger than they actually were? You might have been the only person freelancing from home in slippers and a bathrobe, or one of the very few people in a small design agency, but that profound "we" made the company sound more serious, and hence more trustworthy, didn't it? We've pretended to be somebody else to get projects we wouldn't be entrusted with otherwise – and I'll be the first to admit that I am as guilty of it as everybody else.

These days, when so many things around us are exaggerated and deceptive, authenticity remains one of the few qualities people genuinely connect to. Too often, however, it's not exhibited through a website at all, regrettably creating a vague image of yet another obscure entity covered with corporate stock photos and meaningless jargon. When every brand promises to disrupt or be different, nothing truly feels disruptive or any different, and this causes alienation and skepticism.

Humans can genuinely connect to brands they trust, but brands need to earn that trust first. Obviously, it comes from reliable recommendations and positive experiences. But as designers communicating on behalf of companies, how do we efficiently elicit trust in people who aren't yet aware of the brand? As it turns out, trust can also come from the appearance of the brand, which can be influenced by its values, beliefs, principles, and activities. It isn't easy to fall in love with a company or organization without knowing somebody who admires it almost contagiously. It's much easier to connect with *people* whose values you support, and with *people* who stand behind their beliefs and principles.

If humans connect best to humans, perhaps if our interfaces reflected the values of the people creating them, we might be one step closer to triggering that desired emotional connection. We've been there before, of course, and so that's why we show the people working in the company on a "Team" page or in the footer of the front page, right? Well, let's look into it from a slightly different perspective.

What if you were asked to describe the personality of your brand? What adjectives would you use? Think about it for a minute, and write them down.

Ready? Chances are high that you've come up with common and predictable answers. Perhaps words such as "simple," "clean," "strong," "dynamic," "flexible," or "well-structured" have come to mind. Or maybe "attentive to details," "focused," "user-centric," and "quality-driven."

Can you see a problem with these answers? These words describe our *intention* rather than our *personality*. While the former is usually very specific and stable, the latter is usually very fuzzy and ever-changing. The qualities outlined above don't provide a good answer to the question, as they describe *how we want to be perceived*, but not necessarily how we actually *are*. In fact, usually we don't really know who we are or how we are perceived outside of the comfortable company bubble we find ourselves in.

Instead, what if you asked your colleagues and customers a slightly different question: what they care about most in their work, and what they value the most about the company or the product. Maybe they care about the diversity of talented, motivated co-workers who are knowledgeable and experienced, yet also approachable and humble?

Maybe it's the fact that the company is actively contributing to pro bono projects for non-profit organizations that make a real difference in the world. Maybe because it supports schools and newcomers to the industry by providing an annual scholarship. Or because it ties in the profits with a fair salary bonus for all employees. Or just because it allows you to play with the latest fancy technologies and crazy experiments, and contribute to open-source in five percent of your working time. The company doesn't need huge ambitions, idealist goals, or a fancy working environment to stand out.

> *Note:* Designing humane experiences means being kind and humble, and emphasizing qualities that matter to the company and to users. That means highlighting privacy, respect, ethics, and transparency, but also reflecting the personality of people working on the product.

Here's an example. Your company could care deeply about diversity, data privacy, accessibility, and transparent pricing. That would mean your interface is accessible and honest, you publicly take a stand against giving away customer data to third parties, and you include features that support pricing comparison without pushing your agenda over the edge. You could highlight those values prominently along with the competitive pricing tiers, and measure the outcome.

Now, can you spot a similar thread among all of the statements above? Because they come from personal experiences, they seem much more human and relatable than more general and abstract terms you might come up with initially.

MailChimp's interaction design just before and just after an email campaign is sent out.

slack

Add custom loading messages just for your team

Loading ...
If nobody comes back from the future to stop you, then how bad of a decision can it really be?

Go to my.slack.com/customize/loading to set your own

Slack's loading messages reflect the personality of the brand and the people working there. That's the power of copywriting at play.

That's why companies like Slack or MailChimp feel so much more tangible than brands like Uber or General Electric. They employ quirky and informal microcopy and illustrations that reflect their human side.

They don't shine through a mission statement or press releases, but through the quirks in the interface and how they communicate publicly, via email, or in social channels. That's the underlying foundation of a character deeply integrated into the user experience.

Cats have become one of the key figures in Smashing Magazine's branding. The Smashing Cat reflects the character and attitude of people working behind the scenes.

To avoid a generic appearance, you need to **define your personality first**. That means asking the right questions and finding accurate answers. When conducting user interviews with our readers, we quickly realized they had a quite different perspective on the Smashing brand than we did. We confidently described the brand by listing all the usual suspects, the qualities you probably came up with initially. The truth was baffling, though: we couldn't have been further away from how the brand was actually perceived.

We always wanted the magazine to be a professional, respectable publication with a strong voice in the industry, highlighting important work done by members of the community. User interviews brought up qualities that didn't really describe that goal in the way we always strived for. Instead, we heard words such as "informal," "quirky," "friendly," "approachable," "supportive," "community," and – most importantly – "cats."

Now, we never wanted our legacy to be cats, but it wasn't really up to us at this point. Back in 2012, our dear illustrator Ricardo Gimenes chose to bring a Smashing cat to life as a mascot for our very first Smashing Conference. There was no conscious decision for or against it. We didn't even properly discuss it, as we didn't know if we'd host more conferences in the future anyway. This small decision put something in motion that we couldn't dismiss years later. Because conferences turned out to become one of our central products, we've been promoting them heavily in our mailings, announcements, release posts, and social media messages.

Over time, every conference had to put up with a cat illustration of its own, and all these cats were facing our customers over and over again for years. Cat illustrations heavily influenced the perception of the brand without us actively fostering or guiding it. So we had to make a decision: either let the cats slowly fade away into oblivion, or integrate them heavily into the new design. You probably have discovered by now what we've settled with. As of this point, we have over 70 quirky and friendly cats freely wandering all over the new Smashing Magazine website.

However, as much as a mascot can help make the brand more approachable, it's rarely enough to convey the full story. Interviews also helped us realize how important the **community aspect** of Smashing Magazine actually was. The words "community" and "people" appeared in user interviews a lot, and not without reason – the magazine wouldn't exist without humble and generous contributions from people behind the scenes. Our design didn't really reflect it, though. So we chose to shift the focus heavily towards highlighting the people behind the scenes – authors, editors, and members of the community. Showing people prominently has become another attribute defining our design signature – and that explains why author thumbnails take up such a prominent position in the design, and why we highlight authors publishing on their own blogs or other platforms on our front page.

What does it all mean for you? Ask questions to surface humane qualities that lie in the very heart of the company first. This will give you a foundation to build a visual language on – a language that would translate your qualities to the interface design. Every company has a unique signature in *some* way, and often it's reflected through the people working there. Ultimately, it's just about finding the time and courage to explore it – and to embrace the fact that our flaws and quirks are a part of it as much as our big ambitions and good intentions are.

Personality Is Never Perfect

As designers, we often take pride in being perfectionists. Every pixel has to be polished, every angle has to be just right, and all components should be aligned to the grid. Remember that never-ending discussion about the perfect border-radius on call-to-action buttons? After an eloquent and long-winded debate, the design team eventually settles on 11px, just to switch over to 13px a few months later, just to move back to 12px by the end of the year. In many companies, these changes are prompted through numerous ongoing A/B tests, in which nothing is left to chance, and everything – from assumptions to design decisions – has to be tested and proved first.

We restlessly strive to reach the most effective, the best performing solution – a solution that's just right. However, aren't we riding our horses to death trying to improve the same tiny component over and over again, just to find a slightly better variant of it, with all those minimal, microscopic changes?

Espen Brunborg, a creative lead for a graphic design agency in Norway, suggests to **never conduct A/B tests alone**.[1] According to Espen, A/B tests help us reach a *local* maximum of the user experience, but often they aren't far-reaching enough to encompass the big picture in its entirety, effectively stopping us from reaching a *global* maximum.[2] That's why in addition to A/B tests (in which microcopy and colors and positions in the layout are tested), they run so-called *A/Z tests*, testing an existing "baseline" design against completely different designs. Their differences lie not only in the shade of a button or copy, but in absolutely different layouts and visual treatments. The branding and the core principles remain the same, but pretty much everything else keeps evolving. This allows Espen and his team to reach new absolute maxima in terms of conversion and KPIs every few months.

In one of our conversations years back, Elliot Jay Stocks, who was involved in the 2012 redesign of Smashing Magazine, briefly mentioned one fine detail of his design process that stayed with me for quite some time. He said that a good design possesses one of two qualities: it's either *absolutely perfect* in every way, with perfect alignment, sizing, and hierarchy (which is usually quite hard to achieve), or it's *deliberately imperfect* in a few consistent ways (which is much easier to achieve). According to Elliot, in a good design there shouldn't be anything in between. In other words, buttons should either be perfectly aligned to the grid, or not aligned at all – offset by 20–30 pixels and more. Being off just by a few pixels would feel wrong, while being off by 20–30px looks deliberate, and hence less broken.

1   In his article "Putting A/B Testing in Its Place" (http://smashed.by/abtests), Jakob Nielsen highlights the limitations of A/B testing. E.g. it should never be the only testing method. Observations of user behavior often generate deeper insights.
2   Bill Buxton was probably the first to discuss this problem in his book *Sketching User Experiences* back in 2007. According to him, designers often end up with a local hill-climbing problem when the design gets plateaued on a local maximum.

So what if, instead of chasing the perfect solution for every single component, we ran and tested various expressions of our personalities? In interface design, it would mean entirely different creative directions. Perhaps a multicolumn layout with bold typography, against a geometric layout with a single accent color? What if, rather than seeking the perfect roundness of a button, you deliberately introduced slight inconsistencies? A custom animation on one of the call-to-action buttons, or a dynamic placement of an image outside of the box in which it's usually supposed to be placed? Or perhaps rotating a subheading by 90 degrees? The personality can be expressed in many entirely different ways, so the task is to discover variations that are promising enough for testing.

A personality is never perfect, and so perhaps our websites shouldn't be perfect either. What if you set up a publicly visible art board in your company, with magnets representing the qualities on one side, and magnets representing components or visual treatments on the other side, and then randomly clashed one against the other to produce a visual direction for the next A/Z test? Apply perfectionism to the level of detail required to produce deliberately imperfect designs.

This approach won't always win, but complemented with A/B tests, it might bring you to new heights you wouldn't be able to achieve otherwise. Ultimately, we want customers to fall in love with their experience and consequently the brand, to form a lasting bond. A deliberately imperfect yet humane interface can help us get there. It requires you to find just one distinguishable quality that nobody else has, and boost it up.

Choose One Thing and Boost It Up

Personality can be expressed through a *design signature* – a recurring visual treatment, the voice and tone of the copy, or an interaction pattern used consistently from one page to another. It might be tempting to explore a diverse mix of sophisticated, non-conventional treatments that would be seen in the interface miles away from the mouse cursor. However, that's a recipe for a disastrous experience that prioritizes a designer's expression over users' intentions. However bold the personality is, its design signature should remain subtle.

When working with Dan Mall on the Smashing redesign, one interesting detail Dan brought up at the very start of the project was the role of the signature in the final outcome. According to Dan, choosing a few distinct, competing expressions of the personality is often too much: it's enough to choose just one little detail and boost it up all the way. In more practical terms, that means picking one pattern and using it consistently, *everywhere*: on every page, and in every user interaction. How do you find that sacred detail? You go back to the roots of the company.

In the very early days of Smashing Magazine, we didn't have any branding at all. We chose a pretty random WordPress theme, placed the name in Arial, and that was it. Eventually, in early 2007 Ryan Denzel from South Africa designed Smashing Magazine's logo, which included a letter S tilted by 11.6 degrees. Despite minor alterations in the shade and colors of the logo, we stayed true to the design for over a decade, and with the recent redesign, we weren't considering changing it. However, when seeking a design signature that would be deeply connected with the brand, we actually took the tilting of the logo very close to our heart – from the very start.

Early design explorations with Andy Clarke used the tilting consistently for every single visual element on the site. This signature carried over to the final design as well. Today, all icons, author images, conference flags, job board logos, illustrations on product panels, and book covers on product pages are all consistently tilted. That tiny detail doesn't break the experience, yet it lends a unique visual treatment to the design that's clearly distinguishable from everything else as a result.

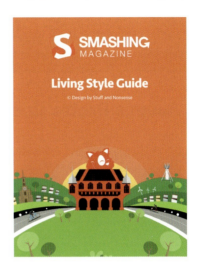

Admittedly, we did redesign the tilting through the process, moving away from 11.6 degrees to 11 degrees, and adding 11px roundness to all components. It was months later that the bold colors and typography and layout came into play, supporting the quirkiness and informal style of the tilted elements – all slowly crawling up into the design mock-ups eventually.

Early design explorations used the tilting element consistently for every visual element on the site. This signature carried over to the final design as well.

At this point you might be slightly worried that you don't really have any distinctive element that could be promoted to become your signature. You might not have the tilting or a particular color palette that stands out. As it turns out, *anything* can become a design signature. In the next sections, we'll explore some examples and ideas you could use for you own particular situation.

Always Prefer Custom Illustrations

Once the qualities of a personality have been identified, the next step is to translate these qualities into a distinct visual language. Initially it happens via color and typography, so when defining the visual style, look out for these qualities in initial color combinations and type families.

Probably the easiest way to come up with your own design signature is by using custom illustrations designed specifically for the brand. Every artist has their own unique style, and unlike stock images or stock photos that often almost enforce generic appearance into layouts, custom illustrations give a brand a unique voice and tone. You don't need to go overboard and create dozens of illustrations; just a few would probably do. Think about replacing all the stock photos you've purchased with custom illustrations – this should give you a good enough baseline to start with.

Atlassian is a wonderful example of an illustrative style applied thoroughly and beautifully at every touchpoint of the experience. The illustrations are more approachable than stock photos. Notice, however, that they rarely appear on a plain background – they are supported by the color palette and typographic choices that complement the illustration style.

Atlassian uses a friendly illustrative style with color consistently used for buttons and headings at every touchpoint of the experience.

Why are custom illustrations not enough to stand out? Because just like many other attributes on the web, illustrative style also follows trends. Compare Atlassian's style to Slack's visual language. Yes, the fine details are different, but the pastel color combinations are similar. The illustrations from these different projects could happily coexist within one single website, and many customers wouldn't notice a difference.

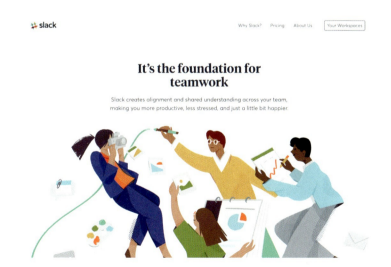

The style of the illustrations on both the Atlassian and the Slack sites look fairly similar. Both illustrations could happily coexist within one single website.

A distinct visual style requires further attention to other elements on the page, primarily backgrounds, typography, shapes, and layout. Notice how all these **elements play together** on *Bond*.[3] They interplay with the background, text colors, and the layout.

Medium uses a collage-like style for all its illustrations on landing pages and help pages. The key is that illustrations are used consistently across pages. They might not make sense to every visitor, but they contribute to the unique visual appearance of the brand.

3 https://bond.backerkit.com/

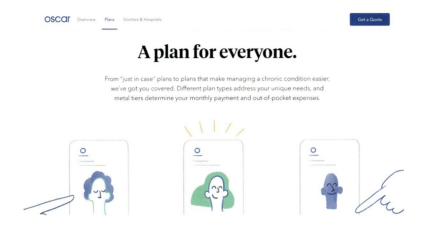

Health insurance is a very competitive and not particularly friendly nor transparent environment for citizens and business. With custom illustrations, subtle animated GIFs, and straightforward copywriting, *Oscar*,[4] a newcomer to the industry, appears more approachable and relatable.

WebConf.asia is a conference website with vivid color combinations and background, and boxy components designed as if they were **three-dimensional**. This is enough to set the design apart. The visual treatment produces depth, which is used for speakers, talks, and main navigation.

4 https://www.hioscar.com/

Bandenjager uses **slanted shapes** and compositions consistently on call-to-action buttons, in the navigation, and even in the quantity selector on the product page. That's their design signature. Notice how even micro-components such as product labels use the same pattern.

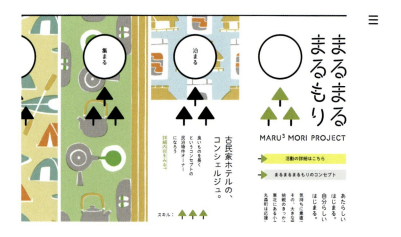

Maru Mori Project[5] is an economic development project initiated by the municipal of Marumori, Japan. The site uses circles and tree shapes everywhere — "Maru" means circle, "Mori" (森) means forest.

5 https://marumarumarumori.jp/

Storytrail is a city guide with interactive maps and videos. Every city has its own signature which is a wavy horizontal line outlining a city's most important landmark. The design uses this signature line for various animations, transitions, and arrangement of items in the layout.

Haufe uses overlapping backgrounds to add more dynamics to the design. The main structure of the grid is derived from the letter H, which is the main character of the company's identity. All components are laid out on the grid to support that personality trait. A nice play of

photos, original compositions, and a variety of geometric backgrounds at once. *Haufe*'s design system[6] beautifully describes the underlying principle of Haufe's dynamic grid.

Another way of drawing attention is by adding randomness to your composition. Rich Cahill's site[7] splits its photos into three vertical parts, randomly offset horizontally and colored with a set of pre-defined colors. It's a nice example of combining predictable parts of the system in seemingly random, unpredictable ways.

6 http://smashed.by/haufeds
7 http://rc3.me/

Lynn Fisher[8] also adds some randomness to her portfolio. The layout changes completely between different breakpoints, creating a totally different experience on mobile and desktop devices. Even the favicon changes dynamically as well.

When considering the visual direction of a site, it's a good idea to consider custom illustration style, backgrounds, typography, and shapes. Establish strong connections between all of these attributes by reusing design decisions, such as the choice of colors and spacing. While doing so, of course, it wouldn't hurt avoiding predictable options used widely everywhere else. One of the effective ways to achieve this is by keeping tabs on ongoing design trends, then pick the most prevalent one and... *smash* it to pieces.

8   https://lynnandtonic.com/

Pick a Trend and Smash It to Pieces

When talking about great design, Yves Saint-Laurent, a well-known French fashion designer, once noted that "Fashions fade; style is eternal." According to Saint-Laurent, to create timeless designs it's important to take note of trends, yet serve an *interpretation* of trends through the lens of your own personal style. That's not what we usually see on the web.

It's almost ironic that it has become trendy to dislike trends these days, and for good reason: usually their primary purpose is visual embellishment, rather than driving a designer's intent, and often they don't add much to the experience beyond friction, confusion, and fancy whistles and bells. No wonder then that designers have started to fight back with "*brutalist designs*"[9] – websites that aim to exhibit the essence of a website in its unstructured form, exposing the website's functions to extremes.[10]

While doing so, designers often deliberately break design patterns, usability practices, and design trends. At first glance they might appear as designs created with the sole purpose of being different, but because they have a striking personality, they draw attention to themselves. Admittedly, sometimes they seem to be too far-fetched in how they deliberately turn their back on well-established design principles. Not everybody can afford it, and not everybody would feel comfortable connecting such non-conventional aesthetics to their brand.

9 http://brutalistwebsites.com/
10 Brutalism in architecture is characterized by unconcerned but not intentionally broken aesthetics. When applied to web design, it often goes along with deliberately broken design conventions and guiding principles.

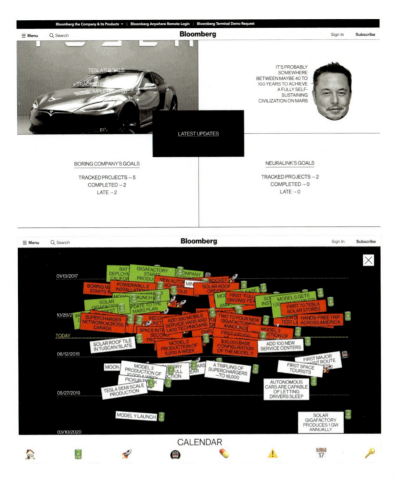

A brutalist design showing up in its glory. A feature on Elon Musk, published by Bloomberg.com, breaks most conventions we've got used to over the years.

A slightly more pragmatic strategy lives somewhere between generic designs and brutalist designs. To get there, you could pick a trend, find a unique perspective and apply your personality to it. For example, if you see many websites using smooth and silky animations, think about how they would fit into your story, and find the twist that would enrich it, and make it more personal. Break down the trend into pieces to understand its mechanics and what's happening behind the scenes, then twist some parts of it, repackage, and integrate into your design.

Dropbox rebranding wasn't received too well. The design is very bold, and very noticeable. As such, Dropbox achieved its goal of being talked about in their redesign.

Instead of bouncy animations, you could use an artificial delay which slows down the appearance of items on a page. If most profile images have a perfect circular shape, try to come up with a different shape that would work well for showing avatars. If most photos are rectangular, think of another shape that might do the job well. Lo-Flo Records[11] uses an artificial delay with geometric placeholders. The website uses geometric placeholders; smooth, well-orchestrated transitions come to life when content is being populated.

11 http://loflorecords.com/

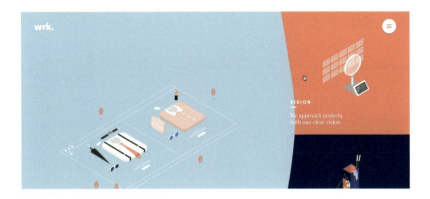

Instead of using off-canvas transitions, think about a particular transition or animation that would reflect your brand best. For more corporate entities, a fast-paced transition might work best; for creative projects, a slightly more playful and slow transition might be a better fit. *Waaark*[12] is a wonderful example of the latter. If all transitions were removed, the portfolio website would look like pretty much any other portfolio site.

Implement Consulting Group uses a short and subtle geometric animation to highlight the featured article on the site. Foreground and background images are a bit offset and animated, with a geometric shape in

12   https://waaark.com

the background and a story preview in the foreground. That's enough to give the experience some personality.

Imagine for a second that you have to redesign your ongoing project, but can't use any basic shapes such as circles, rectangles, or triangles. What would you choose? We all know there is an infinite amount of options, but why is it then that so often we are constrained by highly predictable and heavily used choices? What is neither a circle nor a rectangle nor a triangle? Well, slanted or tilted elements aren't. Neither are letters and large typography. Nor are custom responsive illustrations or iconography. Nor whitespace, audio, and video. Nor transitions and animations. Nor pretty much any other shape created via a polygon, with content embedded via SVG masks. TPS,[13] a Russian real estate agency, uses the shape of its properties for thumbnails, rather than generic squares or circles. Every single property has its own shape. The idea is used consistently for every single property.

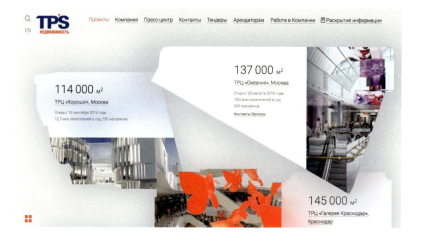

13   http://www.tpsre.ru/

Districtox[14] is a network of decentralized markets and communities. The site uses custom shapes, smooth transitions, and animations to provide a distinct experience. No rectangles or circles. And notice how well the colors, background images, and typography work together on the site.

It's not that all basic shapes should be ignored and dismissed from now on, of course. Avoiding basic shapes deliberately is one of the very first exercises we do when we try to come up with a slightly more original art direction. Once you've come up with a decent idea without basic shapes, you can start bringing them back sparingly when necessary. Chances are high, however, that you might be able to get away without them altogether.

14   http://smashed.by/districtox

Do Make People Think

Why is it that when we are puzzling our way around a foreign city and a souvenir shop owner is desperately trying to catch our attention on the street and push a sale, we pass by in haste; yet we slowly walk into a beautifully designed souvenir store that is silent and humble just around the corner? Perhaps it's because we seek authentic, honest, and respectful experiences, and tend to ignore everything that doesn't fit the bill. In his fantastic book *Blink*, Malcolm Gladwell outlined an interesting phenomenon related to how humans value their experiences.

According to Gladwell, we tend to be more satisfied with our experiences when we feel valued, listened to, and understood. Doctors who take a disproportionate amount of time listening, asking questions, and taking notes with their patients tend to get significantly better reviews and higher ratings despite the fact that other doctors might be as proficient and knowledgeable. They might jump to correct conclusions faster, yet their efficiency doesn't elicit trust and connection in their patients. Of course, primarily we want the problem to be solved, but we also love falling in love with a charming personality, wisdom, expertise, and human kindness.

We know by now that we can enable human connections by embedding compassion into our interfaces. However, these connections don't just happen overnight – they take time. But where does it leave us in the age of instant gratification and invisible interfaces, when it has become the essence of our job to avoid interruptions and distractions, and create a clear path for customers to follow seamlessly? If we aren't supposed to make people think, how do we even get a chance to establish an emotional connection in the first place?

We do so by slowing down. By making people think. Not much. Just a little bit. Just enough to make them feel valued, or smile, or get curious. We do so by adding friction. A few bumps here and there, enough to offer a chance of being directly confronted with the personality infused in our interfaces. It might even mean confusing the customer every now and again just to enable a speedy recovery from that confusion with a dash of positive emotion in their eyes. That's how memorable experiences emerge.

Everything is a *little* off on *BAO London*[15] – the spacing, the color combinations, the form layout, the hierarchy, the buttons, the cursor, the lightboxes, the illustrations. This consistent breaking of predictable patterns makes the website appear interesting and appealing. Breaking things slowly and deliberately, one component at a time. That's not a regular restaurant website.

Everything is *way* off on the Hans Brinker Budget Hostel website[16] and it's done deliberately as well. The hostel was struggling to sell rooms as

15 https://baolondon.com/
16 http://hansbrinker.eu/

CHAPTER 10

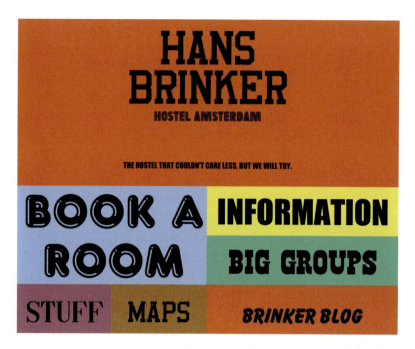

If you can't make it better, make it worse. Even if you don't have a wonderful product to sell, it's always possible to wrap a story around it and make it more interesting.

the competition is quite tough in Amsterdam. Rather than improving the design, they made it worse to fit well within their story. Pretty much every element on the page actively makes people confused – from color combination to typography to interactions. And it worked – they are expanding to Lisbon now. Not everybody will like it, and some people will find it annoying, confusing, misleading, childish, or just over the top. Very much like we find it difficult to connect to some people, we might experience the same issue with an interface that attempts to show its human side. But isn't it worth it? Perhaps in times when everything is remarkably similar and doesn't really stand for anything, it's worth striving for our product to be genuinely loved by many people for the price of being genuinely disliked by some people, rather than eliciting no feelings at all.

In his *How I Built This* interview on NPR,[17] Mike Krieger, the co-founder and creative mind behind Instagram, mentioned that rather than spending a significant amount of time trying to understand why people abandon the service, one of the fundamental principles that drives growth is focusing on customers who deeply love your product and stay around for years. By prioritizing existing customers and what they truly love about your product, you might not only attach them to your product, but also boost the word-of-mouth marketing that's infinitely more effective than traditional landing pages.

It doesn't mean, though, that we shouldn't take good care of experiences customers have when abandoning the product, or – even worse – that we should make it harder for them to leave. The humane qualities of the interface should shine through all the touchpoints of the experience – and it holds true for onboarding as much as offboarding. The latter is mostly deemed as being not *that* important – after all, when the customer will face it, they have almost abandoned the product.

17 http://smashed.by/npr

Offboarding Matters

Just like human relationships sometimes end abruptly and badly, leaving a lasting negative aftermath, so can our relationships with digital products. It's highly unlikely that a person abandoning a product with a mysteriously long-winded journey through cancellation redirects would praise the product to friends and colleagues. People leave for very different reasons, and sometimes it has literally nothing to do with the service or the experience. They might have moved on, or just want to save money for something more important, or perhaps they just found an alternative that better fits their needs.

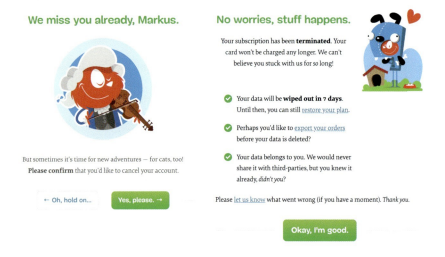

What if at the moment of departure we make them feel deeply valued and understood? Admittedly, with Smashing Magazine's redesign, we didn't spend too much time designing the offboarding UX, but it was important for us that the experience fitted well within the overall personality of the interface. When our customers cancel their membership subscription, we greet them with a respectful and even encouraging notice, providing a little gift for sticking around with us for so long, and explaining what happens to their personal data.

The result was surprising: we discovered that customers who cancel the subscription and go through the offboarding UX, sometimes tend to be even more eager to recommend us to their friends and total strangers than some loyal members who stick around for a long time. They just admire how respectfully and thoughtfully we deal with their decision, and that we don't pull all the shady tricks from the trenches to make it difficult for them to leave.

Make Boring Interesting

It's difficult to introduce playful elements into an experience which is otherwise very much corporate and formal. However, whenever you are designing a particular interaction, be it as simple as hovering a button, or moving from one section to another, or filling in a form, there is always some room to make the experience slightly more interesting.

For example, out of all the wonderful form elements on a given page, what could be less exciting than a "Title" input? Sometimes appearing alongside radio button counterparts or a dropdown, rigorously asking customers for very personal information about their marital status, without any obvious reason whatsoever. And that's exactly the moment when we can make it shine beautifully. A great way of creating memorable experiences is adding a bit of surprise at the point where **it's most unexpected**. Pick the most boring, unnoticeable part of the experience and try to make it interesting. Now, is there a way to make this interaction more interesting?

When creating a new account on *Boden*,[18] customers are dazzled with a quite unusual selection of options, ranging from Admiral to Squadron Leader and Baroness. Who hasn't wanted to be a Squadron Leader at some point in their life? This little design decision elicits smiles, and prompts customers to share this gem with their friends and colleagues. By the way, the list of options is quite lengthy.

Austin Beerworks (see the example on the next page) is just one of many local breweries in the US. When customers enter the site, as always they are prompted with an age check that's supposed to ensure they are over a certain age limit. Most people – honestly or dishonestly – would click on "Yes" and move on, but if the customer chooses to click on "No," they embark on a "choose-your-own-adventure" trip to be guided to a video that best describes their personality.

18 http://bodenusa.com/

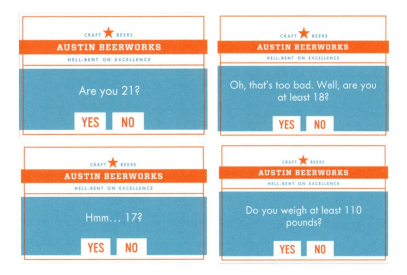

Who doesn't love disliking a pop-up? However, pop-ups can be made interesting too. *Volkshotel*[19] uses the most annoyingly delightful pop-up out there, beautifully illustrated as a person holding a sign in front of the website. As the visitors hover over it to close it, the pop-up sneakily moves away a little bit, making it just a tad more difficult to close it. Personally, I wish every single website had a pop-up like that.

19   https://volkshotel.nl

Tympanus' 3D Room Exhibition[20] doesn't look particularly exceptional until the visitor chooses to interact with it. When moving from one exhibition detail page to another, rather than just loading another page, the user is moved from one room to another within a 3D space.

What's a common interaction on the web? Forms, in all their different flavors and appearances. In fact, chances are high that you have some sort of a login and password input on your site, and, of course, that's a pretty boring interaction. Adding a character responding to a user's input might spice things up a little. As a result, people might spend more time interacting with the form before signing in. That's better engagement at hand. Darin Senneff's Yeti character[21] (see image on the next page) does just that.

The strategy is simple: choose one predictable, boring pattern, study user expectations and... break them mercilessly by adding something unexpected and uplifting to it. Please note that it doesn't mean breaking usability just for the sake of breaking it; rather, it's about making a handful of boring elements more interesting by adding some unconventional treatments to their design.

20 http://smashed.by/tympart
21 http://smashed.by/yetiform

Darin Senneff's Yeti form (http://smashed.by/yetiform) responds to input actions such as revealing a password or typing in an email.

Find a Pain Point and Solve It Well

Can you hear restless voices of skepticism whispering from the corner of the room? Not every corporate setting will sustain a funky custom illustration, a quirky animation, or an unconventional interaction. A striking visual identity might not really fit into your digital presence, custom illustrations might not be within the budget, and you might not want to break customer's expectations anyway. In these cases, you might want to explore a slightly different route. If you can't convey your personality through unconventional aesthetics or interaction, an alternative is to convey it through superior problem solving. It means you need to uncover painful moments of interaction – when customers are annoyed or disappointed or confused – on similar sites, and sweep through experimental and seemingly far-fetched solutions to try to trump the experience that your competitors provide. Take on a problem, and tackle it meticulously, head on.

Surprisingly, most of the time these pain points aren't particular features; it's the perceived complexity of the interaction and the lack of transparency. Too many form fields; too much time investment; too slow an interaction; too many repeated questions; too many unnecessary requirements. The angle is to find a way to make seemingly complex interactions deceptively easy, hence surpassing expectations.

SBB Mobile is a Swiss trip planner app that allows customers to check the schedule of trains and purchase train tickets. On its own, it's a trip planner like every single similar app out there, except for one thing. The app provides a "touch timetable." Customers can define their common destinations and arrange them on a grid. To purchase a ticket from Zurich to Lausanne, for example, it's enough to draw a line on the grid connecting Zurich and Lausanne and then confirm the selection. Booking tickets has never been that fast and easy. That's a great example of making a conventionally complex interaction straightforward, especially for people who commute frequently. Also, it's a unique design signature that nobody else has (yet).

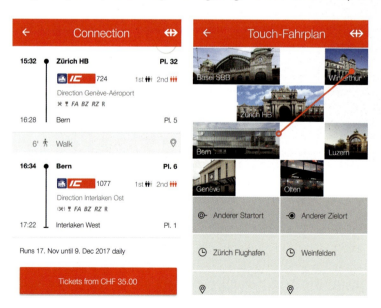

What would it take to provide a remarkable video-playing experience? It might sound as simple as designing a track and a thumb with a few ticks on the track for quick jumps. However, if you study common problems users experience frequently, you'll find one particular issue that stands out. People tend to pause videos and then continue watching later, yet restoring the state of where things were left off is unnecessarily complex in many video player UIs. In fact, you might encounter people writing down the exact time stamp when they paused the video, just to return to it later on another device – but then again, in most UIs it's impossible to jump precisely to a particular second, and most of the time you have to guess and tap the position of a thumb on the track correctly. In the same way, jumping back and forward by 30 seconds or even by a few minutes can be remarkably challenging, especially on mobile, as most interfaces aren't designed around that particular case.

Not only does YouTube provide fully accessible controls for navigation, it also contains a keyframes preview with thumbnails appearing on hover, and navigation via keyboard – and it stores the current state of the video, allowing customers to save a particular time stamp with a unique URL to continue watching later. YouTube also contains many lengthy videos, like documentaries or tutorials, so users can slide up the thumb vertically to adjust the scale of the track and hence jump to the point of interest more precisely. Unfortunately, only a few users know of the feature, and the interaction isn't particularly self-explanatory, but those who *do* know of it, use it frequently. One pain point, solved well.

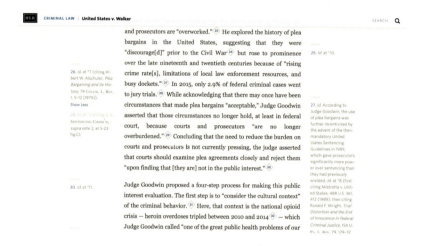

Most academic publications contain dozens of endnotes, footnotes, and references, listed in the order of appearance. If a reader is interested in a particular footnote, they have to jump to the end of the article to read it, and then jump back to continue reading the article. This experience might be a bit too tedious for frequent use, yet it's the default experience we all are accustomed to.

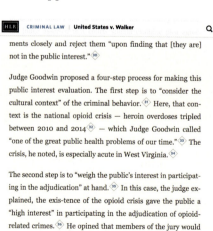

The *Harvard Law Review* solves this problem in a different way. References are always located right next to the point where they are mentioned. Every side note and footnote either appears on the sides on larger screens, or displayed inline via an accordion. Once a user has tapped on the footnote, it expands in its entirety, while the footnote turns into a "close" button. A simple problem solved well.

Imagine you want to book a wonderful vacation with your family, but you haven't picked your dates yet. You have an idea of when you'd like to go, and you have some flexibility regarding the dates for your next vacation. *DoHop* allows its users to choose a flexible date for traveling; for example, particular months of the year, or a particular season, (winter or fall, perhaps). It then suggests dates and a time span with the best price. And if you have a public holiday weekend coming up in a few weeks, and you'd love to make a plan, *RoutePerfect* (see the screenshot on the next page) suggests a route based on your preferences. That's a real problem case solved well. Most traveling websites ask for specific dates for inbound and outbound flights.

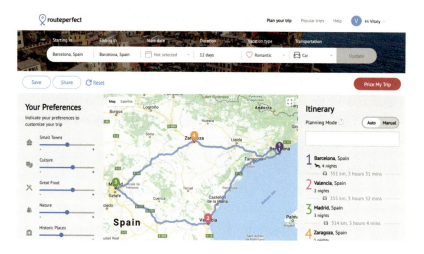

Good solutions require time and focus. They require us to *really* understand what pain points users experience first. Users might not be very good at articulating those paint points, so we developed a simple technique that helps us get to the root of the problem.

We ask testers to complete a particular task on a competitor's website, and record their session on video, along with a webcam, using the device that they are used to. It could be as easy as finding an item in a catalog, or checking out in a retail store, or finding a particular section in the navigation. Of course, we observe their behavior and ask questions if something appears to be unusual, but too often many things that happen during the sessions go unnoticed – they are just too difficult to spot right away. That's why we **rewatch recorded user sessions in slow motion**, often slowing down the playback five or six times.

We look for repeated movements and imprecise hits, as well as negative facial expressions and gestures. More specifically, we search for *little moments of despair* – fleeting moments of confusion when movements or gestures don't make any sense: circling around a button or a link over and over again; focusing on a particular interactive element for far too long; selecting the same text a few times in a row and then continuing to navigate without acting on it. The playback sessions usually happen right after the test, so we still have an opportunity to ask questions and to check our assumptions with the participant. Even a few recordings can provide actionable insights — and they don't require a lot of effort or resources. Should you not have the time to run these tests, it's also a good idea to ask the support team about common complaints.

Once we've identified some issues, we explore solutions that would provide more clarity and ease the interaction, sometimes by designing without any particular visual language in mind. The point is to find an interaction pattern that would be way more superior to the experience customers had on the competitor's sites. We then produce a digital mock-up and invite the same customers to try to solve the same tasks, along with a new group of testers who haven't seen both interfaces yet. We measure the time needed to complete an interaction and ask them to choose which interaction they find more straightforward and useful, and why. Surprisingly, faster interactions aren't necessarily perceived as being faster, and slower interactions aren't necessarily perceived as being slower. Based on that, we iterate and evolve those prototypes. In many ways, those pain points become the heart of our experience that we tackle first and radiate the entire experience out from. That's why sometimes, instead of running a test on a competitor's website, we test our own solutions in the same way.

Good solutions trigger an emotional attachment with or without non-conventional aesthetics or interaction. The more pain points you can address well within your interface, the more likely the difference in experience is to be noticed. Only a few websites make it to customers' browser toolbars, so think about that one pain point and the one solution that would make them do just that.

Exceeding Expectations by Default

Here's another question for you: of all the hotel experiences you ever had, which ones are the most memorable? Think about it for a moment. Think about what made them so special and why they stayed with you all the time. It might have been an extraordinary natural backdrop, or remarkably attentive personnel, or a lavish breakfast buffet. Or something entirely different. In fact, for many of us it could have been a pretty average dormitory as much as an exquisite 5-star chalet in the Swiss alps. The environment matters, but it's not the environment *alone* that matters.

The reason why these experiences are memorable is because they aren't average.[22] In fact, they are the very opposite of average in *some* way, as *something* was exceptional about them. It's not necessarily the hotel itself – it's the timing and the people we happen to spend these experiences with. A good hotel provides a setting that enables wonderful experiences, and so does a good website interface. A *memorable* hotel adds a fine detail to the experience that exceeds our expectations, and it does so without telling us up front. And so do *memorable* websites.

As Brené Brown, a research professor at the University of Houston, so beautifully expressed in her books on empathy, "good design is a function of empathy, while non-empathic design is self-indulgent and self-centered." The key, then, is to empathize with customers both in their negative and positive experiences, rather than pushing your own agenda. To our customers, that extra fine attention to a few little

---

22 According to Daniel Kahneman's peak-end rule (http://smashed.by/peakend), we judge experiences based on how we felt at its peak (the most intense point) and at its end, rather than the total sum of experiences and whether it was pleasant or unpleasant. That means we can tap into very negative and very positive parts of the experience, and tweak them to create an emotional connection.

details can make all the difference in the world. So we could sprinkle a little bit of human kindness here and there, adding extra value silently, without even mentioning it. That fine detail could be as simple as a custom-designed profile illustration, based on the photo the customer has uploaded. It could be a handwritten thank-you note, signed by the entire team and sent via good ol' snail mail. It could also be an unexpectedly straightforward resolution of a problem after a mistake has been made.

In an eCommerce setting, it could mean the ability to modify or cancel a finished order within five mins after the successful checkout. It would both help a customer avoid a time-consuming interaction with the support team as they can edit an order without any extra charges, even if they realize after checking out that something was wrong with the order details.

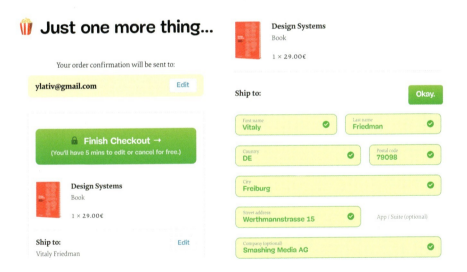

A mock-up we're currently exploring in Smashing Magazine's checkout to allow inline editing of data on the review step and editing of the order within 5 minutes after the purchase.

In the same way, an interface could suggest to a signed-in customer to use a use a coupon code saved in their dashboard as it's about to expire soon, or inform them about a similar – and hence potentially duplicate – booking made a while back. The personality of the brand shines best in those little moments when it helps customers prevent mistakes. By acting on behalf of the experience rather than business every now and again, the interface makes the customer feel genuinely valued, respected, and helped, and that works much better than any ingenious interface copy ever would.

One way of preventing mistakes is by writing adaptive and helpful error messages. That's one of the most obvious points of frustration for customers, and it's remarkable how little effort is put into recovery experience, often falling back to generic and abstract messages. Admittedly, these messages don't necessarily cost a sale but they can damage the long-term perception of the brand. People who experience unrecoverable issues during one of the key interactions on a site tend to not use it in the future at all as they expect the issue to creep out in other interactions too.

Shipping Address — You are entitled for FREE shipping!

| First name |
| ⚠ No Cat is an island. |

| Last name |
| ⚠ Tiger is a common Cat's last name. |

| Country |
| ⚠ Uh-oh! Where in the world are you located? |

| Postal code |
| ⚠ Also known as ZIP code. |

| City |
| ⚠ Probably the best place in the world if you live there! |

Error messages deserve slightly more credit than they are usually given. They appear at the point where the customer's progress is blocked, and when they have to slow down and pay full attention to resolve a problem. We can use the situation to our advantage to infuse a bit of personality into the experience. Every single time an interface fails to meet expectations, it's an opportunity to create a memorable impact in the process of speedy recovery. If we manage to turn an annoyance into the feeling of being valued or understood, we might be heading off on the right track.

One of the very first things I started working on when we embarked on the redesign was filling elaborate spreadsheets with alternate wordings for our checkout error messages. It wasn't done with the intention to A/B test the "best performing" error message; it was done primarily to discover better expressions of the personality through the interface. On their own, error messages don't really make sense, but they fit well within the story being told throughout the site. Once an error has occurred, we try to use both adaptive and playful copywriting to address the issue while also raise the occasional smile.

Voice and tone are the main pillars of a personality. MailChimp has built a dedicated voice and tone style guide (http://smashed.by/voicetone) to align designers, customer support, and everybody else in the way they communicate to customers.

Seek critical pain points that customers often experience on the site by looking into customer support logs and user interviews, and design these experiences with extra care and attention. It goes without saying that a quirky personality won't help much if the customer isn't able to solve a problem, so take care of the basics first. Ultimately, it doesn't take that much effort to turn negative experiences into positive ones – it's just a matter of having it on your to-do list when designing an interface.

The Two Sides of Personality

As much as we love sharing our experiences and showing our better side to people around us, we can't stand that one person spending the entire evening talking about themselves. In our interfaces, every time we add yet another parallax transition or a slow bouncy animation to people who have seen it a dozen times already, we are essentially letting the interface highlight its fanciness without helping the user along the way. Eventually, after a few visits, all those whistles and bells that achieve a strong first impact become annoying as they add too much friction.

Nobody loves self-centered characters, and so a website shouldn't be self-centered either. The design signature should never take the leading role in the user experience as it's never the main reason why people access the website. It should be humble and remain in the shadows, noticeable but not obstructing the smooth flow frequent visitors have got used to.

In her talk on *Designing Meaningful Animations*,[23] Val Head, a fantastic designer from Pittsburgh, suggested using prominent animations

23 http://smashed.by/designanimations

very sparingly, as they should be reserved for very special occasions, while subtle micro-animations could accompany the user all along the way. Val suggests using animation only for key compositions of your story, like sending a marketing campaign, or favoriting an item, or seeing a successful purchasing page, while everything else should remain calm and normal. With this idea in mind we could think of designing our interfaces with two kinds of interactions: the prominent "showroom" ones, used rarely; and subtle "workhorse" ones, used frequently.

Reserve special visual treatments and interactions for special occasions, but also embed subtle treatments used consistently across the entire site. Twitter, for example, uses an elaborate animation when a user "hearts" a tweet. Facebook displays a confetti animation when you congratulate a friend on their birthday or a wedding. In Smashing's case, we use vibrant colors and cat illustrations as our showroom signature, while tilting, hover-animations, and shadows beneath them make up our workhorse signature.

We are used to the idea of our designs adjusting to the viewport or network conditions, but it might be worth looking into adjusting the design based on the frequency of usage, too. This technique is called *progressive reduction*,[24] a dynamic simplification of an interface as users become familiar with it. You identify the main features of an interface, and assign levels to them. Then, track your user's usage by monitoring the frequency of use within a certain time period and create proficiency profiles for the user. Based on the current level, you cam adjust these UI components to reduce hand-holding.

24 http://smashed.by/progreduct

As Allan Grinshtein pointed out,[25] a user's proficiency in a given product decays over time without usage (also known as *experience decay*), so if a user's frequency of use and usage volume have gone down, then *their* interface should regress a level or two, depending on how far down their numbers have dropped. This automatic regression is necessary to balance progression; without it, you lose the ability to fully respond to dynamic changes in user behavior.

The more often customers visit the site, the less likely they want to be confronted with anything that would slow them down. Therefore, it might be a good idea to slowly fade out showroom signatures with growing frequency of use, perhaps removing parallax-effects or speeding up transitions for returning users. In the end, it's all about the choreography: don't be that person at a dinner party filling the room with an extensive story of their life.

The Signature at the Heart of the Design

The design process is a mythical creature. Everybody somehow manages to come up with their own workflow, tooling, and processes, yet it's very rare that anybody is *really* satisfied with it. When it comes to infusing personality into the design, when and where would be the right point to include it in the design process?

In one of her talks from 2014,[26] Patty Toland, a senior UX designer from Filament Group in Boston mentioned the hierarchy of priorities the team uses when designing and building responsive experiences. The main goal of the process is to create the "leanest, fastest-loading, most optimized page." The main foundation is and has always been a

25 http://smashed.by/designanimations
26 http://smashed.by/pattystalk

fully accessible experience, in which text, images, data, charts, audio, video, forms and so on are all broadly accessible and function fully in their default form. Applied to the context of the design process, it means meaningful markup and properly defined relationships between components.

Patty Toland, Filament Group, "Design Consistency for the Responsive Web." (http://smashed.by/pattystalk)

With accessible components ready to be served, the next step is taking care of the scale of the design. That's where the decisions about grid, content size, order, and arrangement, as well as breakpoints, come into play. Often the proportions will be defined using *content wireframes*: low-fidelity mock-ups with gray boxes; the height of each box in proportion to others defines its weight in the layout. Sometimes we add notes about the personality across the content blocks, and then reflect them when it comes to visual design.

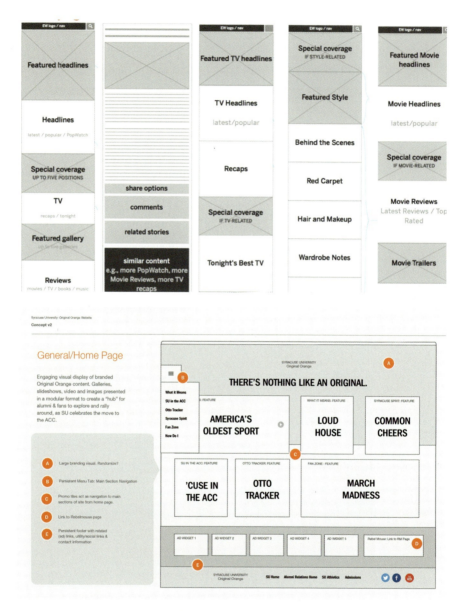

Content wireframes in action. At the top the wireframe of Techcrunch redesign (http://smashed.by/techcrunch) and below the wireframe of the Original Orange redesign by Adjacent (http://smashed.by/adjacent). You can follow the progress of the latter in the screenshots on the next pages, too.

With low-fidelity prototypes in place, the next step for the design is to gain style, with logo, brand colors, custom fonts, transitions, and animations added to the mix. Sometimes this hierarchy will be perfectly mapped in the order we write React components and CSS properties with Sass. Even *BEM naming* for classes will happen in that order as well. The prototypes will gain abstract utility classes first, and more elaborate relationships will be reflected through more specific class names throughout the process. The process establishes a clear separation of responsibilities for modules.

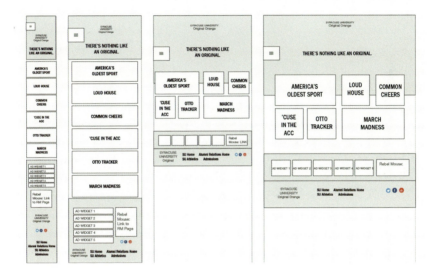

This process seems plausible but it raises a very critical question: *what pages to design and prototype first?* When we start designing, we design the *heart* of the experience first: the most critical and impactful part of the experience. More specifically, we try to capture the very essence of the experience by exploring key interactions, then break it down into reusable components, and then radiate outwards from that essence. For an online magazine, it would be reading experience and typography first. For a landing page, it would be the pricing plans and a feature comparison first.

For an ecommerce site it means looking into the components that would make up an extraordinary relevant and useful product page first. That means large image thumbnails, concise copywriting, transparent pricing, exposed ratings and testimonials, psychological anchors, and call-to-action buttons. The visual design decisions made there are then translated to other parts of the interface, specifically forms and labels and error messages in the checkout.

Only then, eventually, we reach the category pages and the FAQ pages living on the far outer edges of the experience spectrum. Somewhere in between we explore the front page, but usually we design it late rather than early in the process – at the point when we've established a strong identity already, so we use the front page to amplify and explore it prominently, potentially with a bold design that would exhibit the main qualities of the personality.

Remember overarching connections mentioned earlier in the chapter? A critical part of the design process is to connect modules, so they don't appear as standalone solutions when put together in the interface. When we have enough modules to build the first prototype, we jump into the browser and build mobile-first. It's in this process that we finally decide on the grid and the layout and the structure, and implement the connections between modules. In fact, for us, the signature is that magical bond that ties things together.

That's why we start thinking about the signature of the design when we start designing the heart of the experience, and sometimes even before that. Spreadsheets exploring error messages, visual experiments around shapes and colors and type, as well as user interviews help us get there. Eventually, decisions made for the first prototype can be reused for other pages, yet sometimes we need to run the process from the start again – as some pages clearly will be one-offs, such as the landing page or a front page. They will still exhibit relationships to everything else because they are designed and built using the personality traits that have been solidified by this point.

It's these relationships that would then lay the main foundation of a design system, along with components and examples of the interface in use. Too often style guides show a component in isolation, along with Sass class names and a code snippet, without including how that component should appear and behave in relation to other modules on the page. Contextual examples matter both for designers and developers, and they give a good reason to both visit and keep the design system up to date in the long-term.

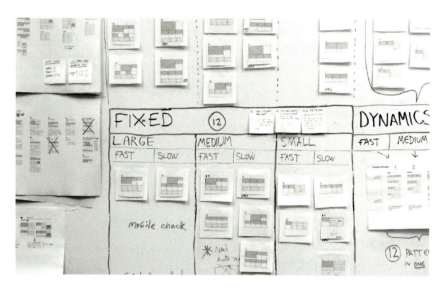

A storyboard with components. Each component also has a speed and level of dynamics attached to them. Image courtesy: Andrew Clarke.

We often create user journey maps to understand the flow users go through to accomplish their tasks, and with personality traits in mind, we could even complement them with storyboards, adding some personality highlights at different points of user experience. Besides, in the context of design systems, we could explore not only components in isolation, but also how the design language can use components to slow down or speed up the experience, or provide greater or lesser impact, as well as dynamic and static layout compositions – very much like we do with showroom and workhorse interactions.

You could even print them out and put them as magnets on a storyboard, just like Sipgate did in the earlier example, so designers can freely move them around and thus explore ways of combining predictable components in unpredictable ways. That's what Andrew Clarke does when embedding art direction and storytelling in his designs – very much like comic strip designers arrange the frames according to narrative dynamics and impact when laying out a comic story.

The design signature lies at the very heart of the design. It's a strand that connects the components in the interface, and it's what helps designers stay on track when maintaining or evolving a design language. Deciding on the personality traits first helps drive the direction of the design, and can be just a good enough constraint to dissolve initial intentions and goals into tangible, distinguishable attributes that could eventually become the heart of the experience.

Wrapping Up

As much as we could get seduced by the charm of a website, in the end, the main purpose of it shouldn't be self-indulgence. Expressions of the personality of the site enable emotional connections with customers and visitors, and because they are human by their nature, they outline a path to authentic, honest, and respectful interfaces. It's up to us to figure out how to shape that path and the outcome ahead of us.

Now, it might not be for everybody, and perhaps not every site needs a personality in the first place, or perhaps it should be subtle and express itself in little nuances here and there. I hope that in either of these cases, once flipping over the last page of this book, you'll have a good enough tool belt of ideas and techniques to create unique and humane experiences – experiences people could fall in love with.

I'd like to express my gratitude to Jen Simmons, Rachel Andrew, Andrew Clarke, Dan Mall, Espen Brunborg, and Elliot Jay Stocks for inspiring work, contributions, and help in discussing the idea of art direction on the web, and making the web more diverse and experimental. I'd also like to thank Marko Dugonjic, Alberta Soranzo, Sashka Maximova, Lilia Zinchenko, Stefan Bucher, Benoit Henry, Nils Mielke, Thord D. Hedengren, and Bertrand Lirette for reviewing the chapter, as well as our fantastic community, which has shared techniques and lessons learned from its work for everybody to use.

About The Author

Vitaly loves beautiful content and complex challenges, and does not give up easily. He co-founded *Smashing Magazine* back in September 2006 and since then spends pretty much every day trying to make it better, faster and more useful. He runs responsive design training and workshops and loves solving complex UX, performance and front-end problems in large and small companies.

Index

0-RTT	245	CSS Grid fallback	117
3D	443	CSS Grid tracks	107
accessibility	48, 173	CSS Object Model	240
adaptive congestion	249	CSS variables, Custom Properties	138, 178
align-content	108	defer	272
align-items	103	design patterns	475
AR	432	design process	345, 524
art direction	470	design signature	486
async	58, 180, 194,	design systems	12, 23
(asynchronous loading)	201, 218,	design trends	496
	264, 271	error message	520
		fallbacks (CSS Grid, Flexbox)	117, 134
		feature policy	314
audio	457	feature queries	123, 180
automated testing	75	Fetch API	194
background content	63	fetch events	195
Background Sync API	230	fetch handling	185
Box alignment	102	Flexbox	84, 89, 121,
buttons	56	focus management	57
caching	197, 289, 307	focus styling	55
calc()	140	font-display: swap	284
Channel Messaging API	221	font subsetting	298
chatbot	342, 366	footnotes	514
client hints	251, 296	forms	331, 510
colors	446	FOUC, FOUT	180, 268,
Compression API	290, 310	(flash of unstyled content, text)	284, 315
content security policy	313	fr unit	88
content sizing	93	frameworks	278
conversational experience/ interface	325, 345, 388, 403	HTML processing	239
		iframe	312
copywriting	354, 480, 521	illustration	488
creativity	470	image formats	297
critical CSS	180, 263	image gallery	127
critical JavaScript	269	image optimization	294
critical rendering	240	intents	374
CSS Grid	82	interactivity	451

`IntersectionObserver`	281	responsive images	295
latency	306, 316	Sass	133, 149
lazy loading	263, 280, 312	semantic CSS	167
length units	85	separation of concerns	220
media queries	112	server-side processing	253
`minmax()`	98	service workers	184, 313
motion	176, 339, 522	single-page app (SPA)	48
network latency	306	`sizes`	296
network strategies	212	Smashing Book 7	2020
non-critical CSS	263	`srcset`	295
notification	68	Storyboards	530
offboarding	506	style guides	24, 41, 78,
offline	204, 310		474, 487, 521
offload	308	subsetting	298
OKR	29	SVG	163
pattern library	12	tabindex	54
percentage sizing	87	tables	121
performance optimization	184, 232, 458	testing	75, 484
personality	350, 470	the fold	156
physics	463	theming	158
plotting	441	third-party content	304, 311
`preconnect`	248	unused content	288
predictability	332, 476	user testing	516
`preload`	232, 266, 286	variable-width images	296
priority hints	261, 279	versioning	215
progressive disclosure	476	`vh` unit	102
progressive enhancement	270	viewport width	124, 171
progressive loading	267, 439	VR	432
progressive reduction	523	`vw` unit	296
Promises	186	wearables	415
prototyping	362, 420, 525	web fonts	284, 298,
		web packaging	292
Push Events	225, 229	WebP	297
push notification	225	WebXR Device API	436
QUIC	246	wireframe	525
refactoring	168	workflow	12
responsive design	112, 155	XR	432

More From Smashing Magazine

- *Apps For All: Coding Accessible Web Applications*
  by Heydon Pickering

- *Art Direction For The Web (Oct. 2018)*
  by Andy Clarke

- *Design Systems*
  by Alla Kholmatova

- *Digital Adaptation*
  by Paul Boag

- *Form Design Patterns (Oct. 2018)*
  by Adam Silver

- *Inclusive Design Patterns*
  by Heydon Pickering

- *Smashing Book #4 : New Perspectives on Web Design*
  Written by Harry Roberts, Tim Kadlec, Mat Marquis, Addy Osmani, Aaron Gustafson, and Rachel Andrew.

- *Smashing Book #5: Real-Life Responsive Web Design*
  Written by John Allsopp, Daniel Mall, Sara Soueidan, Bram Stein, Zoe M. Gillenwater, Tom Maslen, Ben Callahan and Andy Clarke.

- *The Sketch Handbook*
  by Christian Krammer

- *User Experience Revolution*
  by Paul Boag

Drop by smashingmagazine.com/printed-books/ to see all Smashing books.